Mexico's Economy

Other Titles in This Series

Brazil: Foreign Relations of a Future World Power, Ronald Schneider

The Future of Brazil, William Overholt

Westview Special Studies on Latin America

Mexico's Economy: A Policy Analysis with Forecasts to 1990
Robert E. Looney

Robert Looney identifies the forces underlying Mexico's high rate of economic growth in the 1960s and early 1970s in order to determine if economic expansion can be resumed in the 1980s. He differs from other writers primarily in that his analysis indicates that most of the favorable conditions associated with the growth of the 1960s are not self-limiting. The major conclusion of his study is that the prime sources of Mexico's postwar expansion are indefinitely sustainable, while many of the adverse side effects associated with that growth are remediable.

Dr. Looney analyzes the Echeverría administration's economic policies and their role in the events leading up to the 1976 crisis, and examines the new economic strategy of the López Portillo administration in light of its ability to cope with the devaluation of the peso and to restore the economy to a path of stable growth. An analysis of Mexico's recent development experience leads to quantification of the effects of government policies on economic growth. The study concludes with a discussion of such essential components of government action as taxes; measures to attract foreign investment; exchange rates; and the fiscal, monetary, trade, and wage policies needed for a comprehensive development strategy.

Robert E. Looney, associate professor of economics at the Monterey Institute of Foreign Studies, is also senior economist at Systan, Inc., in Los Altos, California, and formerly taught at the University of Santa Clara. Dr. Looney is the author of six books on economic development.

Mexico's Economy: A Policy Analysis with Forecasts to 1990

Robert E. Looney

Westview Press / Boulder, Colorado

Westview Special Studies on Latin America

Published in 1978 in the United States of America by
  Westview Press, Inc.
  5500 Central Avenue
  Boulder, Colorado 80301
  Frederick A. Praeger, Publisher

Library of Congress Cataloging in Publication Data
Looney, Robert E.
  Mexico's economy.
  (Westview special studies on Latin America)
  Bibliography: p.
  Includes index.
  1. Mexico—Economic conditions—1918-1970. 2. Mexico—Economic conditions—1970- 3. Mexico—Economic policy—1970- 4. Economic forecasting—Mexico. I. Title.
HC135.L614   330.9'72'82   78-3132
ISBN 0-89158-093-X

Printed and bound in the United States of America

For Anne

Contents

List of Tables xiii
Preface xv
Acknowledgments xvii

1. Introduction 1

   Methodology 2
   Nature of the Problem 3
   Four Alternative Strategies 5
   Conclusions 8

2. The 1940-1970 Period 9

   1940-1945: The Mexican Economic Takeoff 12
   1945-1954: Period of Industrialization 13
   1954-1970: Period of Stabilizing Growth 15
   Negative Aspects of Government Strategy 18
   Attractions of the Strategy 22
   The Role of Investment in Mexico's Growth 22
   Conclusions 24

3. Increased Difficulties in Applying Monetary Policy 27

   Evolution of the Financial System 28
   The 1945-1954 Period 31
   The 1955-1970 Period 32
   Conclusions 41

4. Increasing Fiscal Constraints on Growth 43

   Difficulties in Applying Fiscal Policy 44
   Role of the Government in Development 45
   Government Revenues and Expenditures 47
   Savings and Investment 53
   Difficulties in Using Fiscal Policy for Stabilization 54
   Conclusions 58

5. Economic Growth, 1970-1973 61

   Strategy of Development 61
   Priorities of the Echeverría Administration 63
   Overview of Growth during the Echeverría
      Administration 64
   Patterns of Development 71
   Conclusions 81

6. The 1974-1975 Disequilibrium 83

   Macroeconomic Overview 84
   Sources of Inflationary Pressure and Imbalance 88
   Evaluation of Government Policies 101
   Conclusions 103

7. General Observations on the Echeverría Administration 105

   Accomplishments under Echeverría 106
   Conclusions 108

8. The 1976 Devaluation of the Peso 109

   The Government's Stabilization Program 109
   Impact of the Government's Policies 113
   President Echeverría's Views on Stabilization 116
   Appraisal of the New Strategy 119
   Conclusions 120

9. Problems Facing the López Portillo Administration 123

   Condition of the Economy at the End of 1976 123
   The Tasks Facing President López Portillo 124
   Events Following the Devaluation 125

Problems Facing López Portillo Stemming from the
  Devaluations 129
  Conclusions 130

10. The Economic Policies of the López Portillo
  Administration 133

  The Alliance for Production 134
  Investment by Industry 135
  The Short-Term Program 136
  The 1977 Budget: Overview 137
  Impact on the Economy 138
  Inflationary Aspects of the Budget 141
  Conclusions 142

11. Patterns of Development, 1976-1990 145

  Evaluation of Mexico's Macro Alternatives 146
  Conclusions 155

12. Potential Obstacles to Accelerated Growth 157

  Natural Conditions for Growth 157
  Major Obstacles to Accelerated Growth 158
  Problems Posed by the Expansion of Population 159
  Water Shortage as a Constraint on Growth 160
  Energy Shortage as a Constraint on Growth 163
  Constraints Associated with Increased Difficulty in
    Attracting Foreign Capital 165
  Conclusions 175

13. A Long-Term Development Strategy for Mexico 177

  The Need for Immediate Reforms 177
  The Need for a Long-Term Development Strategy 178
  Long-Term Demand Management 179
  Measures to Attract Foreign Direct Investment 182
  Conclusions 187

Appendix: A Macroeconomic Forecast of the Mexican
  Economy 189

A Monetarist Model of Income Adjustment in Mexico 189
Simple Keynesian and Simple Quantity Theory Models
   of the Economy 192
Implications of the Models 196
A Forecasting Model of the Mexican Economy 197
Statement of the Model 210

Notes 219
Selected Bibliography 231
Index 243

Tables

1. Mexico: National Income Accounts, 1950-1970 10
2. Mexico: National Income Accounts, 1950-1970 11
3. Mexico: Balance of Payments, 1956-1970 20
4. Mexico: Sources of Growth 23
5. Mexico: Government Subsector Income, 1940-1970 48
6. Mexico: Federal Government Tax Revenues, 1955-1970 50
7. Mexico: Federal Expenditures, 1940-1970 . . . . ,52
8. Mexico: Tax-GDP Responsiveness, 1940-1970 57
9. Mexico: Gross Domestic Product by Sector, 1960-1976 66
10. Mexico: National Income Accounts, 1970-1975 67
11. Mexico: National Income Accounts, 1971-1975 68
12. Mexico: Balance of Payments, 1970-1976 70
13. Mexico: Deviations from Trend, 1960-1975 73
14. Mexico's Private and Public Sector Imports, 1971-1975 86
15. CONASUPO's Farm Support Prices 91
16. Mexico: Domestic Cost Pressures Induced by World
    Inflation, 1970-1975 97
17. Economic Changes in Mexico and the United States,
    1970-1975 98
18. Mexico: Public Expenditure and Borrowing, 1972-1977 140
19. Mexico: Ex Ante Macroeconomic Forecast, 1975-1982 149
20. Mexico: Ex Ante Macroeconomic Forecast, 1983-1990 150
21. Mexico: Ex Post Macroeconomic Forecast, 1976-1982 151
22. Private Foreign Loans and Bond Issues 167
23. Sources of Foreign Capital, Non-OPEC LDCs 168
24. Eurocurrency Borrowing 169
25. Foreign Direct Investment Compared with GNP for
    Selected Countries 173

26. Mexico: Simple Keynesian Income Determination
    Model, 1960-1974 193
27. Mexico: Impact Matrix of Simple Keynesian Model 194
28. Mexico: Simple Monetary Model (1960-1975) 195
29. Impact Matrix for Simple Monetary Model 196
30. Mexico: Money Multiplier, 1955-1975 202
31. Mexico: Incremental Capital Output Ratio, 1955-1975 209
32. Mexico: Structural Equation Estimates, 1956-1975 211
33. Definitions and Identities 212
34. Mexico: Simulated and Actual National Income
    Accounts, 1957-1968 214
35. Mexico: Simulated and Actual National Income
    Accounts, 1970-1975 215
36. Mexico: Impact Matrix of Structural Equations 216

Preface

In the spring of 1976, I had the privilege of serving on a Stanford Research Institute team engaged in examining various facets of the Mexican economy. That study provided the opportunity to visit many government ministries and talk with some of Mexico's leading economists. These professional experiences stimulated me to undertake full-scale research on the growth potential of the Mexican economy, a subject in which I had long been interested and on which I had written from time to time, beginning with my book *Income Distribution Policies and Economic Growth in Semi-Industrialized Countries: A Comparative Study of Iran, Mexico, Brazil, and South Korea.*[1] The present volume might be regarded as the culmination of this endeavor.

The methodological approach here is partly descriptive and partly empirical—illustrative formal models are built on both qualitative and theoretical foundations. To sharpen the issue and put the Mexican economy in perspective, international comparisons are made throughout.

The book offers an analysis of what I consider to be the fundamental forces that govern the constraints on, and the speed and pattern of, Mexican economic growth, not only at present but in the decades ahead. I have found myself differing from other writers primarily on the nature of the obstacles to that growth, and therein lies the major justification of a book of this sort. I have freely entered Mexico's growth controversy here, indicating where and why I dissent from the views held by a number of Mexican economists and policymakers.[2]

In contrast to the many pessimistic statements coming out of Mexico concerning the economy's ability to regain the growth momentum built up in the 1960s,[3] the analysis developed here indicates that most of the favorable conditions associated with that growth are not, as commonly believed, self-limiting. In fact, the major conclusion of the study indicates that the major sources of Mexico's postwar expansion are indefinitely sustainable and that many of the adverse side effects associated with that growth are remediable.

In particular, the maintenance of relative price stability and equilibrium in the balance of payments is not only compatible with the economy's return to rapid and sustained development progress but is, in fact, an indispensable prerequisite for Mexico's continued economic advancement. At the same time, satisfactory progress toward fulfilling the legitimate aspirations of the Mexican people for higher living standards is equally essential to the preservation of monetary equilibrium. In broader perspective, economic development and monetary equilibrium in Mexico are shown to be very closely interrelated, and any attempt on the part of policymakers and economists to treat them as competing policy objectives is inevitably misleading.

Within this context, the Mexican economy of the 1970s affords a unique opportunity to observe and analyze a dualistic pattern of economic development. Its economic structure still retains many traits of a developing economy while rapidly acquiring the characteristics of a mature and affluent society. As such, the economy is instructive to both the underdeveloped and the advanced sectors of the world economy. Due emphasis is given to the underlying role of determinants of growth as well as to the functional role of measurable growth variables. Clearly, such a dynamic institutional-psychological complex as the Mexican economy calls for a comprehensive political economy approach within a rigorous technical structure. Accordingly, I have endeavored along the way to stimulate broader discussion by making a number of hypotheses and testing them for their empirical validity.

The book is directed primarily toward development officials, scholars, and businessmen outside Mexico. But I am hopeful that my Mexican friends will also find it informative. It is certainly immodest for an outsider to presume to tell Mexicans about themselves. Yet sometimes an outside observer who is familiar with, but not a regular participant in, the Mexican development effort is able to identify trends, forces, and implications that are not easily perceived by those who are continuously involved in the development process.

Acknowledgments

The individuals in Mexico who assisted me are so numerous that I cannot mention all of them. During my field work, a number of economists were kind enough to make time for me in their crowded schedules. In particular, Claudio Terrein, Pablo Aveleyra, Enrique de Bayle, Alejandro Medina Mora, and Manuel Zapada of Banco Nacional de México; Redvers Opie, economic chancellor to the American Chamber of Commerce; and Peter Schearer of the World Bank.

In the United States, Dr. Robert Davenport, Dr. Timothy Smith, and Peter Duncan of Stanford Research Institute all provided valuable insights and information on the Mexican economy.

I benefited immeasurably from the assistance, encouragement, and suggestions of many people, particularly Dean Charles Dirksen of the University of Santa Clara, but I should make clear that I assume full personal responsibility for the final results of this effort.

Finally, I must give special recognition to Christine Tapley, who used her profound editorial skills to provide highly professional assistance on my manuscript, and to my wife Anne, who processed the many versions of my draft manuscript with patience, efficiency, and good cheer.

Robert E. Looney
Monterey, California

1
Introduction

Economic and social policies in Mexico have for a long time raised considerable interest abroad—an interest quite out of proportion to the size of the country (in economic terms). This is largely because Mexico has a higher standard of living than many of its Latin American neighbors and because many trends and problems have occurred earlier there than in other Latin American countries, except possibly Venezuela. Of further interest is the fact that the economic and social policies in Mexico have been rather pragmatic and experimental. As a consequence, Mexico might be regarded as a laboratory for economic and social experiments which may be of interest for other countries as well.

Mexican public officials have provided much information about Mexico abroad, often in apologetic reports that have communicated intention and rhetoric rather than reality to foreign audiences.[1] Furthermore, foreign writers writing about the Mexican scene have relied primarily on official documents and statements, though some foreign books and articles have given fresh and interesting insights into particular aspects of Mexican society and, although not altogether uncolored, into Mexican economic policy.[2] As a result, those abroad often have a picture of Mexican economic and social policy that is much less interesting than is really the case.

In surveying Mexican economic policy, four phenomena in particular are analyzed: (1) the economic trends, especially developments in the economy after 1970; (2) the economic policy pursued; (3) the problems confronting this policy; and (4) some suggestions that have been discussed for solving these problems.

In examining a country, these relationships are usually dealt with in economic terms; the justification of abstracting economic analysis from political context is that this simplification of factors allows for greater rigor of analysis. Insofar as this enables economists to make better predictions of the outcome of economic policies, it can be justified; but as some recent writings on the Mexican economy have shown, analysis that eliminates situational or institutional factors often fails to provide predictions or instruments whereby the desired conditions can be achieved.[3] The juxtaposition of rigor and realism has been spurious. It is possible, however, to incorporate both political and institutional factors in the analysis of economic policy.[4] This is the methodology adopted in our examination of the Mexican economy, and for this reason, the study falls into the area of political economy.

Methodology

A review of the literature on the economic policy of Mexico reveals surprising facts and many inconsistencies. Mexican economic policy has not been examined systematically; at best it has been examined only partially, for the formulation of economic policy in Mexico is so closely tied to the goals of the 1910 revolution and to nationalism that it is not easy to separate them. Yet by going to the bottom of the policy choices made, one can see the various interests at play—both the ideological positions and the price that the community must pay for them.[5]

This kind of connection is illustrated in the case of the Mexican government's policy of "development with monetary stability" (*desarrollo estabilizador*) of the 1960s. Although the authorities were very successful in achieving high rates of growth, these same policies resulted in greater income inequalities, larger foreign indebtedness, and a strengthened veto power of the domestic financial community over national policy.

It is not our purpose to prove that economic growth with monetary stability in Mexico was a failure even though the government had touted it as a big success. Nor is it to admonish policymakers that they must solve all problems—planning and structural reform, monetary stability, and income redistribution—at the same time. Instead, our purpose is to unravel the indirect consequences of a given policy in order to understand how certain actions—in spite of their apparent success—have resulted in decreasing returns. It is hoped that analysis along these lines will serve to sensitize opinion to needed modifications in policymaking.

Nature of the Problem

By 1970 the Mexican economy seemed well on its way to becoming another of the postwar economic miracles. And the miracle seemed all the greater since this was a genuine example of development, rather than reconstruction, as was the case in Germany, Italy, and Japan.

The prospects for Mexican economic, social, and political development, however, have become much more uncertain than they seemed only several years ago. Even though at that time most observers with a sense of elementary prudence did not venture outright predictions, they were fairly confident that the country faced some clear-cut alternatives. In one direction lay the road to greater social justice, which would in turn lead to economic advance and a more stable and participatory political system. In the other, the road led to economic stagnation, political decay, and greater social inequalities.

Events since 1970 have shattered both the confident view of economic progress held by most Mexican policymakers in the 1960s and the pessimistic outlook of structural stagnation held by many in the first year (1971) of the Echeverría administration. Common to both views was the idea that without social progress (to be achieved through various reforms and redistribution of income and wealth), the country was condemned to economic stagnation. Although the policies of the Mexican government in the 1950s and 1960s were built on the premise that "all good things go together," the theory of structural stagnation attempted to prove that all bad things go together and was thus the mirror image of the former premise.

Both of these ideological positions could not but succumb to the blow they received from events in the early seventies. A glance at developments under President Luis Echeverría left no doubt about what should have been obvious: economic growth and social progress do not necessarily go hand in hand. In particular, it appeared to some observers in the early days of the Echeverría administration that Mexico was a faded success story.

To them, the apparent economic miracles of past decades of growth had thrust the country (in 1971) into a recession and created misery and destitution behind a veneer of industrialization and modernity. Or as one of the administration's spokesmen noted in 1972:

[The present regime] has resolved to modify the strategy of our

development in view of the evident bankruptcy of the growth structure
that shaped the country during the past three decades. . . . We would no
longer continue to travel the old beaten path that has led to
disproportionate concentration of income, growth in unemployment,
inflation, and dependency. We chose to change the course when all the
signs pointed to an imminent social crisis of serious proportions.[6]

By the end of 1976 and after Echeverría tilted policy toward increased
income and social equality, however, the economy appeared on the
verge of total collapse and was characterized by:

1. an accelerating inflationary spiral
2. slack demand for many key productive activities, which in turn
   resulted in disappointing overall production levels
3. rising national indebtedness
4. failure of the manufacturing industry to achieve substantial
   increases in exports despite the recovery of the U.S. economy
5. contraction of growth in private sector investment, which the
   federal government—in contrast to most of the postwar period—
   was unable to offset with its own spending programs
6. unprecedented purchases of foreign currencies by the saving and
   investing public, a development that along with the government's credit-restricting policies prevented banks from covering
   the credit needs of industry and the consuming public
7. a deteriorating income distribution, with as high as 45 percent of
   the labor force classified as unemployed or underemployed

Mexico's confidence, built gradually since 1940, had been eroded in six
short years. The culmination of these events was the precipitous decline
of the Mexican peso at the end of 1976 from 8 cents per dollar to 4 cents or
less in a matter of months, combined with a massive outflow of funds
from the country, which marked one of the most serious disorders in the
Mexican economy in decades. The dimensions of the capital outflow
will probably never be accurately measured, nor will the sources of the
many rumors that circulated in Mexico and abroad about peasant
invasions, attempted land redistribution by outgoing President
Echeverría, and the recriminations and counterrecriminations between
the president and representatives of business, finance, and agriculture.[7]

In examining the Mexican economy, this study attempts to ascertain
the degree to which the causes of the 1976 crisis were a result of the
underlying structure of the economy, the society, and the political

system that Mexico has uniquely developed over the half-century since the revolution. In doing so, we shall determine the likelihood that the underlying economic problems, of which the peso crisis was only a symptom, will continue into the López Portillo administration. Finally, we shall evaluate the extent to which these factors bear on the long-run growth potential of the economy through the 1980s.

Inevitably this will entail some consideration as to the various strategies open to Mexican policymakers and an evaluation of the strategy and associated policies that will be best suited for obtaining the government's economic and social goals.

Four Alternative Strategies

As Mexico approaches the 1980s, it is at a critical point in its history. It will undoubtedly follow one of four major approaches toward economic policy.[8]

Growth with Coercion

This strategy and its associated policies have as their major goal rapid rates of growth in the present and near future, with social policies relegated to a later time. At that time, presumably, the basic structure of the economy will have increased several times through high rates of savings and investment. This strategy implicitly involves a tight income policy on wages so as to maximize the return of capital, favors reinvestment in the private sector, and channels income to upper-income groups to encourage savings. The high level of income achieved through this strategy will, it is hoped, make it possible to improve income distribution without sacrificing growth.

Mexico's performance during the Díaz Ordaz administration (1964-1970) best exemplified the strategy of growth with coercion—as leaders of rural and urban guerrillas were pursued relentlessly by the military, opposing political factions of the far left were intimidated, often by hoodlums of the right (with police acquiesence), and student leaders were arrested and in extreme cases shot.

At the same time, the authorities allowed the income distribution to remain highly skewed. Little change took place in income distribution from the mid-1950s through the end of the 1970s, except for slight gains in the share of the poorest 10 percent of the population and slight declines in the share of the richest 10 percent.[9] Social policies were at best token measures; economic policy focused on growth first, distribution and associated fiscal reforms later.

Growth with Co-optation

The second alternative, though also growth-oriented, provides for some measure of social change. In this case, the government usually undertakes a variety of highly visible social projects to create an atmosphere of change. However, there is no significant alteration of its basic policy mix; it still favors concentration of wealth in the upper-income groups, maximization of private savings of these groups, and the encouraging of domestic and foreign investment to produce the commodities that the groups consume.

But the co-optation strategy differs from the first strategy, although the two are comparable and may even be combined in various ways. That is, part of the proceeds of growth are drawn through taxes and other contributions into a pool that the authorities use to buy off opposition whenever it is present. For those groups unwilling or unable to accept these payoffs, the policymakers must then resort to coercion.

The political implications of these first two strategies are that the previously existing power structure, both political and economic, is not unduly threatened and that major changes in decision making are not necessary. There is some evidence that during the first three years of the Echeverría administration, Mexico apparently pursued this second strategy.

This second strategy, as adopted in Mexico, tended to draw on nationalistic sentiment in an effort to oppose foreign business interests. Clearly, a number of contradictions developed, since one of the essential elements in the growth-oriented strategy was the reliance on foreign capital to supplement domestic investment.

The Echeverría regime became trapped in a number of inconsistencies: it made rhetorical speeches about social reform but never designed a set of comprehensive policies to regulate foreign investment. The result was speculation and uncertainty approaching hysteria in some private quarters, and a tendency toward capital flight, balance-of-payments problems, and a deceleration in both growth and social change. This strategy could not last very long without major instability and political-economic chaos; by late 1976, in fact, the country had already come to this stage.

Social Change toward a Different Growth Path

The third possible strategy would be a distinct break with past policies. Because of its potential mass markets, Mexico has an opportunity—unique among developing countries—to embark on a new strategy of development that will encompass the broad spectrum of the population. It includes fiscal reform in terms of both taxes and expenditures: increased revenues are to be used for expenditures on those activities that will increase the wages and wealth of the working class.

It would favor investments in those activities that draw on widespread diversification of ownership, that produce commodities that facilitate the direct investment of the lower-income groups in housing, small business, small-scale agriculture, education for productive employment—especially training in technical skills for agriculture and industry, rather than professional education of the elite. In addition, the financial sector could be utilized to attract savings from the working class to be invested in such enterprises; that is, high and subsidized interest rates for their savings could be offered, thus permitting market forces to be used as a basis for shifting the monetary assets over time from the rich toward the poor.

The López Portillo administration (1976-1982) is in a position to gain support for implementing this strategy by appealing to labor organizations, rural interest groups, and progressive members of the business community. Indeed, the premise of this approach is that the Mexican economy has a comparative advantage for growth, relative to the more developed regions of the world and relative to most developing countries.

For this strategy to be successfully implemented, monetary and fiscal policies must be used to assure significant returns to investment while requiring a high rate of taxation on noninvested profits, higher taxation of personal income at sharply progressive rates, and higher relative prices for consumer goods of upper-income groups vis-à-vis wage goods.

Several programs consistent with this strategy have already begun. The problem is that President López Portillo and the Partido Revolucionario Institucional (PRI) have not achieved a coalition of support for a viable integrated program, which should include a program of mutually supporting tax, expenditure, and regulatory policies essential to its implementation.[10]

President Echeverría was unable to initiate policies consistent with this strategy because of the lack of a progressive coalition of business, financial, labor, agricultural, and other interest groups. Also lacking was cooperation of such groups in the discussion and formulation of a viable set of policies at the regional and national level. As a result, the Echeverría administration was left with the worst of both worlds: the destabilizing rhetoric of change and the regressive programs and policies of the past.

Revolution and Radical Reform

The fourth option, which is espoused by many members of the

academic community, intellectuals, and the rural and urban poor, is a radical change in economic policies and socioeconomic institutions. This strategy would follow the Cuban pattern of development. Most observers discount the likelihood of such a radical change in the foreseeable future. Those who keep this philosophy alive in Mexico represent a variety of opinion groups. Some see it as a sophisticated technique of motivating reform through terror. Others wish a polarization of the political process and military dictatorship, hoping that this will ultimately bring about mass repudiation and armed revolution.[11]

Conclusions

The shock produced by the 1976 economic collapse could not fail to have its effect on Mexico's intellectual climate: one senses in Mexico today a new willingness—even in official circles—to explore, almost from the beginning, the interactions among the economy, society, and the state. The economic policies chosen in the near future will largely determine the strategy that will characterize Mexican development for some time to come.

Although a solution currently out of favor with academic economists and politicians in many countries of the Third World (including Mexico), this study points to controlled foreign private investment as one of the most effective methods of raising the general living standard of the country. This in turn requires the creation of a favorable investment climate, the removal as far as possible of noneconomic uncertainties, and the cultivation of a greater mutual trust between the public and private sectors. The need for greater harmony among various interests is a key element in the implementation of the third strategy of social change, and one whose merits are strongly emphasized throughout the study.

2
The 1940-1970 Period

Between 1940 and 1970 the Mexican economy expanded at an average annual rate of growth of 6 percent—equivalent to approximately 3 percent per capita. The most notable feature of Mexico's growth during this period was its general stability. The lowest rate of increase was 3.3 percent (in 1952) and the highest increase over 8 percent (in 1963 and 1964). Annual variations were, however, generally greater in the first half of the period than in the second; i.e., the standard deviation of GDP growth in constant prices was 3 percent in the years between 1940 and 1954 but only 2 percent between 1955 and 1970.

The growth of current price GDP was less consistent over time than was real growth. The rate of inflation in the first half of the period—1940 to 1954—was much faster than in the second half—1955-1970. In the former subperiod, the annual rate of inflation exceeded 10 percent; in the latter, the annual rate was less than 5 percent (Tables 1, 2).[1]

The 1940-1970 period encompasses the regimes of Manuel Ávila Camacho (1940-1946), Miguel Alemán (1946-1952), Adolfo Ruiz Cortines (1952-1958), Adolfo López Mateos (1958-1964), and Gustavo Díaz Ordaz (1964-1970). Compared to the administration of Lázaro Cárdenas (1934-1940), these presidents all represent a swing to the right, although Alemán and Díaz Ordaz are considered to have been more conservative than the others.

Economic policy, though conservative throughout the period, was not static; the government's orientation toward the economy underwent a number of subtle changes. This together with several exogenous factors, enables one to identify three distinct subperiods: (1) 1940-1945, the Mexican economic takeoff; (2) 1945-1955, industrialization drive; and (3) 1955-1970, the period of stabilizing development.

TABLE 1

MEXICO: NATIONAL INCOME ACCOUNTS, 1950-1970

(Current prices, billions of pesos)

	1950	1955	1960	1965	1970	Average Annual Rate of Growth 1950-1960	1960-1970	1950-1970	1965-1970
Gross National Product	43.96 (99.09)	87.8 (99.43)	149.4 (99.27)	249.8 (99.13)	411.6 (98.30)	13.11	10.67	11.88	10.50
Net Factor Income From Abroad	-0.4 (0.91)	-0.5 (0.56)	-1.1 (0.73)	-2.3 (0.91)	-7.1 (1.70)	10.65	20.50	15.5	25.29
Gross Domestic Product	44.0	88.3	150.5	252.0	418.7	13.09	10.77	11.92	10.69
Imports	6.1 (13.86)	13.9 (15.74)	19.3 (12.82)	26.0 (10.32)	42.4 (10.13)	12.21	8.19	10.18	10.28
Exports	6.2 (14.09)	14.7 (16.65)	17.0 (11.30)	24.4 (9.68)	34.0 (8.12)	10.61	7.18	8.88	6.86
Total Resources	44.0	87.4	152.8	253.6	427.1	13.26	10.83	12.04	10.99
Private Consumption	35.9 (81.59)	67.0 (75.88)	113.1 (75.25)	187.2 (74.29)	312.6 (74.66)	12.16	10.70	11.43	10.80
Government Consumption	2.1 (4.77)	4.5 (5.10)	9.5 (6.30)	17.7 (7.02)	32.6 (7.86)	16.29	13.12	14.70	12.99
Total Consumption	38.0 (86.36)	71.5 (80.97)	122.6 (81.46)	204.9 (81.31)	345.2 (82.45)	12.43	10.91	11.66	11.00
Savings	5.6 (12.73)	16.3 (18.46)	26.8 (17.81)	44.9 (17.82)	66.4 (15.86)	16.95	9.50	13.16	8.14
Private Investment	3.0 (6.82)	10.6 (12.01)	19.8 (13.16)	30.3 (12.02)	58.9 (14.07)	9.4	11.52	10.43	14.22
Government Investment	3.0 (6.82)	5.4 (6.12)	10.4 (7.30)	18.4 (5.52)	23.1	2.7	8.31	5.54	17.30
Total Investment	6.0 (13.13)	16.0 (18.12)	30.2 (20.07)	48.7 (19.33)	82.0 (19.58)	6.49	10.50	8.48	10.98
Domestic Resource Gap	-10.5 (23.86)	-6.5 (7.36)	-3.4 (2.25)	-3.8 (1.51)	-15.6 (3.73)	-10.66	16.46	2.00	32.64

Source: Banco de México, Informe Anual, various issues.

Note: ( ) = percentage of Gross Domestic Product.

TABLE 2

MEXICO: NATIONAL INCOME ACCOUNTS, 1950-1970

(Constant 1960 prices)

	1950	1955	1960	1965	1970	Average Annual Rate of Growth			
						1950-1960	1960-1970	1950-1970	1965-1970
Gross National Product	86.0 (98.96)	113.4 (99.47)	140.4 (99.27)	210.5 (99.15)	291.6 (98.31)	5.68	6.92	6.30	6.74
Net Factor Income From Abroad	-0.9 (1.04)	-0.7 (0.61)	-1.1 (0.73)	-1.9 (0.90)	-5.1 (1.72)	2.03	16.58	9.06	21.83
Gross Domestic Product	86.9	114.0	150.5	212.3	296.6	5.65	7.02	6.33	6.92
Imports	13.9 (16.00)	16.4 (14.39)	19.3 (12.82)	20.7 (9.75)	31.7 (10.69)	3.34	5.09	4.21	8.90
Exports	10.0 (11.51)	13.0 (11.40)	17.0 (11.30)	20.3 (9.64)	26.8 (9.04)	5.45	4.66	5.05	5.71
Total Resources	90.9	117.4	152.8	212.7	301.5	5.33	7.03	6.18	7.23
Private Consumption	70.5 (81.13)	89.0 (78.07)	113.1 (75.15)	157.2 (74.05)	217.6 (73.36)	4.84	6.76	5.80	6.72
Government Consumption	4.2 (4.83)	6.3 (5.53)	9.5 (6.31)	15.3 (7.21)	21.4 (7.22)	8.50	8.46	8.48	6.94
Total Consumption	74.7 (85.96)	95.3 (83.60)	122.6 (81.46)	172.5 (81.25)	239.0 (80.58)	5.08	6.90	5.99	6.74
Savings	11.3 (13.00)	18.1 (15.88)	21.8 (17.81)	38.0 (17.90)	52.6 (17.73)	9.02	6.98	7.99	6.72
Private Investment	8.1 (9.32)	14.6 (12.81)	19.8 (13.16)	25.0 (11.78)	44.8 (15.10)	9.35	8.51	8.93	12.37
Government Investment	8.0 (9.21)	7.5 (6.58)	10.4 (6.91)	15.2 (7.16)	17.6 (5.93)	2.66	5.40	4.02	2.98
Total Investment	16.1 (8.53)	22.1 (19.39)	30.2 (20.07)	40.2 (18.94)	62.4 (21.04)	6.49	7.53	7.01	9.91
Domestic Resource Gap	-4.8 (5.52)	-4.0 (3.51)	-3.4 (2.26)	-2.2 (1.04)	-9.8 (3.30)	-3.39	11.17	3.63	34.82

Source: Banco de México, Informe Anual, various issues.

Note: ( ) indicates percentage of gross domestic product.

1940-1945: The Mexican Economic Takeoff

The short period of five years between 1940-1945 marked the turning point in Mexico's development and its beginning as a self-sustained economy. The country's economic transformation was a product of the interplay of many elements laid down in the period following the revolution. During the 1940-1945 period, growth was largely the result of two main forces: one exogenous and the other domestic.

The exogenous force was World War II, which presented Mexico with unparalleled opportunities for further economic growth. The primary impulse toward expansion came from the increase in the country's exports after 1941, although this expansion was not uniform. The shortage of manufactured goods from the industrial countries opened markets for Mexican manufactured goods in Latin America; textile exports, for example, which had been virtually nil in 1939, reached $42.5 million in 1945.

Agricultural exports such as cotton, coffee, and tomatoes also increased in both volume and in price, but exports of minerals decreased. Fortunately for Mexico, this shift in the composition of exports actually increased the country's foreign exchange earnings, since the commodities in which the greatest increases occurred were produced by Mexican firms rather than by foreign firms.[2]

In addition to the sharp increase in the exports of goods, foreign receipts from tourist expenditures and from the remittances of Mexican workers employed in the United States increased significantly. These increases in foreign receipts on current account, plus the inflow of foreign capital, allowed Mexico to increase imports heavily without balance-of-payments problems. In fact, gold and foreign exchange reserves increased during this period.

After 1944, the inflow of capital goods increased rapidly. The index of the volume of capital goods imported was 118.3 in 1943, 191.2 in 1944, and 320.3 in 1945. (By 1947 the index had increased to 772.5 only to fall to 560.0 in 1949.)

The other new force (of a domestic character) was the organization of the national banking system. The purposes of the reorganization were twofold: to meet the increasing inflow of foreign capital in a manner that was stabilizing to the economy, and to divest funds into investments considered desirable by the authorities. In 1941 the first postrevolutionary public loan was negotiated; a series of loans followed, enabling industrialization to proceed rapidly. With regard to the channeling of savings, in 1941 the central bank was given discretionary control of private bank operations, and increased regulation of direct foreign investment began.[3]

In 1940, Nacional Financiera (the national investment bank and the country's official intermediary for foreign loans) started to channel and absorb resources from the country's capital market, at the same time giving control and guarantees to foreign lenders.

To summarize, the impetus to development from 1940 to 1945 came from the increase in the availability of imports, particularly capital goods. Higher levels of imports were coupled with a high level of domestic demand and the absence of exports of consumer goods from the market. The foreign market for Mexican manufactured goods, however, disappeared after the war with the reentry into these markets of goods from prewar suppliers; but this did not stop the industrialization process in Mexico. There was a slowing down in 1947 and 1953, but this was only temporary.

1945-1954: Period of Industrialization

After the war the country began to industrialize by taking advantage of:

1. the politically mature and independent status of the government, which made it possible for the public sector to reach a clear agreement with the private sector as to the areas reserved exclusively for private sector investment and those under the responsibility of the public sector;
2. the popular acceptance of the economic intervention by the government in areas not reserved for the private sector; this enabled the government to concentrate its funds on high-priority projects while channeling private investment into socially necessary activities;
3. a new group of entrepreneurs who after becoming accustomed to wartime profits were anxious to maintain the momentum built up in the 1940-1945 period;
4. the acceptance of many foreign investors of Mexico as a semiindustrialized country characterized by stability and dynamism—which enabled the government to attract foreign capital on the scale necessary to maintain a high and constant rate of economic growth.[4]

The economic growth of Mexico during the 1945-1955 period was due largely to the coordinated action of private entrepreneurs and the public sector. Top priority was given to industrialization, with the private sector obtaining a wide variety of incentives to invest in manufacturing and import replacement activities. The private sector responded by developing a wide array of consumption and capital goods. In general, these products were not competitive in international markets and were largely produced for the domestic market.[5]

The measures the government used to encourage industrialization were primarily (1) tariff protection; (2) licensing arrangements (which restricted competing imports); (3) government tax incentives and subsidies; (4) the establishment of public enterprises in key sectors; and (5) the provision of electric power, roads, communications systems, and fuel at subsidy prices.[6]

The public sector bore the "unproductive" side of industrialization, receiving only 10 percent of GNP for its 50 percent share in total investment. Its economic intervention was very selective and was restricted mostly to infrastructure (e.g., electricity, transportation, irrigation), the removal of impediments to growth, and strategic enterprises such as petroleum, steel mills, fertilizers, food crop storage, and heavy capital goods.

During the 1945-1954 period the Mexican government undertook this investment through deficit financing which occurred in the context of (1) a low tax ratio (9 percent of GDP), (2) a level of current public expenditure that could not easily be reduced (given the government's commitments to current expenditures in the social sector), and (3) substantial transfers from the federal government to the decentralized agencies, transfers that were primarily designed to allow them to maintain low prices of essential goods and services.[7]

The deficits were both large and difficult to finance abroad. During the war years, the constraint to foreign borrowing was essentially the dislocated world economy, in which international capital movements were severely limited. Thereafter, however, Mexico's status as an international borrower was weak for several years in the aftermath of the nationalization of the hydrocarbons sector in 1938; early improvement in the current balance of payments and the pattern of regular debt repayment established during the administrations of Ávila Camacho (1940-1946) and Alemán (1946-1952) could not compensate for this nationalization. Not until the mid-1950s did foreign credits become generally available.

During this period, the balance of payments was also in deficit, bearing the weight of the disparity between the imports necessary for industrial investments and the inelastic payment capacity of the country.

Deficit financing was severely inflationary. Between 1948 and 1954, the wholesale price level rose at 8.4 percent per annum. Meanwhile, the U.S. price level rose at 2.0 percent per annum. Since the two economies were so closely linked by both trade and financial flows, this widening gap between peso prices and dollar prices was reflected in pressures on the exchange rate. In short, internal imbalance resulting from fiscal policy deficits led to external imbalance and pressures on the exchange rate. The peso was devalued between 1948 and 1954 from 4.85 to 12.50 to the dollar (where it remained until August 31, 1976).

1954-1970: Period of Stabilizing Growth

Mexican real GNP per capita has grown with extraordinary consistency, suffering only three minor setbacks since 1940. But until 1955, inflation at an average rate of about 13 percent per year marred this achievement. The record is also punctuated by devaluations in 1948-1949 and 1954. Since 1955, however, prices have been relatively stable, and the rate of exchange has been maintained. By Latin American standards, this is a history of impressively stable growth. Because of the steady expansion during these years a number of commentators have referred to the period as one of "stabilization."[8]

This stabilizing strategy had as its basic premises an increase in capital accumulation and a reduction in dependency on foreign markets. Measures to increase employment were not directly implemented, since most officials believed the growth process itself would automatically absorb the expanding labor force and permit a gradual improvement in income distribution.

As it evolved over 1955-1970, the main elements of the government's development strategy were:[9]

1. the maintenance of a fixed exchange rate, through controlling domestic inflation at rates equal to or lower than Mexico's major trading partners
2. the maintenance of economic policies that were strongly conducive to the growth of private savings and investment
3. the sectoral allocation of public resources in a way that increased the profitability and hence stimulated the growth of the private sector

The achievements of the period were considerable.

1. Between 1950 and 1970 real gross national product increased at a rate of 6.5 percent per year. On a per capita basis, this translated into nearly 3 percent.

2. Both agriculture and industry, as well as the other branches of the economy, shared in this rapid advance. Agricultural production increased at a rate of 3.65 percent and manufacturing output at 8.36

percent (in current prices), and overall GDP increased by 6.58 percent. Among key sectors, steel production and electric energy expanded in an impressive manner. By 1970, Mexico had for the first time come close to self-sufficiency in many branches of light and medium industry.

3. Capital formation rose sharply, not only in absolute terms, but also in relation to the national product. The share of government capital formation increased and remained high.

4. Capital imports were substantial and increasing, and continued to be of decisive importance in the process of expansion. They are estimated to have aggregated about $10.6 million for the period, equal to about 46 percent of total imports. As to the balance of payments, the heavy increase in tourist income, mostly from the United States, was at least as important. The net foreign exchange earnings from tourism increased from $137.2 million in 1955 to $385.2 million in 1970.

5. The sharp expansion of output, reflecting partly an increase in the economically active population from about 8.3 million in 1950 to 12.9 million in 1970 and partly an increase of productivity per man at a rate of 2.5 percent a year, was accompanied by a relatively stable price level. This is in sharp contrast to the World War II period, during which the price level doubled. Since 1955 wholesale price rises averaged 2.89 percent a year to 1970. The increases were well behind the rise in the international price level until the late 1960s.

6. The dependence of the Mexican economy on foreign trade declined slightly between 1955 and 1970, the combined share of exports and imports to GNP falling from over one-fourth (26 percent) to about one-fifth, only half the proportion that prevailed around the turn of the century. Mexico was not as successful in reducing its dependence on capital good imports. Machinery and other capital goods remained predominant at about four-fifths of total imports.

7. Industrialization and urbanization made rapid strides. Industrial production as a share of national product increased from 21.13 percent in 1955 to 27.09 percent in 1970. Even more striking was the pace of urbanization: for example, cities of 10,000 inhabitants increased their share of the country's population from 31 to 42 percent between 1950 and 1970. Largely as a result of accelerated industrialization and urbanization, there was a relative decline in rural economic activity. The share of agriculture in total employment fell from nearly 50 percent in 1950— not much below the level at the turn of the century—to approximately 40 percent in 1970.

8. The differences between development in the urban and rural sectors were considerable, with income per capita remaining much

lower in the rural areas. In general, income grew more rapidly for those in the upper-income groups, and there was a general tendency for income to become more concentrated for the country as a whole.

9. During this period there also was marked improvement in the major indicators of social welfare. Life expectancy, which had increased slowly from 33 to 38 years between 1925 and 1940, increased to 61.9 years by 1970. The death rate was halved within two decades, falling to 8.6 percent in 1970 from 16.2 percent in 1950. The percentage of illiterates declined from 42 percent to 16 percent over the same period.

10. The rapid expansion in real output and the substantial increase in the price level were accompanied by a commensurate increase in the size of the financial superstructure. Quasimoney (as defined by the International Monetary Fund) increased from 2.13 percent of GDP in 1955 to 4.35 percent in 1970.

This period witnessed the further development, and to some degree the stabilization, of two important characteristics in modern Mexico. The first is the establishment of political control by one party—the PRI, the Institutional Party of the Revolution. This party, however, was flexible enough to avoid the building up of unmanageable pressure by periodic shifts of party control among right, left, and center groups; and popular enough to retain control of the country for over fifty years without resort to dictatorial measures and—an achievement particularly noticeable in Latin America—without giving the military substantial influence over civil affairs.

The second characteristic is the allocation of spheres of activity between the government and government-directed enterprises, on the one hand, and private business—Mexican and foreign—on the other. By 1970 the country had evolved a substantial and dynamic public sector—including the transportation system, the electric power and oil industries, and a considerable proportion of all financial institutions—and an equally dynamic and very profitable private sector which dominated manufacturing, trade, modern agriculture, and real estate activities.

In evolving this successful mixture, Mexico managed to maintain the image at home and abroad of a progressive and even semisocialist country. In actuality the government had managed to stimulate the capitalistic sector to invest through maintaining very low rates of effective direct taxation of incomes and profits. It tolerated monopolistic positions in business and in general created an environment very favorable to profitable private enterprise, particularly for foreign investment.

Negative Aspects of Government Strategy

By 1970 many negative results of the stabilizing strategy became
increasingly evident. These in turn required more severe assessment of
the principles, objectives, and policy guidelines followed by the
government after 1955.

The fact that the main indicators showed better results during this
period than in previous periods conceals several major problems that
sooner or later were bound to produce a crisis. The most prominent
difficulties associated with the strategy were the tendency to run deficits
in the balance of payments and the inability of the government to
balance the budget.

Balance-of-Payments Deficits

The 1955 balance of payments (goods and services) showed only a
slight deficit of 35.6 million dollars (Table 3). The 1960s were a period of
growing deficits, however. The 1960 deficit amounted to $US 174.0
million, or 2.6 percent of the gross domestic product, a figure that
declined gradually up to 1962. But beginning in 1963, the current
account deficit displayed an upward trend, with minor fluctuations,
accentuating sharply in 1969-1970 to $US 908.8 million, or approxi-
mately 3 percent of GDP.

The deterioration in the balance of payments resulted from the fact
that exports of goods and services (excluding payment to external
factors) lagged behind imports. During the 1960s, net payments to
external factors rose rapidly as a result of growing remittance of profits
on foreign investment and the payment of interest on external private
and public debts. The net payments to external factors came to about
$US 160 million at the start of the 1960s, or 1.3 percent of GDP,
increasing thereafter to more than $US 670 million or 2 percent of GDP
in 1970.

This rising external indebtedness in relation to the problem of the
balance-of-payments current deficit was reflected in an increase in the
rate of service on the public debt, particularly those loans with a
maturity exceeding one year. The debt-service ratio (ratio of interest and
amortization payments divided by exports) amounted to nearly 16.3
percent at the beginning of the decade and increased steadily to about
23.2 percent in 1970.

Public Sector Deficits

The other major macroeconomic problem that had developed by the
end of the 1960s was the extent of the public sector's deficits and

associated public sector debt. In large part, the deficit reflected the growing expansion of public investment as part of the state's increasing role as promoter of development and redistributor of income. In 1966, government net indebtedness amounted to nearly 2.6 percent of GDP; in contrast, by 1970 the ratio had increased to about 3 percent. This increasing dependence on deficit financing can be traced to the fact that current savings by the public sector grew more slowly than public investment levels. In 1966 public sector savings accounted for 3 percent of GDP. This percentage fluctuated steadily around that parameter, amounting to only 3.2 percent in 1970, which, combined with the more active expansion of gross fixed investment by the public sector in relation to GDP (from 4.1 percent in 1966 to 5.4 percent in 1970), generated the rise in net total indebtedness.

By 1970 the overall deficit of the public sector was beginning to restrict the level of public activity. In addition, it created additional pressure on the balance of payments (since an important component of public spending was financed with external loans and since these were becoming comparatively larger than the government's traditional source of domestic financing, the country's banking system). The high level of public debt, particularly from external sources, had great significance for the development strategy adopted by President Echeverría (1970-1976), since that strategy assigned a major role to the expansion of public investment.

Related Problems

Several related problems were associated with the government's strategy:

1. The government's industrialization policy failed to make full use of the economy's economic expansion capacity. This deficiency was due in part to insufficient and inadequate imports of production goods.
2. The government's policy centered on the sector competing with imports of production goods and almost entirely neglected the export sector.
3. The import substitution strategy aimed chiefly at producing finished consumer goods, though rarely capital and intermediate goods. This increased the need for an ever larger, inflexible flow of foreign purchases of materials and equipment to maintain and expand the industrial plant and led to almost complete neglect of technological research and development, making it impossible to create a scientific and technological infrastructure.

TABLE 3

MEXICO: BALANCE OF PAYMENTS, 1956-1970

(Million dollars)	1956	1957	1958	1959	1960	1961	1962	1963	1964
Balance of Bonds and Services	-35.6	-154.2	-181.6	-31.7	-174.0	-62.4	-93.7	-206.0	-406.5
Exports of Goods and Services	1420.4	1406.3	1361.1	1456.9	1520.3	1630.4	1586.8	1709.2	1836.2
Imports of Goods and Services	1456.0	1560.5	1542.7	1488.6	1694.3	1692.8	1680.5	1915.3	2242.7
Errors and Omissions	-113.9	-55.4	4.2	-66.5	-25.9	-247.1	-63.9	72.0	-138.5
Long-Term Capital	153.1	192.0	181.6	140.8	122.1	285.5	260.9	301.4	513.8
Short-Term Capital	56.9	-10.2	-91.2	9.2	69.3	2.5	-86.5	-57.7	62.7
Variation in Reserves	60.5	-27.8	-87.0	51.8	-8.6	-21.5	16.9	109.7	31.6

(Million dollars)

	1965	1966	1967	1968	1969	1970
Balance of Goods and Services	-375.7	-391.0	-506.3	-632.2	-472.7	-908.8
Exports of Goods and Services	1989.1	2159.2	2292.7	2506.3	2976.1	3147.7
Imports of Goods and Services	2364.8	2550.2	2799.0	3138.5	3448.8	4056.3
Errors and Omissions and Short-Term Capital	182.5	110.4	200.1	302.2	-172.2	505.5
Long-Term Capital	172.3	286.7	346.0	379.0	692.9	460.1
Variation in Revenues	-21.0	6.1	39.8	49.0	47.9	102.1

Source: Banco de Mexico, Informe Anual, various issues.

4. The government's development strategy favored the formation of a completely distorted market; i.e., an appendage of the productive consumer structure of the Western capitalist economy, particularly the United States, was superimposed upon the traditional Mexican economy.
5. Geographic concentration of economic activities was intensified.

Attractions of the Strategy

The great attraction of this strategy was industrialization, the consequences of which were neither planned nor foreseen. The approach was predicated on the premise that new job opportunities derived from industrialization would act to enlarge the small domestic market and offer investment incentives as well. Hence market expansion was regarded by government officials as an inevitable outcome of enlargement of the productive apparatus. But this, of course, is not a natural outcome. It is one thing to create markets for the nonessential requirements of a small part of the population with purchasing power, and another to expand the market for all types of goods. Critics of the government's strategy often claim that the government's policies were effective only in the creation of restricted markets for a limited number of goods.

It is still too soon to evaluate completely the government's policy. Statistics can be misleading and some results will be seen only in the long term. Government action in recent years has modified important areas in which the stabilizing strategy had concentrated its efforts. Although it is difficult to judge whether the government's policies were good or bad, it is possible at this point to gain some insight into their nature by examining the determinants of growth during the 1940-1970 period.

The Role of Investment in Mexico's Growth

Several of the more important factors responsible for Mexico's growth in the 1940-1970 period include: (1) high levels of investment and domestic savings (primarily private); (2) the availability of relatively inexpensive labor; (3) the importance of technology; and (4) the growth of domestic and, in some important cases, foreign demand.

Certain studies have been undertaken specifically for Mexico employing the Denison method.[10] These studies have attempted to estimate the contribution made to economic growth by increases in the supply and use of various types of productive factors. By this method, the

TABLE 4

MEXICO: SOURCES OF GROWTH

(percent)

	Period	GDP Growth Rate	Capital	Labor Force	Annual Contribution to Growth Rate			
					Maintenance of education component	Improvement of Education	Hectares of land cultivated	Remainder
M. Selowsky	1940-45	7.37	0.71	0.35	0.52	---	---	5.92
	1945-50	5.84	2.73	0.37	0.55	0.01	---	2.18
	1950-55	6.16	3.04	0.37	0.56	0.21	---	1.98
	1955-60	6.31	3.28	0.48	0.71	0.29	---	1.55
	1960-64	6.22	2.79	0.58	0.87	0.51	---	1.47
	1940-45	7.37	0.61	0.42	0.63	-0.16	---	5.97
	1945-50	5.84	2.41	0.45	0.67	0.01	---	2.30
	1950-55	6.16	2.60	0.46	0.69	0.25	---	2.16
	1955-60	6.31	2.71	0.59	0.89	0.36	---	1.76
	1960-64	6.22	2.31	0.71	1.06	0.63	---	1.51
C. Reynolds	1940-50	6.7	0.70	2.51	---	---	.18	3.3
	1950-60	6.1	1.37	2.17	---	---	.15	2.5
H. Bruton	1940-45	9.0	0.85	1.4	---	---	---	6.75
	1946-53	5.0	2.41	1.3	---	---	---	1.25
	1955-59	5.7	2.1	1.55	---	---	---	2.05
	1960-64	6.2	2.1	1.25	---	---	---	2.85
H. Correa	1950-62	6.0	2.8	1.4	---	0.5	---	1.30

Sources: M. Selowsky, Education and Economic Growth: Some International Comparisions (Chicago: unpublished Ph.D. dissertation, University Chicago, 1967); C. Reynolds, The Mexican Economy, Twentieth Century, Structure and Growth (New Haven: Yale University Press, 1970); Henry Bruton, "Productivity and Growth in Latin America," American Economic Review (December, 1967); and H. Correa, "Sources of Economic Growth in Latin America," Southern Economic Journal (July 1970).

amount of growth not accounted for by the direct inputs of capital and labor is a residual comprised of changes in technology and in efficient use of resources (Table 4).

The empirical work on the contribution of various factors to Mexican economic growth indicates that the postwar Mexican economic expansion was made possible largely through capital formation. These studies also indicate that there was plenty of room to expand and sustain growth through the continued increase in the availability and utilization of additional capital and labor or through increasing the profitability of such resources by reassigning them among the major sectors of the economy, particularly in the agricultural sector.

The high contribution of capital formation to growth tends to support the government's position that throughout the decade and a half from the mid-1950s, the growth of external public borrowing was wise. External resources were used primarily for the development of infrastructure and public sector industry; the yields of these projects were apparently generally adequate to cover the costs of debt financing or in any case enabled the country to sustain a high and constant rate of growth. External savings thus made a significant contribution to economic growth and to financing more public investment than could have been accomplished solely on the basis of public sector and domestic savings mobilized through the banking system.

The orientation of the country's monetary and fiscal policies toward raising the level of savings—both internal and external—and toward facilitating the noninflationary financing of the public sector deficit would also seem to be correct.

Both the means chosen to finance public investment (having a heavier fiscal burden in order not to have an adverse effect on private savings and investment) and the end (providing infrastructure and developing public utility industries) were thus associated with the growth of the private sector, from which the main thrust of GDP growth was derived.

Conclusions

A number of elements underlie Mexico's post-1940 development success, particularly the 1955-1970 period: (1) the local presence of a wide variety of national resources on which to build a development effort; (2) the imaginative and far-reaching role played by government through economic planning through the development policies and strategies it adopted and implemented, through its massive infrastructure investment, and through the establishment of state or public enterprises; (3) the vigorous response of both domestic and foreign private enterprise to development opportunites and incentives; and (4) external forces such as the rapidly growing United States market and the ability to attract large amounts of foreign loans and investment.[11]

One basic element that aided Mexico's development efforts was the emergence of a national consensus in the late 1930s and its development after World War II into a well-developed doctrine of growth, the essence of which was that Mexican government should take deliberate and affirmative action to promote development. In this respect, Mexico's experience paralleled that of a number of less developed countries.

When a national consensus for a development drive was formulated, the country already possessed a favorable mix of factors that could support that drive. Unlike many other countries that have been committed to some ideology, such as private capitalism, free enterprise, or socialism, Mexico has never for long placed itself in an ideological straitjacket. At certain times and in relation to specific events, such ideologies as nationalism, socialism, and communism have attracted popular support. Yet rigid adherence to ideology or doctrine has rarely hindered Mexico's development drive.

Pragmatism permitted the private sector's development drive to take place with little hindrance from the government. It also resulted in a nondoctrinaire approach to reliance on private versus government enterprise and encouraged periodic reexamination of and changes in economic planning approaches and strategies. Admittedly, pragmatism has resulted in substantial numbers of failures, but more importantly it has stimulated an impressive series of imaginative innovations in economic development.

The broad objectives of public investment policy after 1940, and particularly during the period of stabilizing growth, were to develop physical infrastructure (roads, railroads, telecommunications) and public utility industries concerned with the production of electricity, hydrocarbons and water, in order to provide the public sector (both domestic and foreign) with assured supplies of low-cost inputs. Social investment, although there was some expansion toward the end of the period, was generally less important than investment in infrastructure or industry, and only limited resources were allocated to rural development, education, housing, and other social programs; the resources of these sectors were, however, to some extent supplemented by selective credit controls and by the operation of trust funds established by the Bank of Mexico.

The government's economic strategy during the 1940-1970 period, though in large part successful, had several limitations. First, the public sector did not explicitly address the problems of Mexico's poor. The solution to these problems—as evidenced by the highly skewed income distribution in 1970—was becoming urgent. Second, although the government emphasized the development of industry through public investment, the expansion of certain sectors, particularly heavy industry (steel, petroleum, and electricity), lagged increasingly behind domestic demand.

By 1970 agricultural growth began to lag and the social sectors were also becoming a major constraint to the country's continued expansion. The economy was beginning to show signs of strain. The low level of public expenditure and taxation, which had presumably enabled the private sector to achieve relatively high rates of profits, was responsible for many of the bottlenecks impeding future growth. Public sector investment grew at an annual real rate of 4 percent during 1965-1970— a sharp contrast to the annual real rate of growth of 13.4 percent of private sector investment during the same period.

By the end of the 1960s, several other long-term issues were beginning to confront the Mexican monetary authorities. (1) Credit requirements appeared likely to increase at a faster rate, particularly if Mexico's overall development was to maintain and increase the momentum built up in the mid-1950s and throughout the 1960s. (2) The ability of the Mexican system to adjust to changes in international capital markets appeared limited, and therefore the inflow of foreign savings, vital to the country's growth, seemed to be becoming increasingly volatile. (3) There were certain risks of an unstable debt profile stemming from the practice followed successfully during the 1960s of financing long-term and fixed assets out of short-term savings instruments. (4) Mexico's low level of tax revenues and the resulting need for substantial amounts of government deficit financing through the banking system could be sustained without inflationary pressures only so long as banking liabilities were able to increase at a satisfactory rate—and this was by no means a certainty.

3
Increased Difficulties in Applying Monetary Policy

Some degree of governmental regulation of money and financial institutions has become generally accepted throughout the world. Furthermore, it is not uncommon for a government to make special provisions to try to provide credits, perhaps at a "low" rate of interest, for certain purposes. In Mexico, monetary policy has developed so that the government is now deeply involved in providing direct finance for a wide variety of structural, industrial, and commercial activities, in influencing the distribution of private banking funds to various sectors of the economy, in maintaining the solvency of the banking system and the individual banks, and in improving the financial markets.[1]

The principal aim of Mexico's monetary and credit policy through most of the postwar period has been to assist the country's overall development effort within the framework of a monetary and price stability and a productive allocation of credit supply. The public ownership and control of Mexico's key financial intermediaries affords the government considerable opportunity to influence the direction and content of economic behavior through monetary and exchange policy. Yet it should be noted at the outset that monetary policy in Mexico, as in most of the developing countries, is not as effective as it is in the West because of the limited scope of modernization in the economy, the absence of a well-developed capital market, and until quite recently the relatively small number of financial institutions.[2]

Monetary and credit policy in Mexico, especially since the mid-1950s and up to 1970, was based on the theory that monetary stability and economic development were complementary goals, not two independent policy objectives that could be pursued separately. The basic assumption underlying Mexican monetary policy was that monetary stability could not be maintained in the long run if the country's economy became stagnant. Similarly, the monetary authorities designed policy on the presumption that the high rates of economic growth achieved during the war and the immediate postwar period could not be maintained in an environment of monetary instability.

There has not been a consensus in Mexico as to the overall orientation of monetary policy. One of the most prominent Mexican economists during the 1950s, J. Noyola, argued very strongly that in the Mexican context monetary policy could be effective only when it reduced economic activity, increased unemployment, or retarded development; i.e., monetary policy could only counteract the economy—it was not a powerful enough tool to expand the level of economic activity.[3] Similarly, Noyola contended that fiscal policy and controls on prices and wages were infinitely preferable alternatives to monetary policy— again since monetary policy only began to be effective the moment it checked economic development. To Noyola and other structuralist writers, monetary policy should be passive and inflation not a cause of concern to policymakers.

Criticisms of monetary policy along the lines of Noyola, though interesting, are weak because they confuse the use of monetary policy as an anticyclical device to counter short-run income changes with the use of a conservative policy in a stable economic environment.[4] Under certain conditions it certainly is true, as Noyola argues, that a severe restriction of the rate of growth of the stock of nominal money balances by the central bank may lead to a sharp recession. But this in itself is not a valid argument against pursuing a conservative monetary policy over a long time period. As the experience of several countries has demonstrated, control of the rate of growth of the money stock in a manner that yields a rate of inflation of just a few percentage points per annum can be very conducive to high and sustained rates of economic growth.[5]

Clearly, any evaluation of Mexican monetary policy must be founded in fact. In this regard it is important to examine monetary policy's effectiveness in: (1) regulating or controlling aggregate demand—its role in short-run stabilization of the level of economic activity; and (2) controlling prices, the balance of payments, and economic growth over long periods of time.

Evolution of the Financial System

Mexico's financial system has developed its current structure relatively recently.[6] The Constitution of 1917 called for the establishment of a modern banking system to replace the structure that had been largely destroyed by the revolution. Not until 1925, however, was the central bank, the Bank of Mexico (Banco de México), established as a dependency of the Secretaría de Hacienda y Crédito Público (Treasury). The bank had little real power until the 1930s, when it finally asserted its authority and became the country's exclusive issuer of bank notes. Legislation in 1936 finally endowed it with its present broad powers. The second major institution is Nacional Financiera, the principal government bank. Founded in 1934, it functioned on a modest scale until 1940, then grew rapidly during World War II. Ever since, it has played a central role in financing Mexican industrial development. Surrounding these two institutions are some twenty public financial institutions—principally specialized development banks—and over 200 private financial institutions.[7]

In many ways the growth of the Mexican central bank was similar to that of the Federal Reserve System of the United States. Yet some significant differences exist. The Federal Reserve Act of 1913 was designed to establish the Federal Reserve System as an agency semi-independent from the government, but the Bank of Mexico was set up and remains an integral part of the federal government. Thus, the federal government and bank policies are considered synonymous for Mexico, and the central bank may be viewed as an essential arm of the federal government's overall policy objectives. In this regard it conducts policy in close consultation with other government agencies, but particularly the Hacienda and Nacional Financiera.

Institutional Basis of Monetary Policy

In general, Mexican monetary policy is determined by the director general of the Bank of Mexico and the secretary of the treasury. The former in turn is aided by the advice and counsel of the bank's Monetary Policy Commission. In addition, as with most central banks, there is close day-to-day cooperation with Treasury officials.[8]

The Monetary Policy Commission of the Bank of Mexico is charged with analyzing all data relative to the national and international economic situation, and upon the request of the director general of the bank, its members study monetary policy measures and evaluate the existing ones. After examining the work of the commission, the director general dictates appropriate measures and, if necessary, makes suggestions to the Treasury. Although the Organic Law of the Bank of Mexico gives the bank the power to issue certain rulings, the bank is not allowed to interpret the law when it is not clear.[9] Therefore, the bank occasionally asks the federal government, through the Treasury, for credit directives clarifying certain legislation and regulations in force.

These credit directives are then utilized by the bank in issuing regulations designed to enforce precise and formal compliance on the part of the commercial banks.[10]

The Bank of Mexico works in close cooperation with the Treasury in order to coordinate monetary policy with fiscal and debt management policy. Article 71 of the Organic Law of the Bank of Mexico gives the Treasury the power to veto the resolutions of the Bank of Mexico on important matters directly affecting the country, but since the Bank of Mexico and Treasury cooperation has always been very close, this veto power has rarely if ever been used.[11]

The complex and extensive set of controls that the Bank of Mexico imposes on the private financial system is generally justified on two grounds: to foster economic growth and to enhance public confidence in the financial system. The development of viable and resilient money and capital markets requires financial institutions that enjoy the confidence of the public. One means of cultivating confidence in financial institutions has been the government's unwritten law, clearly understood by investors, that there will be no bank failures.[12]

The partnership between the Bank of Mexico and the other government agencies was highly successful through the late 1950s and 1960s. By the late 1960s (and certainly the early 1970s), however, there were indications that this partnership was becoming strained. In part, the difficulties were caused by worldwide inflation and economic instability. More importantly, however, changing official attitudes outside the bank made the partnership less tenable. The institutions surrounding the bank and the financial system built up over the years seemed ill suited to meet the new demands placed on it by the authorities, particularly by the president of Mexico. The ability of policymakers to restore monetary policy to an effective force in economic growth will, in large part, determine whether the country will enter the 1980s with renewed hopes for attaining higher levels of real income.

Changes in the Orientation of Monetary Policy

Mexican monetary policy has not been static and in fact has been very adaptable to changing economic environments. Since the end of World War II, monetary policy—like the general pattern of economic development in Mexico—has gone through three distinct phases. The first phase, from 1945 to 1954, was characterized by inflation and an expansive monetary policy used to finance the nation's economic development. This phase saw rapid price increases force several devaluations of the peso. In general, the period was one of instability in national and sectoral growth.

The second period began with the 1954 devaluation. It encompassed the period of "stabilizing development" from 1955 to 1970. During this time, the authorities pursued what must be considered a conservative monetary policy, supportive of the government's goals of import replacement, rapid economic growth, and a stable exchange rate.

Since 1970 a third (final) phase has developed. It has been marked by increased government debt, financed by the central bank; expanded foreign borrowing; several devaluations of the peso; accelerated inflation; and a decrease in real economic growth. This final period suggests that the policies characterizing the period of stabilizing development were increasingly difficult to maintain. It also suggests that the cost of returning to a stable growth pattern under import replacement while maintaining present (post-1970) federal government fiscal policy may not be impossible but will certainly be difficult. Whether the pursuit of the highly successful monetary policies of the late 1950s and 1960s will be possible without a wholesale series of economic reforms is an issue that is dealt with in succeeding chapters.

The 1945-1954 Period

The peso, which had been devalued after the hydrocarbons sector was nationalized in 1938, was again devalued in 1948 (by 45 percent), largely due to balance-of-payments problems. Another devaluation occurred in 1954 in the context of a sharp increase in public expenditure and excessive debt financing by the Bank of Mexico. In general, the period was one of rapid inflation, which in turn discouraged domestic savings and made the attraction of foreign savings extremely difficult. The relatively low level of savings and its preemption for investment in land and foreign exchange speculation greatly circumscribed the government's ability to borrow from the private sector.[13]

Domestic investment, however, produced by official policy, continued to expand well in excess of the possibilities of voluntary domestic savings, and since access to foreign capital was rather limited, Mexico's economic expansion after the war was financed by inflationary means. The official monetary stance reflected the desire to maintain the flow of resources to the economy rather than considerations of price stability.[14]

In 1948 and 1949, the Bank of Mexico introduced a system of selective credit controls under which reserve requirements were selectively applied to commercial banks according to the different categories of borrowers, thus giving the authorities an additional means of channeling credit to key sectors of the economy. However, little was accomplished in restraining overgrowth of credit; central bank financing of the budget deficit expanded rapidly. These introductions of high-power money into the system allowed for a rapid expansion of bank credit to the private sector. Because monetary policy aimed at supplying credit for public spending and industrial expansion with little regard for stability, the money supply expanded rapidly.[15]

Whether or not there were options for deficit financing other than that of increasing the money supply, the latter course was clearly inflationary. Between 1940 and 1954, the stock of money increased by an average of 17.8 percent per annum, but from 1955 to 1970 it rose by a yearly average of only 12.2 percent. As in the case of the period after 1955, this trend and that of the price level were closely linked.

The 1955-1970 Period

In the years after the 1954 devaluation, the authorities introduced a new system of finance based upon price and exchange rate stability. In general, the rate of price increase was substantially reduced and the country was able to maintain a satisfactory rate of growth of output. Although the process of stabilization was continuous, the period of devaluation from 1955 to 1970 can conveniently be broken into two parts. The years 1955 to 1958 can best be understood as a transition period during which the basis of a system of noninflationary growth was established;[16] after 1958, development proceeded with the pattern of noninflationary growth already established.[17]

Goals of Monetary Policy

The aims of Mexican monetary policy as set forth in the Bank of Mexico's annual reports during this period were almost always stated in broad, general terms. The bank's major goals were: (1) to maintain internal monetary stability; (2) to channel credit primarily to industrial, agricultural, and livestock activities and secondarily to commerce; (3) to guard the liquidity and solvency of the banking system; and (4) to promote a sound development of the securities market. In the international field, the Bank of Mexico followed a policy of maintaining unlimited convertibility of the peso, an action that had a major influence on the bank's conduct of monetary policy.

The government felt that a stable rate of exchange must be maintained if it was to attract the savings (domestic as well as foreign) needed for development. Since foreign and domestic savings were relied upon to provide the required savings for financing private and public investment, dependence upon the central bank for deficit financing was reduced. Thus the Mexican government's strategy after 1955 was governed by a set of rules that were designed to maintain steady growth in public and private investment without excessive inflation, with increased capitalization, and with the maintenance of fixed exchange rates.

The need to preserve monetary stability as a necessary condition for growth was interpreted by the monetary authorities in a relative sense and within the limits set by the international monetary system, the movements in world prices, and the psychological reactions of the public. During the whole postwar period up to 1970, however, monetary stability was never the sole aim of the authorities—for the simple reason that they realized that any attempt on their part to maintain price stability at all costs would be futile; i.e., Mexico's price level to a large extent depends on the rates of inflation in its major trading partners, particularly the United States.

Within this general approach to policy, the monetary authorities sought to control excess demand arising from unwarranted increases in domestic expenditures—demand that very often resulted in mounting balance-of-payments deficits. On the other hand, the authorities made certain that efforts by private enterprise or the government to invest in fields conducive to the development of the country were not hindered by lack of funds.

The following rules, though not legislated, were followed by the government authorities during the 1955-1970 period: (1) the government would increase its deficit spending only at a rate that was equal to or just greater than the rate of real economic growth; (2) public investment would grow at a rate equal to or slightly greater than the rate of real growth; and (3) money supply expansion would take place at a rate only slightly greater than real economic growth.

These rules provided the framework for economic policy during the 1955-1970 period, allowing monetary policy to be used in financing government deficit without excessive money creation. The policies resulted in stable real growth with low levels of inflation approximating the world rate. Thus the economic development plan of the period required emphasis on a dynamic fiscal expenditure policy and a monetary policy complementary to the role of government in development.

Further, the rules could easily be followed, since the Treasury required low levels of domestic credit creation to service the government debt or to satisfy money demand. Maintenance of these three rules of monetary and fiscal policy was probably the most important factor contributing to economic growth without major resource misallocation and periodic economic distributions, which marked much of Latin

American economic activity during the period.

Policy Instruments

During the 1955-1970 period, Mexican monetary policy operated largely through the regulation of credit and the direction of bank resources to sectors considered by the authorities to be essential to the national interest. In the pursuit of its major goals, the Bank of Mexico and the financial authorities used various instruments of monetary policy, adapting them to the special conditions that marked the evolution of the Mexican financial market.

An attempt was made to fit such instruments both to the general factors that affect the long-run development of the Mexican economy and of the banking and financial system as well as to factors of a temporary nature. Similarly, these instruments were adapted to the particular traits of the economy.[18]

Monetary policy was conducted within a financial structure that dictated to a large extent the measures that could be used by the bank in achieving its major objectives. The major elements of the system included:

1. The important role played by government financial institutions. These institutions (excluding the Bank of Mexico, usually development banks), accounted for about one-third of the assets of all financial institutions by the late 1960s and occupied a crucial position in the long-term financing of the economy.
2. The dominant position occupied by a small number of financial groups, each centering on one of the large commercial banks, but also controlling the most important private development—savings and mortgage banks.
3. The great importance of liabilities of private and public financial institutions, particularly development banks—liabilities that were legally medium-term or long-term but that were in effect redeemable on demand and yielded high interest rates.
4. The relative unimportance of publicly offered and traded securities held outside financial institutions. Fixed interest-bearing securities outside financial institutions in the late 1960s amounted to only a little over one-half of the total outstanding and were equal to less than one-fifth of all claims against financial institutions held by the public. Most of these securities were issued by the central government or by government agencies.[19]

Since the major instrument of monetary policy is the money supply, the authorities, in controlling the volume of money, must control the monetary base. The principal ways in which the level of the base were affected during the period were: (1) the amount of rediscounting given to the private banks; (2) alteration of the commercial bank's reserve requirements; and (3) the quantity of credit extended by the central bank to the government and private sectors of the economy. Although these measures were used to alter the quantity of money, they also affected the composition of output—primarily by the central bank's varying the rate of inflation, changing the reserve requirements, and directing various financial institutions on the composition of their assets.[20]

The first method the central bank used to influence the monetary base was the amount of paper it rediscounted to the private banks. The discount rate of the Bank of Mexico was (and still is) the official rate at which the bank makes loans to banks. The rate for commercial and industrial paper remained unchanged at 4.5 percent throughout the period. From 1940 to 1952, the discount rate of agricultural paper was 3 percent and from 1952 to 1970, 4.5 percent. However, these rates were simply nominal, and in practice the bank can (and does) charge whatever rate it wishes for rediscounting. Similarly, it reserves to itself the right to discount and can vary the extent of its loan and rediscounts according to the dictates of policy.

The bank used rediscounting during this period to achieve two of its major goals. First, it provided subsidized credit to small and medium-sized farmers. Short-term loans made by deposit banks to finance such crops as maize, beans, wheat, and sorghum could be rediscounted at the central bank at a low rate of interest. The bank's policy therefore required the banks themselves to make the original loans at a rate substantially below the fair market rate. Second, the Bank of Mexico was prepared to rediscount paper and make short-term loans to deposit banks that had experienced an exceptionally heavy drain on their reserves due to such crises as crop failures or loss abroad of short-term capital. Here the bank's action was intended to reduce the frequency of bank failures and instill public confidence in banks, on the one hand, and on the other to smooth out sharp changes in the stock of high-powered money (and, in turn in the money supply itself).[21]

Reserve requirements were the main instrument of monetary policy throughout the entire period. All banks but the mortgage companies were (and are still) required to hold a minimum cash deposit with the central bank. The cash reserve requirement varies depending on whether it is a deposit, savings, or investment bank, whether it is domestic or foreign currency, whether it is on total liabilities or marginal liabilities, and whether or not the banks are within the Federal District.

The power of the Bank of Mexico to require 100 percent reserves for increments in deposit liabilities (both demand and time deposits of all private intermediaries) and to specify the financial claims that qualify as reserves enabled the Bank of Mexico to prevent multiple expansion of the money supply, which would ordinarily result from the open-market operations necessary for maintaining the liquidity of bonds.[22]

The reserve requirements system of the Bank of Mexico are complex, that is, the banks are directed by the central bank as to how much lending they can make to various private sector activities such as agriculture, exports, and housing and how much must be invested in official government securities at various rates of return. In addition, these reserve requirements vary on the margin; i.e., a new deposit in a financial institution may be subject to a different rate than are existing deposits.[23]

The final instrument used by the monetary authorities to control the money supply—the quantity of credit extended by the central bank to the government and private sectors of the economy—is closely related to the first two. As far as the sectoral allocations of credits granted by financial institutions are concerned, the central bank took action in order to regulate their use in accordance with the requirements; its means were selective credit control clauses or the specification of the distribution of the portfolio, favoring agriculture, industry, and the public sector. It thus exerted pressure for the extension of loans to these activities in volumes and under conditions that were not considered sufficiently attractive by commercial banks, but that were important from the standpoint of general economic development and stability.[24]

By means of this measure, the government attempted to make the supply of goods and services more flexible: (1) there was a reduction in the relative share of credit to the commercial sector and a more direct contact between banks and industrial firms; (2) banks were forced to use new techniques in lending in order to make loans to activities that, though profitable, had been neglected; (3) the commercial sector was not affected adversely, since its self-financing capacity was higher than that of other sectors; (4) finally, agricultural and industrial entrepreneurs were given access to credit that was equivalent to a reduction in their borrowing rates of interest.[25]

During this time, the monetary authorities found that the environment in which monetary policy was conducted largely precluded the use of the instruments traditionally employed by central banks in more developed countries. The weak and unorganized securities market, for example, reduced the efficiency of open market operations. Moreover, the rather irregular and high rates of interest in other countries made variations in the discount rate ineffective as a monetary tool. Mexico's central bank therefore applied its policy of credit control both quantitatively and qualitatively by means of many indirect measures, but basically by changes in the reserve requirements.[26]

Growth of the Financial System

Monetary policy was conducive to a very rapid rise in gross banking system liabilities (the public's savings). In fact, these liabilities were one of the most essential building blocks of the country's impressive performance during the 1955-1970 period.[27] Although the proportion of banking system liabilities to GDP had remained fairly constant in the lower 20 percent range between 1940 and 1957, it began to rise rapidly thereafter and by 1970 had reached almost 50 percent.

The increase in banking system liabilities also reflected the public's growing preference for peso savings rather than cash or foreign currency (clearly indicative of the confidence associated with a convertible foreign exchange system and strong economy). The 17 percent annual rise in gross banking system liabilities during the 1960s can also be attributed to the high profit rates in the advanced sectors of the economy, the public's gradually increasing willingness to deposit savings in banks, and substantial foreign inflows. Although it is difficult to estimate the role of foreign inflows on the basis of banking statistics, it is estimated that the inflows represented between one-sixth and one-fifth of the annual 17 percent average increase in banking system liabilities during this period.

Among the banking institutions, investment banks *(financieras)* have played a particularly important role in the mobilization of savings. Investment bank liabilities increased at an average annual rate of about 22 percent during the 1960s and by 1970 represented about 45 percent of total banking system liabilities. The growth of *financieras* was dynamic, because the monetary authorities allowed them to pay higher interest rates on their savings instruments than were permitted other financial institutions. In addition, their growth was aided by the fact that some of their liabilities—though of medium-term maturity—could be redeemed on sight at no loss to the investor. The combination of high yield and liquidity proved extremely attractive to savers both domestically and abroad.

Borrowing by the public sector averaged about 3.5 percent of GDP in the latter 1960s. About two-thirds of the borrowing was from internal and one-third from external sources. On what was still a thin financial base, this ratio of borrowing might have created stability problems. But in Mexico, because of the rapid growth of nonmonetary financial assets, the banking system was able to provide total financing averaging 6 percent of GDP per annum. This expansion in the monetary liabilities of the banking system was correlated with the growth of nominal national income.

Time and savings deposits, deposits in foreign currency, obligations *(pagares)* denominated in pesos and in foreign currency (U.S. dollars), and bank bonds rose from 3.4 billion pesos to 162.33 billion pesos in the period 1950-1971—a compound annual growth rate of 20.5 percent— largely as a result of innovations in the banking system. The relative shares in the savers' portfolio of banking liabilities of the classical savings forms—time and savings deposits—were fairly constant over the 1950s and 1960s, but those of bonds and obligations denominated in both pesos and foreign currency (U.S. dollars) increased by 220 percent.

This growth was mainly the result of the central bank's policy of permitting private finance companies *(financieras)* to pay interest rates higher than those existing in other financial centers. The liabilities (primarily bonds, one-year obligations, and peso-denominated 180-day to 360-day time deposits) of these institutions had de facto liquidity and could be redeemed on demand at par plus accrued interest.

At first glance, interest rates in Mexico during this period seem surprisingly high when one considers that the liquidity afforded most securities was high, that the rate of inflation was moderate, and that the financial system was becoming relatively large and diverse. Rates on government securities were generally below the prevailing market rate and were sold to and through the assistance of the Bank of Mexico and other national credit institutions. In the early 1960s, rates of 10 to 12 percent on short-term business loans were not uncommon. These rates were, however, not high enough to eliminate the excess demand of credit by private investors.[28]

The Use of Monetary Policy for Stabilization

The fundamental task of monetary and credit policy as it evolved in Mexico during the 1955-1970 period was to provide the greatest possible assistance to the government's development effort within the necessary environment of monetary equilibrium. In pursuing this general aim the monetary authorities were faced with two major problems. (1) They were often faced with conflicting trends in the level of activity in the various sectors of the economy and were consequently prevented from following a single corrective policy. Monetary and credit policy also had to be particularly flexible so that the authorities could evaluate the financial requirement according to the priority given each sector by the government. (2) To be effective in stabilizing the level of activity, monetary and credit policy had to exert an effective quantitative influence on income. Owing to the nature of the financial system, the traditional monetary instruments employed in advanced economies (e.g., open market operations, discount rate adjustment, viable reserve requirement) were inadequate.

Despite these difficulties, the monetary authorities were largely successful in their efforts to stabilize the overall level of economic activity.[29] The stability was in large measure a result of the offsetting movements in public expenditure and private autonomous expenditure. The burden of adjustment, however, was mainly carried by investment under the manipulation of the monetary authorities rather than by public expenditure. The level of private investment was controlled by the authorities by altering the level of reserves that private financial institutions were required to deposit in the central bank. This manipulation was based on the bank's "monitoring" of two key economic variables: the rate of growth of the money supply and the rate of change of foreign exchange reserves. Because of the structure of the economy, these two variables generally gave consistent, meaningful, and timely signals for policy change.

For the 1955-1970 period, public and private expenditures generally moved in offsetting ways. Because the movements were not only in contrary directions but also of comparable magnitude, "good luck" can probably be ruled out. Given the inflexibility of the fiscal system, it is unlikely the authorities could manipulate government taxes and expenditures in a manner precise enough to offset private sector expenditures.[30] If fiscal policy is ruled out as a factor contributing to the stability of the period, then the successful pursuit of monetary policy must have accounted in large part for the observed patterns of output and prices.

Clearly, inflation was not prevented exclusively by the judicious use of monetary policy. The responsiveness of agricultural output to the growth in overall demand must surely be attributed in large measure to public investments in irrigation and roads; the absence of uncontrollable cost-push inflationary pressure must be due in part to the manner in which union demands for higher wages were restrained by the government; export growth allowing for the augmentation of domestic supplies was due in part to public investment in active promotion of tourism and border industries.

Financing the Government Deficits

Given the growth of the financial system and the availability of funds within the financial community to satisfy the public debt, the central bank and the monetary authorities created a system of reserve requirements that would transfer funds from the private and semiprivate institutions. A critical element in this process was the stipulation that a percentage of the reserves held against deposits could be held in the form of government bonds. These bonds were low-interest-bearing and could be used instead of deposits at the central bank for reserves.

Bonds could be utilized for a percentage of the reserves on hand at the bank, the percentage to vary depending upon the type and date of deposit, type and location of institution, and whether the deposit was in pesos or in another currency (usually dollars). In essence, these bonds acted as a transfer of money from the private to the public sector. The transfer could be regulated by the central bank's utilizing the required reserve rates.

There are several important points related to this type of financing.[31] First, since deficit spending depended on transfers of funds from the private to the public sector through the banking system, the government became more and more dependent upon the private and semigovernmental banking system for funds. Second, if any policy of the government disturbed the amount of savings captured by the banking system, the system was less able to feed the investment portfolio of the government.

Third, if the rate of growth of the deficit was greater than the savings rate, private investment liquidity was less available. Fourth, and perhaps the most important aspect of this system, the Mexican reserve mechanism did not affect the monetary base and did not produce the traditional money multiplier associated with reserve requirements.

The effect of the high absolute level of reserve requirements imposed by the monetary authorities on commercial banks was to reduce the value of the money supply multiplier. The requirement that the banks hold not only cash but also interest-earning government debt, which could only be exchanged with the central bank, in effect made the banks hold a higher ratio of reserves to deposits than they otherwise would have held. This requirement had the same effect on the money supply as that of a high cash reserve requirement but with the central bank paying interest on a certain proportion of the reserves.[32]

As a result, changes in reserve requirements were not on the average particularly important throughout the whole period in leading to changes in the money supply.

The main function of reserve requirements and in particular their extensive and complex character, therefore, was to enable the government to alter the composition of output. By insisting that the banking system and other financial intermediates hold certain assets and make certain loans at interest rates below those prevailing in the market, the government was effectively subsidizing the activities of various sectors and taxing those of others. This is seen particularly in the extent to which the financial system was required to lend to the public sector. During this period, Mexico, despite a highly developed financial system, found itself in the position where the government was still unable to sell sufficient debt to finance its deficit. Reserve requirements as an instrument of policy were therefore substituted both for a relatively limited fiscal base and a relatively weak market in government debt.

Clearly, given the structure of the Mexican banking system, a dramatic rise in government spending that would call for greater than available savings would entail a decrease in private liquidity and investment. Or, if domestic credit were increased to supplement private liquidity, the result would cause pressure on the balance of payments through an outflow of short term capital. Any disruption in the Mexican financial structure, therefore, implies a loss in captured savings. The movement by one sector from equilibrium begins a cycle that is difficult to break. The major difficulty with the financial system was that toward the end of the 1960s, it was becoming less able to satisfy the goals of monetary policy—stability and growth with the government's need for larger and larger volumes of borrowed funds.

Conclusions

During the period 1955-1970, Mexico's development plan was consistent and well developed, and there was little doubt that because of government action, particularly its monetary policy, the country had achieved substantial economic growth. At the same time, it was relatively free from many of the monetary problems faced by most Latin American countries. Government planners implemented their development plan with tenacity. Monetary and fiscal policy were clearly complementary.

Whether one agrees or disagrees with Mexico's concentration on an import-replacement policy is not an issue for debate at this point. Mexico chose this policy, and it is clear that it was able to develop a series of monetary tools and use them in a manner consistent with the goals of import-replacement development. Given inadequate revenue levels, a policy for the capturing and utilizing of private resources had to be

formulated. The resulting monetary policy responded with noninflationary federal financing through expansion of the financial intermediaries.

During the 1955-1970 period, the government was able to maintain
and achieve its three goals for monetary policy. The first goal was to
maintain a stable exchange rate and a stable growth of national income.
The second goal was to finance government debt, not necessarily
through excessive increases in domestic credit but through transference
of funds from the financial intermediaries to the government by reserve
obligations to *financieras*, savings banks, mortgage banks, and
commercial banks. The third goal was to increase relative growth in
those sectors of the economy viewed as strategic to maximizing
economic growth. Admittedly, however, the liquidity that the banking
system provided to the government reduced the amount available to the
private sector for investment.

The most important feature of this period of development was the
strict adherence to general guidelines. As long as the stated goals of
development were met with consistent policy and as long as policies
could be generated that would carry out these long-run goals, the process
was sustainable. However, any breakdown of the rules or a disruption of
the plan itself would have been disruptive to the entire system. The
complementary nature of the policies and the development process
generated a system that was viable. As we shall see for the period after
1970, this was not the case.

By 1970 several long-term issues were beginning to confront the
Mexican monetary authorities and place a strain on the financial system.
(1) Credit requirements were beginning to increase at a fast rate, as
overall development maintained its high momentum. (2) The ability of
the Mexican financial system to adjust to the vagaries of international
capital markets was limited, making it difficult to regulate precisely
inflows of needed foreign capital. Moreover, and most importantly,
foreign savings inflows are potentially volatile. (3) There were certain
risks inherent for longer-run growth, stemming from the practice
followed successfully throughout the 1960s of financing fixed assets out
of savings instruments largely redeemable on sight. (4) The low level of
taxation and the resulting need for substantial amounts of deficit
financing through the banking system could only be sustained without
inflationary pressures so long as banking liabilities increased at a
sufficiently rapid rate. (5) Even if savings continued to increase at a
satisfactory rate—and this to a significant extent is related to point 2—
government reliance on banking credit was beginning to entail an
avoidable budgetary cost in the form of interest payments.

4
Increasing Fiscal Constraints
on Growth

In Mexico, one of the most outstanding social phenomena of the twentieth century has been the extension of the functions of the public sector. The government's expanded role has required it to obtain more revenues, particularly since it has broadened its economic role in providing investments in infrastructure and has extended its range of action in the production of goods and services which previously had been provided almost exclusively by the private sector. The government has grown largely through the creation of a network of decentralized agencies, state enterprises, and enterprises with state participation.

The public sector in Mexico is therefore composed of an extremely diverse set of institutions, which include the different levels of government: central (or federal), state, municipal, and also all those institutions that carry out specialized administrative functions (such as social security institutions) or that carry out publicly owned investments (which the government determines and classifies either as central or local).[1]

The public sector's growth is evidenced by the fact that government outlays increased from 4.1 percent of GDP in 1952 to more than 13 percent in 1970. Similarly, the public sector's share in gross domestic fixed capital investment increased from 35.9 percent in 1952 to slightly over 38 percent by 1970 (in 1975 government expenditure had reached 17.2 percent of GDP and 42 percent of total investment). In addition, the federal government's fiscal policy has been playing an increasing role in the country's economic growth.

Fiscal policy between 1940 and 1970 had four major objectives, varying in relative importance according to the president in office at the time:

1. to maintain the basic machinery of government and to procure such services as deemed desirable for the achievement of the country's basic socioeconomic objectives
2. to promote economic development, either by direct government action, such as the construction of highways, or indirectly through the combined effect of taxation and expenditures on the economic system
3. to improve social and cultural conditions, including not only specific purposes (such as education and public health) but also broad social objectives (such as a distribution of income) to ensure a balanced growth of the economy (these goals have been pursued through the government's tax and expenditure policy)
4. to stabilize the economy insofar as possible to offset fluctuations in general business activities and to maintain full employment

Difficulties in Applying Fiscal Policy

In carrying out its tax and expenditure plans, the government has had many problems. First, there is no general economic framework existing in the more advanced countries that can be conveniently utilized to study the precise impact that alternative fiscal policies may have on various segments of the economy. Second, the data that are readily available to the authorities are often not of the form that could provide a realistic picture of the problem at hand.

Lack of Overall Framework for Analysis

The Mexican economy can best be described as an economy in disequilibrium.[2] That is, the economy comprises a number of markets, some of which experience periods of excess demand while others simultaneously experience excess capacity. Because of these conditions, the neoclassical analysis developed for the more advanced economies, which relies on assumptions of relatively instantaneous adjustment of markets to marginal changes in the conditions of supply and demand, is difficult to apply.

Similarly, it is difficult to adopt Keynesian models of the economy based on the implicit assumption of underemployment in all markets. During most of the postwar period, a number of markets have experienced chronic excess demand (such as the market for investable funds, owing to the fixed interest rate policy of the central bank),[3] so that increases in public expenditure have not been able to alter their performance. In general, some markets have experienced changes in real output and employment, with expansionary fiscal policy, and others have simultaneously faced production shortages and the need for rationing in the short run if price increases were to be avoided. The disequilibrium that characterizes the Mexican economy, therefore, inhibits the use of fiscal policy along the lines perfected by the more advanced Western economies.[4]

Applicability of Data

The second major problem—the applicability of the available data[5]—includes:

1. Discrepancies between ex post and ex ante tax and expenditure policies. This is most clearly evidenced by the growing gap between planned and actual budget levels, making both quantitative and qualitative assessment of fiscal performance extremely difficult to determine.
2. Ambiguities in official figures of such vital statistics as growth and net investment, the functional and personal distribution of income, and foreign trade.[6] Reliable data are essential in determining both the incidence of income and the effects of taxation and government expenditure on various facets and groups in the economy.

Despite these difficulties, several useful insights can be gleaned from an examination of trends in taxes and expenditures. This will permit some tentative conclusions as to why the government had increasing difficulties in the late 1960s in pursuing its stabilization policies *and* in creating an environment conducive to long-range economic growth without inflation.

Role of the Government in Development

Until the postwar period, most of the economic activity in Mexico was generated by the private sector. Although the public sector was important in setting the strategy for development, by international standards it had very low levels of revenues and expenditures.[7] Mexico also suffered from insufficient fiscal administration and uncoordinated financial planning. The tax system had strong regressive features, and tax enforcement was inadequate. Furthermore, the low tax rates that resulted from this situation necessarily reduced the potential of fiscal policies and incentives and discouraged the efficient use of available economic and financial resources. Finally, the scarcity of financial resources and the constraints on administrative capacity resulted in inadequate levels of government investment in social and economic infrastructure and held back economic development severely.

In the mid-1950s, when the Mexican government elected to play a more active role in development, the situation began to change. At that time, government strategy called for substantial growth in public sector investment, an expansion and improvement of government services at all levels, a reorganization and revitalization of local governments to involve them actively in development efforts, and increased economic activity by publicly owned corporations, agencies, and enterprises.

In general, public finances were managed prudently during most of the period up to 1970, although they were relatively inflexible in adjusting to economic circumstances. At that time, too, a number of signs indicated that the long-standing weakness of the revenue system was impinging on the country's economic growth and that the government would have to take more direct action in this area. The country's glaring fiscal weaknesses resulted from a failure of revenues to grow automatically at a faster pace than did gross domestic product. They thus made recurring borrowing by the government—from both the domestic financial system and international lenders—necessary simply to maintain the public sector's already low share of national reserves.[8]

The dilemma facing policymakers in 1970 was somewhat similar to the one confronting the country in 1940, when the government had to choose between mobilizing resources through a major tax effort or through inflationary finance (mainly borrowing from the central bank). Throughout the war and up to the 1954 devaluation, they chose the latter.

Commentators have been at odds over the necessity and wisdom of inflationary fiscal policy during the 1940s and early 1950s. One group is critical of the government's action: it takes the position that although a number of developing countries are susceptible to inflation in times of rapid growth, growth and inflation need not coexist in Mexico. If the public sector had pursued a balanced budget policy by increasing the rate of taxation, therefore, capital mobility and profit rates in Mexico would have been even higher than obtained through inflationary finance. Inflationary financing of government expenditures, according to this line of argument, was dictated not by necessity but by unwise government policies that were in effect a tax on money holdings; it thus channeled savings from lower-income groups to investors indirectly rather than channeling savings from industry and commerce directly into public investment through a high effective rate of taxation.

This alternative interpretation of the proper conduct of fiscal policy assumes the existence of supply inelasticities in the domestic economy.[9] These rigidities in both industry and agriculture necessitate a high degree of protection and internal price rises so as to stimulate private investment. Those who stress the existence of rigidities in the economy argue that the wartime and postwar inflation were essential elements in permitting rising rates of return of capital in the private sector.

Underlying this argument is the assumption that higher tax rates could have been absorbed by the economy without substantially lowering the rate of private savings and investment. Most Mexican officials of the period were convinced, however, that sharp tax increases would have been disruptive and that private investment would have fallen off to such an extent that its decline would have offset any gains from increased government investment.

Although observers attracted to this line of reasoning do not condone inflation stemming from fiscal deficits, they contend that in the long run the investment would permit expanded production, which would eventually eliminate the excessive inflationary demand; i.e., inflation would be eliminated by the process of development itself. This prophecy was fulfilled in the following decade, but this was partly due to substantial increases in tourism revenues, which could not have been readily predicted in the late 1940s.[10]

Regardless of one's views on the workings of the economy, by 1970 Mexico found that its neglect of fiscal reforms was constraining all aspects of its development effort. The problem had become so great that a number of leading Mexican economists began to argue that the federal government, which had depended upon transfers of savings from the financial sector to pay for government expenditures, should no longer do so.[11] They contended that the cost to the economy as a whole and to the banking system in particular arising from this type of financing was becoming increasingly high and that the marshaling of resources through the tax policy was becoming of paramount importance if Mexico were to maintain its strategy of stabilizing growth.

Government Revenues and Expenditures

The Mexican system, like the revenue system of any other country, is the product of a slow process of growth and adaptation to the changing economic structure of the country. By the late 1960s, the public sector revenues came from two major sources. Taxes and fees comprised about 70-75 percent of the revenues, and "other incomes," largely revenues from the so-called decentralized agencies and enterprises with state participation, comprised the rest. The federal government collects the

TABLE 5

MEXICO: GOVERNMENT SUBSECTOR INCOME, 1940-1970

(million pesos)

	1940	%	1950	%	1960	%	1970	%	Average Annual Rate of Growth			
									1930-1940	1940-1950	1950-1960	1960-1970
Federal	577.0	71.4	3,640.8	79.4	19,457.6	78.6	33,868.2	74.6	7.17	20.23	18.25	5.70
State	115.5	14.3	487.9	10.6	2,172.8	8.8	5,544.2	12.2	6.28	15.50	16.11	9.82
Federal District	72.6	9.0	303.2	6.6	2,434.6	9.8	4,205.1	9.3	8.07	15.37	5.62	9.51
Municipal	43.0	5.3	151.7	3.3	702.6	2.8	1,780.8	3.9	2.56	13.44	16.57	9.75
Total	808.1	100.0	4,583.6	100.0	24,767.6	100.0	45,398.3	100.0	6.80	18.95	18.38	6.25

Source: Secretaría de Hacienda y Crédito Público and Dirección General de Estadística, Secretaría de Industria y Commercio.

major share of funds and municipalities the lowest share (Table 5).

In general, the government's total revenues have kept pace with the increase in gross domestic product, an increase that is more or less in line with similar developments in other countries and that is partially accounted for by the rise in population and national income and wealth during the same period.

But the tax revenues have not increased in line with expenditures; they have been traditionally below the taxable capacity of the country.[12] In this respect, in the late 1960s, Mexico ranked sixty-sixth of seventy-two countries in terms of the ratio of tax revenues to GNP—with 9.9 percent. In this regard it also ranked below most Latin American countries. Brazil's ratio was 21.4 percent, Uruguay 21.8 percent, Chile 20.9 percent, Argentina 20.1 percent, Peru 16.0 percent, and Colombia 10.9 percent. France ranked highest with a ratio of 37.7 percent.

However, Mexico's tax effort may not be quite as poor as international comparisons seem to indicate. Traditionally the government has subsidized a number of firms, particularly the public enterprises, by not taxing them. This process is somewhat different from that followed in a number of countries where firms often receive subsidies and are also taxed. To calculate the true extent of taxation, therefore, the government should estimate how much tax it would collect—at given tax rates— from these institutions.

The heavy reliance of the government on decentralized agencies and enterprises for its revenues has great significance for the Mexican economy. These companies were originated (or absorbed) by the government with the basic object of promoting economic development. That the public sector depends on them so heavily for revenues means that with very few exceptions (such as the National Railways System and CONASUPO), the prices charged for the goods and services produced and sold by these companies must be economically sound; i.e., they must cover costs and expansion. This is an extremely important point in understanding the Mexican economy, particularly the increasingly important role the government's decentralized agencies and majority-owned enterprises play within the overall economy.[13]

Patterns of Tax Revenues

Over the 1955-1970 period, total taxes received by the federal government increased from 6.156 million pesos to 29,900 million pesos; at the same time, the income tax increased its share in the total from 32.3 million pesos to 58.1 million (Table 6). The sales tax also increased in importance, and taxes on imports and exports declined somewhat.

During the same period, several reforms of the income tax were

TABLE 6

MEXICO: FEDERAL GOVERNMENT TAX REVENUES 1955-1970

(million pesos)

	Income Tax	%	Import Tax	%	Export Tax	%	Sales Tax	%	Natural Resources Exporta-tion Tax	%	Industry and Commerce Produc-tion Tax	%	Other Taxes	%	Total
1955	1,985	32.3	915	14.8	1,446	23.5	642	10.4	299	4.9	796	12.9	73	1.2	6,156
1956	2,565	36.8	998	14.3	1,253	17.9	727	10.5	222	3.2	934	13.5	267	3.8	6,966
1957	2,720	39.7	1,013	14.8	1,045	15.3	775	11.3	131	1.9	937	13.8	215	3.2	6,836
1958	2,758	35.2	1,313	16.7	1,023	13.2	879	11.2	134	1.7	979	12.6	739	9.4	7,825
1959	3,056	37.9	1,554	19.2	946	11.9	973	12.1	214	2.6	1,188	14.7	129	1.6	8,060
1960	3,628	38.8	1,753	18.7	923	9.9	1,102	11.8	261	2.8	1,314	14.2	355	3.8	9,345
1961	4,070	40.5	1,641	16.4	807	8.0	1,286	12.8	296	2.9	1,466	14.6	484	4.8	10,050
1962	4,727	42.3	1,688	15.1	863	7.7	1,449	13.0	244	2.2	1,802	16.2	391	3.5	11,163
1963	5,475	41.0	1,949	14.6	872	6.4	1,532	11.5	263	2.0	1,934	14.5	1,335	10.0	13,360
1964	7,262	46.0	2,411	15.1	880	5.6	1,860	11.7	271	1.7	2,211	13.8	1,024	6.5	15,919
1965	8,630	47.9	2,651	14.7	876	4.8	2,108	11.7	325	1.8	2,463	13.7	974	5.4	18,018
1966	8,625	45.3	2,412	12.8	783	4.2	2,389	12.7	340	1.8	2,533	13.4	1,753	9.3	18,835
1967	10,170	49.9	2,630	12.9	565	2.8	2,627	12.9	338	1.6	2,892	14.2	1,154	5.7	20,376
1968	11,700	50.9	2,600	11.3	600	2.6	3,300	14.4	330	1.4	3,400	14.8	1,070	4.7	23,000
1969	13,700	51.3	2,500	9.4	500	1.9	3,800	14.2	350	1.3	3,700	13.9	2,150	8.1	26,700
1970	15,500	58.1	3,100	10.4	400	1.3	4,300	14.4	390	1.3	4,300	14.4	1,910	6.4	29,900

Source: The Federal Public Finance Account; Secretaría de Hacienda y Crédito Público.

undertaken. For example, there were seven separate income tax schedules in 1960. The tax reform of December 1964 replaced the multiple schedules with two global categories for personal and corporate income. The main reasons for this major reform were undoubtedly to enhance the government's ability to increase its total revenue to reduce reliance on indirect taxes and to strengthen the potential value of the tax system as a tool to redistribute wealth.

In 1965 another important reform took place, this time with respect to business income tax. The schedular system was changed so that the income from all firms was taxed on a global basis and at a progressive rate, rising to a marginal rate of 45 percent. Before 1965 there were nine tax schedules and three complementary tax surcharges; but under the 1965 reform there were two groups of taxpayers—enterprises and persons. Personal income was in turn taxed at different rates, depending on whether it was derived from labor or from capital.

As to the respective contributions of the remaining taxes to government receipts, the outstanding development of the 1955-1970 period was the gradual and almost uninterrupted decline of the importance of import and export taxes as major sources of revenues. In 1955 the export tax was the second leading source of revenue behind the income tax. By 1970 it was only a minor tax, accounting for only 1.3 percent of federal government tax revenues. Import duties have shown a decline but not nearly as spectacular as that in the case of exports. The relative decline in import duties, however, is in line with developments in many other countries whether industrialized or not.

A reflection of the reasoning behind the diversification of the Mexican tax structure is the absolute and relative increase in receipts from the miscellaneous or "other" tax category. This group includes several internal consumption taxes, which have become more important in recent years.

Expenditures

Although the total expenditure of the federal government grew in relation to the gross domestic product, several other trends were equally noteworthy: (1) capital expenditure as a proportion of total outlay rose during most of the period; (2) expenditures on social projects (e.g., health, education) increased markedly over the years and by the late 1960s were nearly equal to expenditures on economic projects in the general budget (Table 7); (3) defense and security expenditures decreased sharply as a percentage of total expenditure; and (4) the share of interest payments in total expenditure rose somewhat, reflecting the government's decision to increase the level of its international and domestic borrowing.

TABLE 7

MEXICO: FEDERAL EXPENDITURES, 1940–1970

(percentages)

Year	President	Administrative	Military	Economic	Social	Debt
1941–1946	Ávila Camacho	10.7	16.6	39.2	16.5	17.0
1947–1952	Alemán	9.7	9.7	51.9	13.3	15.4
1953–1958	Ruiz Cortines	8.7	8.0	52.7	14.4	16.2
1959–1963	López Mateos	9.8	6.0	39.0	19.2	26.0
1964	López Mateos	9.7	5.4	39.4	21.1	24.4
1965	Díaz Ordaz	8.1	4.3	42.5	18.2	26.9
1966	Díaz Ordaz	10.1	5.3	40.7	22.4	21.5
1967	Díaz Ordaz	8.8	4.4	37.6	20.3	28.9
1968	Díaz Ordaz	11.3	5.0	40.4	21.6	21.7
1969	Díaz Ordaz	10.9	5.1	42.3	21.3	20.4
1970	Díaz Ordaz	12.0	4.6	40.1	22.0	21.3

Sources: James W. Wilkie, The Mexican Revolution: Federal Expenditure and Social Change Since 1910, 2nd ed., University of California Press, Los Angeles, 1970; Statistics and National Policy, University of California, Latin American Center, Los Angeles, 1974.

Savings and Investment

The trends in public sector expenditures and revenues combined to yield a distinctive pattern of savings and investment in the 1940-1970 period. During this period, total public sector investment exceeded public sector savings. The resulting deficit was financed in part with domestic resources and in part with funds borrowed abroad. There was a sharp difference between the first (1940-1954) and second (1955-1970) halves of the period, however, in that external financing became important only in the latter half.

Domestic private savings accounted for the largest part of total savings—an average of about 70 percent in years 1940-1970. Federal government savings amounted, on the average, to about 14 percent of total savings, and those of the decentralized public agencies to about 16 percent. The ratio of fixed investment to GDP rose from 9.5 percent in the early 1940s to 19.6 percent in 1970, having fluctuated downward in the late 1950s.

Several problems were becoming acute in the late 1960s. Although the federal government had increased its savings from 4.5 billion pesos in 1966 to 7.6 billion in 1970, the financing gap of the public sector as a whole rose to nearly 13 billion pesos over the 1968-1970 period. This deficit amounted to about 3 percent of GDP and over 40 percent of public investment. The public sector's high financing requirement was due in large part to the failure of the decentralized agencies to improve their savings performances markedly: their investment increased from 7.6 billion pesos to 11.6 billion from 1966 to 1970, but their savings only increased from 4.3 billion in 1966 to around 5 billion in 1969 and in 1970.

During the 1955-1970 period, government action to increase domestic and external private savings was based on the assumption that savings would be responsive to the real rate of interest. The nominal rate was left unchanged, and the level of inflation was a partial determinant of the real interest rate; but action was taken to reduce taxes on the yields of fixed-income securities up to a limit of 7 percent and to tax, at slightly progressive rates, up to 10 percent.

These conditions were designed to be attractive not only to domestic but also to foreign savers—although in the latter case an important additional aspect was the fact that the nominal rate of interest was considerably higher than that prevailing in other financial centers outside Mexico. Additional internal savings were thus captured by the public sector and channeled to productive investment through the development of the legal reserve requirements system of the Bank of

Mexico, the amounts obtained being related on the one hand to the desired level of public investment, and on the other to the estimated investment requirements of the private sector.

Through these financial innovations, almost 90 percent of the federal government deficit between 1955 and 1970 was financed by internal resources; i.e., voluntary savings of households were transferred to the government through the credit system. The success of the savings incentives was measured in the growth of banking system liabilities. The growth of fixed-income securities—the main instrument for tapping voluntary savings—was particularly strong.

Difficulties in Using Fiscal Policy for Stabilization

In recent years there has been increased interest in the possibility of compensating fluctuations in business conditions and national income by fiscal and monetary means. From the Mexican point of view, the prospects of success in this direction must be viewed with considerable reserve.[14] Most economists feel that a relatively small country, dependent largely upon foreign markets, can do little to protect itself against disturbances in the world economy. Nevertheless, the fact that the government's expenditures fluctuated considerably during the postwar period up to 1970 and that the overall pattern of economic growth during this period was very stable has led some observers to conclude that a stabilizing fiscal policy in Mexico is feasible and that it was pursued extremely successfully, especially in the late 1950s and early 1960s.[15]

The Presidential Cycle

The fact that public and private investments move in offsetting directions seems to indicate that investment was acting to stabilize the economy following an exogenous change (for whatever reason) in the level of private expenditure.

This pattern of government and private investment indicates the need for government expenditures to make up for the lack of private demand and also suggests that the political constraints under which the PRI operates prevents the government from having sufficient fiscal flexibility to permit adequate full-employment policies.

Clearly, the pattern of expenditures could also be explained where government expenditures fluctuated, and private demand could then be adjusted in the opposite direction to maintain a high level of aggregate demand. Government expenditures could fluctuate widely owing to: (1) the high degree of decentralization and lack of coordination among the government's operating ministries; (2) the tendency of planned budgets to underestimate revenues, permitting a high degree of discretion in actual expenditure policies; (3) the changing policy emphasis of each successive presidential administration; and (4) the related shift in the occupational structure of the government bureaucracy every six years resulting in a time lag between decisions on expenditures and their implementation—(the so-called presidential cycle).[16] If in fact the government was actively pursuing stabilization policies, these factors would clearly prevent the smooth implementation of fiscal policy.

Deficient Coordination of Expenditures

Until about 1967 there was no administrative machinery for systematically selecting or financing government investments, and the lack of a consolidated public sector budget meant that some major agencies were able to borrow without effective control by the Ministry of Finance. In 1967, however, the Ministry of the Presidency, working closely with the Ministry of Finance and the Bank of Mexico, began to organize and coordinate agency investment plans and established a Subcommittee for Public Investment Financing to screen and authorize all public investment expenditure. Not until after 1970, however, was complete centralized control over public expenditures achieved.[17]

The Tendency to Underestimate Revenues

The Mexican central government has never been very effective in estimating its income and expenditures. Between 1949 and 1969, it underestimated its income by an average of 55 percent each year. Only once since 1949 did estimates come close to actual collections (in 1953 the government collected only 9 percent more than was projected). The greatest deficiency in government estimates came in the early 1960s when planning was deficient by an average of 76 percent.[18]

Throughout the 1940-1970 period, there was a wide discrepancy between budgetary estimates and actual outlays. Most congressionally approved budgetary forecasts underestimated both revenues and expenditures and were subsequently revised upward at the discretion of the president. For example, in 1970 actual revenues and expenditures were over 109 billion pesos rather than the 72.2 billion pesos approved in the budget.

Deficiencies in the Tax System

Mexico's fiscal policy could undoubtedly have been utilized for stabilization purposes if its tax system had been a better generator of funds. In large part the authorities used the tax system as a means of providing incentives to investment rather than as a major source of revenues.

Fiscal incentives were generous and a source of much revenue loss. They were used primarily to aid the private sector's fixed investment and dated back to 1939, when Cárdenas enacted legislation favorable to private investment in order to allay fears resulting from the expropriation of foreign oil companies a year earlier. Changes were made in this legislation in 1941, 1946, 1955, 1962, and 1964. In general the focus of the legislation was that "new" and "necessary" industries were eligible for taxation relief. "New" industries were defined as industries that were not substitutes for goods already produced. "Necessary" industries were those producing commodities accounting for less than 80 percent of the total quantity bought by domestic consumers or producers. The extent of tax relief during this period varied with the classification of industry into basic, semibasic, and secondary.

One measure of an adequate fiscal policy is the ability of its tax structure to generate proportionately higher revenues both through discretionary action (changes in the tax rate and the tax base), legislative action, improved collection techniques and so forth, as well as through revenue growth that occurs over time in response to increased economic activity.

The record for Mexico during this period was not encouraging. The elasticity of revenue from the tax system was 1.0757 for the whole period, with even a slight decline to 1.0621 in the 1955-1970 period from 1.0762 in the 1940-1954 period (Table 8).[19]

The aggregate data were therefore disheartening to policymakers who believed it was essential to relieve pressure on the financial community through increased tax revenues.

On a more positive note, the traditionally income-elastic personal and corporate income tax receipts increased from 13.6 percent of Mexican tax revenues in 1940 to nearly 60 percent in 1970. This was certainly an indication of the efforts of the authorities to alter the tax base from primary reliance upon indirect sources such as imports and exports to the income tax. The increased weight of income taxes in the structure, however, was still not sufficient to increase significantly the tax elasticity for the system as a whole. In part the fiscal authorities could not offset the loss of import-export levies (a result of the country's import-substitution pattern of growth).

The only area of real improvement during this period was the sales tax, which contributed 7.8 percent of total taxes in 1940, increasing to 14.4 percent in 1970. The relative increase in sales taxes was reflective of

TABLE 8

MEXICO: TAX - GDP RESPONSIVENESS, 1940-1970

(millions of pesos)

	Constant Term			Elasticity			R^2			F Value of Regression		
	1940–1954	1955–1970	1940–1970	1940–1954	1955–1970	1940–1970	1940–1954	1955–1970	1940–1970	1940–1954	1955–1970	1940–1970
Income Tax	-3.81	-3.40	-3.48	1.44	1.35	1.37	0.96	0.99	0.99	311.7	1,472.3	2,861.5
Import Tax	-1.94	-0.79	-1.82	0.98	0.77	0.96	0.84	0.92	0.96	68.9	154.6	689.1
Export Tax	-3.62	6.26	-0.87	1.34	-0.63	0.72	0.79	0.86	0.62	48.8	86.1	49.1
Sales Tax	-3.51	-3.37	-3.17	1.29	1.24	1.20	0.91	0.99	0.98	129.8	2,124.3	1,387.9
Natural Resources Exploitation Tax	-1.55	0.00	-0.33	0.81	0.46	0.53	0.78	0.43	0.90	46.1	13.7	122.9
Industry and Commerce Production Tax	-0.90	-2.48	-1.53	0.76	1.08	0.90	0.91	0.98	0.98	124.6	776.9	1,297.6
Other Taxes	1.03	-6.71	-3.60	0.12	1.80	1.19	0.03	0.76	0.78	0.4	44.7	102.2
Total Tax Receipts	-1.58	-1.51	-1.58	1.08	1.06	1.08	0.90	0.99	0.98	115.6	1,206.7	1,455.1

Source: Computed by Author.

Mexican development strategy, since sales taxes are, of course, easier to collect than those on manufacturing and on income. The increased reliance upon sales taxes may be attributable to the inability of the fiscal authorities to marshal taxes through more income-elastic structures, such as personal and corporate income levies. Contrary to some observations, however, sales taxes in Mexico did not appear as inelastic as one might suspect. The measured rate of increase of the sales tax to GDP was 1.2050 for the period as a whole and 1.2859 and 1.2419 for the 1940-1954 and 1955-1970 periods, respectively.

These figures indicate that built-in exemptions for basic foodstuffs, clothing, and shelter tended to generate much higher revenue-income elasticity for sales taxes than one would expect a priori (at least for a more advanced country). Clearly, the authorities could not collect much tax revenue from small street vendors and traditional marketplace sales, which comprised a large proportion of both money and barter exchange in the country.

The revenue performance in Mexico was therefore poor, because the tax laws were used in large part as an inducement for increased investment (through both favorable income tax treatment and reduced tariffs for capital and intermediate materials imports), and because many low-income groups were impossible to monitor for tax purposes.

In summary, the revenue structure in Mexico was much less income-responsive than one would desire for a country at its 1970 stage of development. As larger shares of the national economy become dependent upon government infrastructure expenditures, and as the need for social goods and services expanded, Mexico was faced with a tax structure that was beginning to finance a decreasing percentage of federal outlays. The government's tendency to avoid this problem through increased borrowing had obvious limitations.

Under the tax system existing at the end of the 1960s, it was increasingly difficult for the government to raise the revenues required to meet the demand for social goods associated with the country's normal pattern of growth. As the development policy of the 1950s and 1960s had been important in creating this tax structure, it was difficult to expect changes in the fiscal revenue collection structure without some change in the country's development strategy.

Conclusions

During most of the 1940-1970 period, but particularly between 1955 and 1970, fiscal policy was used in Mexico primarily to foster private domestic and foreign investment. But its use in stabilization was rather limited, as was its use to achieve a more equal distribution of income.

During this period, the government obtained most of its additional revenues from wage income, indirect taxation (much of which was regressive), and domestic and foreign borrowing. The effect of fiscal policy was for the most part to subsidize capital income, stimulate private savings and investment, and limit consumption by taxing wage income and expenditures. The combined policies of fiscal conservatism and private sector funding of the government through transfers of financial savings (based on increased holdings of government debt by the banks and *financieras*) were a key element in the government's stabilizing development strategy.

The Mexican model received much favorable publicity as a self-corrective means of providing growth with diminishing inflation and without major tax reform. The result of Mexico's apparent economic success, however, was to delay policies that would have permitted the tax base to expand at a rate commensurate with the needs of the economy. Instead, the fiscal performance of the Mexican government lagged far behind that of most other countries at similar stages of development.

A number of problems had also built up, indicating that both internal and external balances were increasingly threatened by the policies of the 1955-1970 period. Internally, much-needed fiscal reforms were delayed, causing the share of government expenditure to remain among the lowest in the world. The fiscal deficit continued to exceed the share of government direct investment in GDP, which had to be financed by domestic and foreign borrowing.

5
Economic Growth, 1970-1973

During the fifteen years before 1970 (1955-1970), the Mexican economy had demonstrated its ability to combine a rate of economic growth of 6-7 percent per year with relative price stability. This impressive performance resulted in large part from a tradition of political stability, institutional continuity, and the government's growth-oriented economic policies backed up by high savings and investment rates. Thus a climate of confidence had developed over the years, both at home and abroad—all of which was reflected in a fully convertible and stable peso.

The economic strategy pursued by the Mexican government after 1955, however, had two major weaknesses. First, given rapid population growth at an annual rate rising to 3.4 percent in the 1960s, economic expansion did not generate sufficient new employment opportunities to absorb the new entrants into the labor force. By the end of the 1960s, about 40 percent of the labor force was either unemployed or (accounting for a much larger proportion) only marginally employed in relatively unproductive and hence poorly paid occupations, mainly but not exclusively in agriculture and in the informal urban sector. Moreover, the policies that produced rapid growth were not comparably successful in spreading its benefits. The incidence of poverty had certainly been much reduced from its earlier levels, but the differentials between rich and poor, and between regions, were apparently spreading.

Strategy of Development

When Luis Echeverría was inaugurated president of Mexico in December 1970, he pledged to maintain the vigorous pace of the country's economic development within a context of price stability. He also pledged to make his administration more responsive to the needs of lower-income groups. Among the nation's priorities he announced a full program of economic measures designed to stimulate rural and regional development.

Although stressing social reform, the goals of his administration were much the same as his predecessor's:[1]

1. continued high rates of noninflationary growth
2. creation of employment both to absorb new entrants and to reduce unemployment
3. decentralization of industry with more active rural and regional development
4. a more equitable distribution of income and the alleviation of poverty
5. increasing Mexicanization of ownership and control of economic activity
6. further improvement in domestic money and capital markets

From the start of his administration, it became clear that President Echeverría would be the most activist president in recent Mexican history. His programs can be compared with those of Franklin Roosevelt or Lázaro Cárdenas.[2] From the outset he sought to restructure the Mexican economy in a process of "shared development," which he hoped would redistribute income in favor of peasants and labor, expand employment opportunities, decentralize industry, improve the balance of payments, and reduce Mexico's dependence on foreign capital and technology.

In carrying out his strategy, Echeverria implicitly assumed, often with no sound empirical evidence, that there would inevitably be conflicts between stability objectives (tolerable levels of unemployment and inflation) and the developmental objectives of "structural change" (a redistribution of income, major changes in the structure of output and employment, a rising level of investment, and reduced external dependence). In each of his six years as president, Echeverria was plagued by what he considered to be the need to sacrifice the social objectives he felt should have top priority in order to achieve what many officials felt was an acceptable rate of economic growth.

Priorities of the Echeverría Administration

Echeverría had given an insight to this strategy in his campaign for the presidency when he had stressed the necessity òf structural change, which included:

1. developing the rural sector in order to provide jobs and to increase the purchasing power of the underprivileged;
2. undertaking educational reform in order to integrate the country's system of training more fully into its development effort, with the goal of providing graduates from all types of institutions with the skills and talents needed for the country's development effort;
3. designing policies to assure that vital national industries— petroleum, electricity, and steel—would remain in Mexican hands. He also gave his support to the existing policy of Mexicanization (majority Mexican ownership of companies). He saw foreign capital as fulfilling only a "complementary" role, and only when combined with national capital would it continue to be welcomed.

Soon after he assumed the presidency, Echeverría announced his plans in more specific terms: (1) greater controls would be placed on foreign capital to assure that it made the maximum contribution to the country's development; (2) serious attempts would be made to alleviate the very unequal distribution of income and wealth; (3) a genuine popular participation in national development by all groups would be promoted; (4) new exports would be developed; and (5) the government would try to achieve the highest rate of growth compatible with the four other goals (which had first priority). Clearly, the president's plans indicated a fundamental shift in Mexico's pattern of development. Echeverría's approach toward economic policy implied that the role of the government in the economy would have to be greatly expanded, even at the expense of the private sector if need be.

During his campaign, he frequently referred to the need for redistributing income, resources, and opportunities in favor of the poor. In his inaugural address, he spelled out the manner in which his new approach to the country's development differed from those of previous administrations:

We cannot exclusively entrust the solution of our problems to the equilibrium of our institutions and the increase of wealth. To encourage the conservative tendencies which have resulted from a long period of stability would be to deny the best heritage of the past.

Grave deficiencies and injustices exist which can endanger our conquests. The excessive concentration of income and the marginalization of sizable human groups threaten the harmonious continuity of development. . . . Although we have liquidated old structural inequalities, others have sprung up in recent years, but they are circumstantial and must be temporary.[3]

The feeling of many officials in the Echeverría administration was that for all its apparent success, the economic strategy of the 1950s and 1960s suffered from two inherent deficiencies. First, the public sector did not command enough financial resources to enable it to address the problems of Mexico's poor. These problems—judging from the apparent deterioration of income distribution from 1960 to 1970—were becoming urgent.

Second, although since the Cárdenas administration industrial strategy had emphasized the development of heavy industry through public investment, the latter proved inadequate to meet the domestic demand for basic industrial inputs—such as steel, petroleum, and electricity—which began to increase rapidly toward the end of the 1960s. The same observation applies to other sectors—including agriculture as well as the social sectors—which were not accorded an important place in the structure of public investment in the 1960s. The inadequate growth of the public sector is probably best illustrated by its investment, which grew at an annual real rate of 4 percent during 1965-1970 as compared with an annual real rate of growth of 13.4 percent for private sector investment during the same period.

Overview of Growth during the Echeverría Administration

For purposes of economic analysis, the Echeverría administration can be broken down into three periods: (1) 1971-1973, the period of austerity and inflationary growth; (2) 1974-1975, the period of international crisis and deterioration; and (3) 1976, the year of devaluation and collapse.

Gross Domestic Product

Under Echeverría's stewardship, Mexico's GDP grew from 419 billion pesos in 1970 to 988 billion pesos in 1975. Because of increasing inflation during this period, the latter figure is equivalent to 552 billion pesos at 1970 prices. This is an average annual growth rate of 5.7 percent in real output, quite satisfactory by world standards. But it is well below the 7 percent rate that had prevailed in Mexico during the preceding decade. It was only adequate—given the high population growth rate of 3.5 percent, as a result of which per capita output for the economy as a whole increased by only 2.2 percent per year.

Preliminary estimates for 1976 indicate that the real growth of GDP was scarcely 3 percent, and for the first time in decades, real product per capita income may have declined slightly. In 1976, however, it stood at about $820, still placing Mexico at the very upper reaches of the underdeveloped world.

To President Echeverría's credit, he kept Mexico's GDP expanding under very difficult circumstances. On the other hand, growth under his administration was, as measured by fluctuations from past trends, very uneven and even erratic (Tables 9, 10, and 11).

Government Expenditures and Inflation

Between 1971 and 1975, federal government expenditures grew from 41 billion pesos to 145 billion pesos. Revenues failed to keep pace, and the deficit rose from 4.8 billion pesos to 42 billion pesos. At the same time, the money supply increased from 53 billion pesos to 118 billion pesos at annual rates from 21 to 24 percent.

Inflation grew at rates of 5.6 percent for 1972 and 12.3 percent for 1973, accelerated to nearly 24 percent in 1974, and fell back to 16.5 percent in 1975. The deficit in the current account of the balance of payments rose sharply, from just over $900 million in 1972 to $4 billion in 1975. Preliminary data for 1976 indicate more of the same: inflation at 21 percent, the money supply increasing at 27 percent, and a federal deficit of 55-60 billion pesos.

Medium-term and long-term public borrowing and investment did accelerate after 1971, nearly tripling again between 1973 and 1975. By 1975, net public borrowing was almost 15 percent of total net capital inflow.

Taxes on business incomes were imposed cautiously for fear of adverse effects on investment, and generous exemptions were given for reinvested earnings. The "fiscal reforms" of the Echeverría administration consisted largely in tightening up business tax deductions, raising marginal tax rates on personal incomes in the highest brackets, imposing taxes on luxury consumption, raising real estate property taxes, and emphasizing improvements in the administration of budgeting and tax collection procedures. Tax officials admit that there was no basic reform.

TABLE 9

MEXICO: GROSS DOMESTIC PRODUCT BY SECTOR, 1960-1976

(Billions of 1960 pesos)

	1960	1970	1971	1972	1973	1974	1975	1976	Average Annual Rate of Growth			
									1960-1970	1970-1973	1973-1976	1960-1976
. Agriculture	24.0 (15.9)	34.5 (11.6)	35.2 (11.5)	35.4 (10.8)	36.1 (10.2)	37.2 (9.9)	37.7 (9.6)	36.9 (9.3)	3.70	1.52	0.73	2.72
. Mining	2.3 (1.5)	2.9 (1.0)	2.9 (0.9)	2.9 (0.9)	3.2 (0.9)	3.6 (1.0)	3.4 (0.9)	3.5 (0.9)	2.35	3.34	3.03	2.66
· Petroleum	5.1 (3.4)	12.7 (4.3)	13.1 (4.3)	14.3 (4.3)	14.7 (4.2)	16.8 (4.5)	18.7 (4.8)	20.3 (5.1)	9.55	5.00	11.36	9.02
· Manufacturing	28.9 (19.2)	67.0 (22.6)	67.9 (22.1)	75.5 (22.9)	82.2 (23.2)	86.9 (23.2)	90.3 (23.1)	91.9 (23.1)	8.77	7.05	3.79	7.50
. Construction	6.1 (4.1)	13.6 (4.6)	13.2 (4.3)	15.6 (4.7)	18.0 (5.1)	19.1 (5.1)	20.2 (5.2)	20.2 (5.1)	8.35	9.79	3.92	7.77
. Electricity, Gas, Water	1.5 (1.0)	5.4 (1.8)	5.8 (1.9)	6.3 (1.9)	7.0 (2.0)	7.6 (2.0)	8.1 (2.1)	8.7 (2.2)	13.67	9.04	7.52	11.61
·Transportation & Communication	5.0 (3.3)	9.4 (3.2)	10.1 (3.3)	11.1 (3.4)	12.4 (3.5)	13.9 (3.7)	15.0 (3.8)	16.0 (4.0)	6.52	9.67	8.87	7.54
· Trade	60.8 (40.4)	94.5 (32.9)	97.3 (31.7)	104.0 (31.6)	112.0 (31.6)	117.8 (31.4)	121.5 (31.1)	125.5 (31.5)	4.51	5.83	3.87	4.63
. Public Administration & Defense	7.4 (4.9)	17.1 (5.8)	18.6 (6.1)	21.1 (6.4)	23.5 (6.6)	25.4 (6.8)	28.2 (7.2)	30.6 (7.7)	8.74	11.18	9.20	9.28
Other Branches	9.4 (6.2)	39.4 (13.3)	40.8 (13.3)	42.9 (13.0)	45.0 (12.7)	46.7 (12.5)	47.8 (12.2)	45.1 (11.3)	15.44	4.44	0.07	10.30
Gross Domestic Product	150.5	296.6	306.8	329.1	354.1	375.0	390.9	398.7	7.02	6.08	2.06	6.28

Source: Banco de Mexico, Informe Anual, various issues; Indicadores Economicos, various issues.

Notes: ( ) indicates percentage of Gross Domestic Product.
1976 data are preliminary.

TABLE 10

MEXICO: NATIONAL INCOME ACCOUNTS, 1970-1975

(billions of 1960 pesos)

	1970	1971	1972	1973	1974	1975	Average Annual Rate of Growth 1970-1975	1970-1973	1973-1975
Gross National Product	291.6 (98.31)	301.4 (97.32)	323.9 (98.24)	347.0 (98.19)	367.6 (97.12)	383.7 (98.18)	5.64	5.97	5.15
Net Factor Income From Abroad	-5.1 (1.72)	-8.3 (2.68)	-5.8 (1.76)	-6.4 (1.81)	-6.8 (1.82)	-7.0 (1.79)	6.54	7.86	4.58
Gross Domestic Product	296.6	309.7	329.7	353.4	374.4	390.8	5.67	5.66	5.15
Imports	31.7 (10.69)	30.4 (9.82)	35.1 (10.65)	38.0 (10.75)	45.2 (12.07)	46.3 (11.85)	7.87	6.23	10.38
Exports	26.8 (9.04)	28.4 (9.17)	32.9 (9.98)	33.9 (9.59)	35.3 (9.43)	30.1 (7.70)	2.35	8.15	-5.77
Total Resources	301.5	311.6	331.9	357.5	384.3	405.6	6.11	5.84	6.52
Private Consumption	217.6 (73.36)	228.6 (73.81)	238.0 (72.19)	255.4 (72.27)	273.9 (73.16)	284.0 (72.67)	5.47	5.48	5.45
Government Consumption	21.4 (7.22)	23.1 (7.46)	25.5 (7.73)	27.4 (7.75)	30.9 (8.25)	37.3 (9.72)	11.75	8.59	16.68
Private Investment	44.8 (15.10)	42.4 (13.69)	44.7 (13.56)	45.3 (12.82)	50.0 (13.35)	49.8 (12.74)	2.14	0.37	4.85
Government Investment	17.6 (5.93)	17.5 (5.65)	22.7 (6.89)	29.4 (8.32)	29.6 (9.61)	35.9 (9.19)	15.32	18.65	10.50
Total Investment	62.4 (21.04)	59.9 (19.34)	67.4 (20.44)	74.7 (21.14)	79.6 (21.26)	85.7 (21.93)	6.55	6.18	7.11
Savings	52.6 (17.73)	49.7 (16.05)	59.4 (18.02)	64.2 (19.17)	62.8 (16.77)	62.4 (15.97)	3.48	5.86	-1.41
Domestic Resource Gap	-9.8 (3.30)	-10.2 (3.29)	-8.0 (2.43)	-10.5 (2.97)	-16.8 (4.49)	-23.2 (6.07)	18.91	2.33	48.96

Source: Banco de Mexico, Informe Anual, various issues.

Note: ( ) indicates percentage of Gross Domestic Product.

TABLE 11

MEXICO: NATIONAL INCOME ACCOUNTS, 1971-1975

(billions of pesos)

	1970	1971	1972	1973	1974	1975	Average Annual Rate of Growth 1970-1975	1970-1973	1973-1975
Gross National Product	411.6 (98.30)	444.4 (98.28)	504.6 (98.23)	605.5 (97.99)	798.3 (98.20)	954.7 (98.20)	18.33	13.73	25.57
Net Factor Income From Abroad	-7.1 (1.69)	-7.8 (1.73)	-9.1 (1.77)	-12.4 (2.01)	-14.6 (1.80)	-17.5 (1.80)	19.77	20.43	18.80
Gross Domestic Product	418.7	452.2	513.7	617.9	812.9	972.2	18.35	13.85	25.43
Imports	42.4 (10.13)	42.6 (9.42)	50.6 (9.77)	63.6 (10.18)	97.0 (11.93)	106.5 (10.95)	20.23	14.47	29.40
Exports	34.0 (8.12)	39.3 (8.84)	46.4 (8.96)	56.6 (9.06)	75.8 (9.33)	74.6 (7.67)	17.02	18.52	14.81
Total Resources	427.1		518.0	624.9	834.1	1,004.1	18.65	13.53	26.76
Private Consumption	312.6 (74.66)	345.4 (76.38)	380.9 (74.15)	453.9 (74.96)	602.0 (74.06)	717.9 (73.84)	18.09	13.24	25.76
Government Consumption	32.6 (7.79)	29.8 (6.59)	35.3 (6.87)	42.6 (6.89)	58.4 (7.18)	80.4 (8.27)	19.79	9.33	37.38
Total Consumption	345.2 (82.45)	375.2 (82.97)	416.2 (81.02)	496.5 (80.35)	660.4 (81.24)	798.3 (82.11)	18.25	12.88	26.80
Private Investment	58.9 (14.07)	58.1 (12.85)	67.0 (13.04)	78.1 (12.64)	108.9 (13.40)	119.4 (12.28)	15.18	9.86	23.65
Government Investment	23.1 (5.52)	24.1 (5.33)	34.2 (6.66)	50.8 (8.22)	64.8 (7.97)	86.4 (8.89)	30.19	30.04	30.41
Total Investment	82.0 (19.58)	82.2 (18.18)	101.2 (19.70)	128.9 (20.86)	173.7 (21.37)	205.8 (21.17)	20.21	16.27	26.36
Savings	66.4 (15.86)	69.2 (15.30)	88.4 (17.21)	109.0 (17.64)	137.9 (16.96)	156.4 (16.09)	18.69	17.96	19.79
Domestic Resource Gap	-15.6 (1.59)	-13.0 (2.88)	-12.8 (2.49)	-19.9 (3.29)	-35.8 (4.40)	-49.4 (5.08)	25.93	8.45	57.56

Source: Banco de Mexico, Informe Anual, various issues.

Note: ( ) indicates percentage of Gross Domestic Product.

Balance of Payments

Between 1971 and 1976, the current account deficit continued to worsen (Table 12). From the 1971 level of $726 million, it reached $3,769 million in 1975, with the trend continuing in 1976. For the period 1971-1975, the deficit increased at a compound annual rate of over 40 percent, owing primarily to a growing gap in the trade account between imports and exports.

Although both exports and imports grew, imports expanded at a much faster pace. During this period, exports increased by 19 percent annually, in large part reflecting the impressive growth of manufactures exported from the border assembly plants into the United States; but imports grew at 23 percent annually. The net effect of these trends in imports and exports was to cause the trade deficit to grow at 27 percent per annum.

Several external forces contributed to the balance-of-payments deterioration: (1) world inflation caused the prices of many of Mexico's major imports to increase, thus contributing to inflationary pressures; (2) the prices of several of Mexico's exports declined; and (3) increased costs of international borrowing further increased the deficit in the balance of payments of the current account; i.e., interest payments on the public external debt rose not so much because of Mexico's increasing indebtedness as because of less favorable terms upon which loans were secured. The net result of (1) and (2) was a deterioration of Mexico's terms of trade—from an average of 95.7 in 1966-1972 (1900=100) to an average of 89.7 in 1973-1975.

Mexico financed the growing deficit in the current account between 1971 and 1976 by attracting, as in the past, fairly large amounts of direct investment. Of increasing importance was a new source of finance—foreign commercial bank loans. Long-term capital inflows increased at 47 percent per year, with foreign loans to government growing from $286 million in 1971 to $3,054 million in 1975 (the same trend continuing through mid-1976).

Even the private sector was forced to rely quite heavily on foreign sources for its capital. Although data on the private sector's foreign borrowing are not as complete as those on the government's borrowing, those borrowings that were registered increased from $61 million in 1970 to $164 million in 1971 and to $424 million in 1975. Interest payments on foreign debt service grew rapidly. However, the accelerated growth of foreign lending to Mexico was so rapid that interest payments as a percent of net capital inflows actually declined during the period.

During the 1971-1976 period, short-term capital inflows (as reflected in the balance of "errors and omissions") followed a pattern much

TABLE 12

MEXICO: BALANCE OF PAYMENTS, 1970-1976

(Millions dollars)

	1970	1971	1972	1973	1974	1975	1976
Balance of Goods and Services	-908.8	-703.1	-761.5	-1175.4	-2558.1	-3768.9	-3023.7
Exports Goods and Services	3147.7	3192.9	3800.6	4828.4	6342.5	6303.0	6971.4
Imports Goods and Services	4056.3	3895.4	4562.1	6003.8	8900.6	10071.9	9995.1
Errors, Omissions and Short-Term Capital	505.5	194.3	233.3	-378.4	-135.8	-406.0	-2119.4
Long-Term Capital	460.1	669.1	753.6	1676.1	2730.8	4339.9	4889.9
Variation in Revenues	102.1	200.0	264.7	122.3	36.9	165.1	-333.1

Source: Banco de Mexico, Informe Anual, various issues.

different from that characterizing the 1960s. During the 1960s, Mexico was able to attract substantial net inflows of short-term capital. Much of these funds were invested in Mexico to take advantage of the country's relatively higher real rates of interest offered on its financial assets. The stable value of the peso also made Mexican securities very attractive to foreign investors. Beginning in 1970, however, several factors combined to cause a deceleration in short-term capital inflows. First, many foreigners (and Mexican nationals) began to look to other foreign (non-Mexican) securities and assets as world interest rates rose relative to those in Mexico. Second, Mexico's accelerating inflation reduced the nominal interest rate on Mexican *financiera* bonds and deposits. Finally, investors began to divest themselves of peso holdings as the likelihood of devaluation mounted.

These factors combined to cause the deficit in the balance of payments on current account to quadruple between 1970 and 1975. In particular, the short-term capital inflows as suggested in the errors and omissions figure of the balance of payments (Table 12) fell from an inflow of $505 million in 1970 to a net outflow of $136 million in 1974.

Patterns of Development

In 1970, the authorities certainly did not anticipate the adverse relationship among government expenditures, external borrowing, inflation, and balance-of-payments deficits. Mexico's new macropattern of growth unfolded gradually and became all too clear only after it was too late to alter.

In order to meet the targets of what the Echeverría administration considered distributive justice and at the same time expand the productive capacity of the economy, the public sector's expenditures had to increase. Unfortunately, neither the revenue base nor the administrative capacity of the public sector inherited by the new administration was adequate to meet these tasks. The wide range of new initiatives undertaken by the Echeverría administration after 1970 inevitably led to the increase in the real size of the public sector; total public current expenditures grew from 8 percent of GDP in 1966-1972 to 10.7 percent of GDP in 1973-1975, and public investment rose from an average of 6 percent of GDP in 1966-1972 to an average of 8.4 percent of GDP in 1973-1975. The magnitude of these changes, given the short time period during which they were effected, would have led to a number of temporary distortions and fluctuations in economic activity whenever they had occurred. However, the distortions were compounded by the fact that the growth of domestic resources, though relatively rapid, was still insufficient to meet quickly and steeply mounting claims on them. These claims, therefore, had increasingly to be met with borrowed resources.

In retrospect, it is clear that the resulting inflation, balance-of-payments deficits, and finally the devaluation of the peso were accepted by the government as the costs of moving toward meeting social and developmental objectives, through a more ample and more direct involvement of the public sector in the economy.

Growth under Echeverría, however, was very uneven as measured by fluctuations of past trends (Table 13). In general, the change in his administration's policies from that of his predecessors was not reflected to any great extent in the leading economic indicators for several years, owing largely to a certain amount of inertia—a holdover from the previous administration's actions.

In this regard, the level of expenditures during the first two years of his administration followed fairly closely the normal presidential cycle of expenditures that has existed in Mexico since the 1930s (noted in Chapter 4).[4]

In accord with this pattern, the previous administration of Díaz Ordaz had (1) already prepared the budget; (2) been reluctant to commit its successor to high levels of expenditures; (3) increased the level of expenditures in its last year in order to complete as many projects as possible within its term (thus straining the resources of the Treasury); and (4) wanted to give the new president a relatively free hand in forming his own economic policies.

Because of the presidential cycle, the last year of the Díaz Ordaz administration (1970) was one of high growth but also one in which inflationary pressures began to appear and balance-of-payments deficits increased.

Developments in 1971

The new administration which took office in December 1970 found itself therefore with the problem of whether to continue the economic growth of previous years, to assume the risk of continued government indebtedness and external disequilibrium, or to slow down the economy by restraining government expenditures even below the level usually associated with the first year of a presidential term. Clearly, the last action carried the danger of reducing external imbalance at the expense of a higher rate of underemployment, a rate that was already considered too high to be consistent with the new administration's policy of "shared development."

TABLE 13

MEXICO: DEVIATIONS FROM TREND, 1960-1975

(Billions of 1960 Pesos)

	GDP	Government Investment	Government Consumption	Total Gov't. Expenditure	Private Expenditure	Total Autonomous Expenditure
1960	0.3	-0.7	-0.5	-1.6	3.1	0.2
1961	-2.1	1.3	-0.2	1.0	0.1	-2.0
1962	-6.1	1.1	0.0	1.0	-0.7	-1.8
1963	-4.6	1.5	0.5	1.9	-2.3	-0.6
1964	3.8	3.4	1.0	4.2	-1.3	2.0
1965	3.4	-1.0	0.3	0.1	-0.2	6.8
1966	3.8	-2.3	0.3	-2.0	3.8	5.1
1967	2.9	-3.8	0.1	-3.8	3.5	1.9
1968	6.3	-0.3	0.5	1.0	0.8	0.0
1969	5.7	-0.2	-0.2	-0.5	3.0	5.3
1970	6.1	-3.4	-1.1	-4.6	6.8	5.6
1971	-0.3	-4.9	-1.3	-6.2	1.2	4.3
1972	-1.8	-1.1	-0.9	-2.1	0.1	3.9
1973	-0.7	4.0	-1.3	2.7	-3.3	-0.1
1974	-3.9	2.5	-0.2	2.4	-2.7	-4.1
1975	-13.2	7.1	3.6	10.7	-7.4	-13.6

Source: Compiled by author.
Note: Total autonomous expenditure consists of private investment plus exports minus imports.

Because President Echeverría opted for austerity, the pattern of economic activity under his administration began in a fashion similar to that of his predecessor, Díaz Ordaz.

The first year of Díaz Ordaz's regime (1965) also saw a sharp fall in the growth rate of the economy, with GDP at constant prices growing at only 5.3 percent compared with 10.2 percent in 1964. In large part, the fall in economic activity in 1971 was due to the presidential cycle; i.e., a new regime in Mexico spends its first year planning expenditures rather than disbursing them. Several special factors also caused the Echeverría government to reduce public expenditures below their usual pattern. The government also had to face unusually severe balance-of-payments and internal inflationary pressures. In addition, the president's style of government—in particular his insistence on public debate of major economic and political issues—was very different from that of his predecessor and resulted in excessive delays in finalizing public expenditures.

In 1971 President Echeverría committed himself to an economic policy of sustained growth and stability. As part of that policy, the government reduced external borrowing in order to correct a deteriorating balance-of-payments situation, and generally restricted its expenditures in order to maintain the stability of the peso. These factors combined with the private sector's reduction in investment—resulting from its uncertainty over the state of the economy and direction of economic policy—contributed to a decline in the rate of growth of expenditures and the money supply.

The results were dramatic. Inflation was controlled to about 5 percent, and the balance-of-payments deficit was reduced. But Mexico suffered a recession. Gross domestic product increased just 3.7 percent in real terms—a rate barely more than that of the population.

The actions of the government in 1971 are clear evidence of its willingness to sacrifice rapid growth in the short run (one year) in order to achieve larger objectives in a six-year administration; they do not indicate a commitment to stability at all costs. Moreover, the measures taken probably had a more drastic effect than was anticipated.[5]

In fact, no such drastic contraction had been expected from orthodox fiscal and monetary measures. The results of his first year in office were clearly a shock for the president. Stability had been achieved at a high and unintended social cost, which could scarcely be tolerated for long.

On the brighter side, 1971 was a period of consolidation, enabling the government to establish a new institutional basis in some key areas to improve the country's long-term development prospects. A new agrarian law was enacted in early 1971 with the intention of gradually transforming the *ejidos* into more independent and growth-oriented productive units. Government investment and subsidies to fisheries and forestry were expected to enhance significantly the output in these sectors. The government also set up several new institutions and introduced other legislative changes to promote exports.

A new banking law was enacted to strengthen the Bank of Mexico's influence on private banks and thus to improve the economic efficiency of the banking system. Finally, the new administration's tax measures were an important step toward putting the public sector on a sounder financial footing. Perhaps more important, the new administration devoted considerable effort to improving economic management, notably in public investment planning and external debt management.

The fiscal reform law approved by Congress in December 1971 aimed at reducing the inequalities in the existing system by taxing income accruing from capital rather than labor. At the same time, it attempted to encourage investment, savings, and production from export. The points that the government stressed were: (1) that the new tax laws (operative as from January 1, 1972) would not affect workers, farmers, and the middle class, but rather those who received rents or those who derived their income from investments or capital assets; (2) that the additional income the government was to receive from the taxes would be used in investments that would increase employment and income in rural areas and also reduce the country's foreign debt; and (3) that no spectacular short-term results should be expected but that the reform was rather a framework on which to build for the future development of Mexico.

The main aspects of the government's tax reform included the following:[6]

1. *Personal taxes.* A progressive rate of taxation was to be applied to all income over 300,000 pesos a year, with the maximum rate being increased from 35 to 42 percent. The latter was to be applied to annual incomes over 1.5 million pesos.

2. *Corporate taxes.* The reforms of these taxes aimed mainly at increasing export and investment incentives: tax rebates on income from exports would no longer be taken into account for purposes of final taxation; income received from exports of technical assistance, royalties, and commissions abroad were not liable to taxation either; maximum depreciation rates were increased in many industrial sectors and would include a 5 percent annual rate for workers' housing provision (under the 1970 Labor Law); and finally, fiscal exemptions would be authorized for capital profits obtained from the sale of fixed assets, as long as the receipts were invested within twelve months in areas the government defined as being of special aid in the country's economic development.

3. *Fixed-interest securities.* For tax purposes, fixed interest securities in Mexico have long held a great advantage over common stock, on which dividends had been taxed at a rate of 15 to 20 percent. Under the new system, taxes on income from fixed interest securities (except mortgage bonds) were to be increased by up to 200 percent in such a way as to bring taxation on these to about the same level as on dividends.

The 1971 fiscal package was discussed in detail with the private sector and was in keeping with the government's aims of encouraging exports and redistributing income to the poorest sections of the community and the less developed areas of the country (the very low income in these areas dictated that fiscal aid could only be given indirectly, since the poorest sections of the population were not taxed).

Developments in 1972

In all fairness to President Echeverría, his policies in 1971-1972 were greatly constrained by the economic situation inherited from his predecessor, a situation characterized by accelerated government investment and increased inflationary pressures. The 1971 episode was a traumatic experience for President Echeverría, and one that gave the remainder of his administration an inflationary bias. In 1972 the government rapidly increased its expenditures to promote recovery, with apparently little concern for the possible inflationary consequent impact of the expenditures.

Government officials were confident that the faster the rate of growth, the more likely that excess demand would pull up wages (presumably faster than profits) and thus increase the share of wages in GNP.

Expenditures by the federal government and the state expenditures under its control were increased 27 percent over their 1971 levels; with large increases for investments and subsidies, the money supply expanded by 20 percent. The policy worked well. Real gross domestic product grew by 7.3 percent, and inflation was held to 5.5 percent, an excellent performance by world standards. Mexico had momentarily recaptured growth with stability. But the objective was achieved at the cost of a rising balance-of-payments deficit, an increase in public foreign debt, and a sharp rise in the burden of debt service.

Despite the economic upturn in 1970, the private sector remained critical of Echeverría's economic policies. In particular, many firms complained of the scarcity and cost of local credit facilities in Mexico. Retailers' organizations argued that although they contributed about 32 percent of GDP and about 65 percent of federal income taxes, they received only 19 percent of local bank credits.

The shortage of local credit and its high cost compared with interest in the world's financial centers, coupled with the strength and convertibility of the peso, had traditionally led many Mexican companies to take up credits from foreign rather than local sources. Normally, creditworthy borrowers have had no major problem in renewing these credits as long as both they and the economy in general continue in good health. As an aftermath of the 1971 recession, many banks refused to extend credit, a move that contributed to a number of bankruptcies.

The government laid at least part of the blame for this situation on the less scrupulous of the many loan brokers and financial agents who operate in Mexico on a commission basis, and who often tend to give clients the impression that their foreign loans are more or less automatically renewable (which of course was not always true). Other government objections to the operations of these intermediaries were that they increased the real cost of credit to local borrowers, thus adding to the country's balance-of-payments difficulties.

Developments in 1973

In the spring of 1973 the economic outlook was good, and there were signs of a real rapprochement between government and business interests. But by the end of the year, inflation had become rampant, new investment had dropped off, and the internal political situation had become uneasy with the resignation of the minister of finance.

In the first months of 1973, prices began to rise much faster than at any time since the early 1950s. By December the annual rate of inflation (measured by the consumer price index) had risen to 21.4 percent, and the mean-to-mean increase was 12.1 percent as compared with a rate of growth of only 5 percent the year before.

In terms of output, economic performance in 1973 was superficially satisfactory with a real GDP growth of 7.6 percent—one of the highest ever recorded. However, there were signs that the economy had begun to move along a different trajectory, influenced by two phenomena that were unprecedented in the recent economic history of Mexico.

The first was the appearance of the negative interest rate differential between Mexican and international (Eurodollar market) interest rates. Together with the new increase in inflation, the result was the lowest level of financial savings in years (8 percent through December compared with an annual rate of 17 percent in 1972). The inflow of private short-term capital ($US 544 million in 1972) gave way to a net outflow (of $US 675 million), and private fixed capital investment stagnated.

The second was the profound economic and financial strains that appeared in the world economy. The dollar was devalued for the second time in fourteen months; floating exchange rates were adopted for major currencies; an energy crisis became acute; shortages appeared in foodstuffs and raw materials; high levels of industrial output generated excess demand; interest rates rose to unprecedented heights; massive speculative movements of short-term funds took place; and world prices accelerated at the highest rates in a quarter of a century.

World inflation and uncertainty intensified domestic economic and political tensions. The government granted an 18 percent increase in minimum wages and a 30 percent increase in the support prices of corn and beans in efforts to protect the income of at least some major groups. In a decision to eliminate future deficits of key government enterprises, prices were raised for electricity and petroleum products.

To defend the peso from the effects of a large outflow of short-term funds, the government raised interest rates and borrowed heavily, so that the central bank was actually able to increase its international reserves by $120 million during the year. The government also arranged a standby credit of $500 million with a consortium of private banks and renewed its standby credit lines with the United States Treasury and the Federal Reserve Bank of New York. Together with reserves, the credits brought the total foreign exchange at the disposition of the Mexican government to $2.7 billion at the end of 1973, an amount that was hoped would forestall fears of devaluation.

Expenditures by the federal government and its enterprises increased by 38 percent over their 1972 level, government borrowing grew rapidly, and public foreign debt increased by 40 percent. Despite an impressive increase of 25 percent in exports, imports expanded by more than one-third, and Mexico's current account deficit rose to a record high of $1.3 billion. The money supply expanded by 24 percent. Although real gross domestic product grew by 7.3 percent, inflation was rampant; wholesale prices increased by 25 percent and consumer prices by 22 percent.

The causes of the 1973 inflation were the result of increased costs and increased demand. On the cost side, everything was up: (1) imported raw materials cost more because of the rapid rise in world commodity prices; (2) domestic inputs cost more owing to the poor agricultural crops in 1972; (3) imported machinery and equipment cost more because they were largely bought either from countries experiencing high rates of inflation such as the United States and the United Kingdom or from strong currency countries such as West Germany and Japan; (4) labor cost more because of normal pay demands and the New Workers' Housing Fund Payroll tax of 5 percent; and (5) the tax on companies' gross turnover had been increased from 3 to 4 percent, which was passed on to the consumer. At the same time, prices were also being pulled up by record levels of consumer and industrial demand, with shortages and delivery delays appearing in many sectors of the economy.

The 1973 inflation hit Mexico at a delicate moment. The hard-won mutual understanding between the business sector and the left-wing government was badly jeopardized, with both sides blaming the other for an inflationary situation that clearly neither wanted, but that given the international situation was almost inevitable. The inflation set off confrontations between the government and leading spokesmen of the private sector, with mutual criticisms going beyond the immediate issue of inflation. Thus the heads of the Mexican Bankers' Association, the Mexico City Chamber of Commerce, and the National Manufacturing Chamber (three of the leading private sector spokesmen in the country) criticized the government for what they considered to be general incompetence in economic matters, no definite economic policies, not consulting them, and spending excessively. The government contended that businessmen were indifferent to social justice and the national interest.

Paradoxically, the widely proclaimed recovery of the Mexican economy in 1972—reflected in higher production levels, better sales, and increased government spending—did not really persuade the private sector that all was well again. Perhaps the main reason was that all through 1972 and into 1973, the government imposed a number of new taxes and restrictions.

More importantly, the government's incentives to industry were no longer intended solely to encourage its growth; they also forced part of a general program to achieve the express aims of equitable and balanced overall development. Many industrialists felt that the government was fundamentally altering the rules of the game under which they had operated all through the postwar period. In large part, the uncertainty created by the government's attitude toward the private sector was responsible for that sector's dismal investment levels.

The 1973 inflation exposed the weak parts of Echeverría's economic policies. For Mexico, continued rapid economic growth was vital, if only because continued rapid demographic growth is inevitable. However, the government could not resort to stern deflationary measures for fear of setting off another recession as in 1971. In addition, the government's leftist leanings committed it to follow through on a number of programs that alienated the private sector to such a degree that this sector for all practical purposes ceased to play a role in the country's development.

Echeverría's huge wage increase of 33 percent to urban workers in

1973 infuriated the powerful private sector of the economy. Mexican businessmen believed the president was constricting both their profits and the nation's economic growth.

In addition, the government passed two closely related laws—the Law on the Transfer of Technology and the Use and Exploitation of Patents and Trademarks, and the Law to Promote Mexican Investment and Regulate Foreign Investment—both of which the private sector and foreign investors considered blatantly antibusiness.

The new foreign investment law (or more strictly the bill to promote Mexican investment and regulate foreign investment) was of much concern to the foreign observers and investors in Mexico. It was approved by Congress on February 16, 1973, and went into effect later in the year. In large part, the law codified many of the regulations and practices that had been applied more or less pragmatically in recent years. The main provisions were:

1. A national commission of foreign investment was to be established. Composed of eight different ministers, it would be in charge of all aspects of authorizing and controlling foreign investment in Mexico. Seventeen different criteria were to be taken into account by the commission when considering applications by foreign investors, but the most important were that foreign investment should (a) be complementary to Mexican capital, (b) not displace local capital, and (c) help Mexico's balance of payments.

2. A national register of foreign investment was to be opened at the Ministry of Industry and Commerce, in which all foreign investors as well as Mexican companies and trusts with foreign shareholders would have to register full details of their investments. Registration must take place within 190 days of the coming into force of the law.

3. Bearer sheets held by foreigners in companies operating in Mexico must be converted into registered shares, within 180 days of the law's coming into force.

4. The prior authority of the commission was required for foreigners to acquire more than 25 percent of a Mexican company's capital or 49 percent of its fixed assets.

5. As a general rule, foreign investors are not to own more than 49 percent of any new company established in Mexico; however, the commission was empowered to allow higher percentages than this in special cases—e.g., for investments in certain geographic areas or types of activity.

6. Foreign participation in the management of Mexican companies should not exceed its share in the capital thereof.[7]

The long-term effects of the law were difficult to predict, but two immediate results were visible at the time of the signing. First, although the law was specifically not retroactive, it obviously worried, if not frightened, existing foreign investors with majority shares in Mexican companies. Second, it caused some prospective foreign investors to delay their entry into Mexico until they could see how the law was applied in practice (and new direct private investment in Mexico had already fallen in each of the previous two years).

Conclusions

President Echeverría's September 1, 1973 report to the nation marked the halfway point of his six-year term. Ideally, a Mexican president should, at this stage of his administration and following the normal presidential cycle, be able to look back on a first year of economic planning followed by a couple of years of solid preparation of a consistent economic program designed to meet its major objectives. The basic strategy should by now have been tested, leaving the way forward clear for its implementation. Overall growth should, perhaps, be steady rather than spectacular, leaving room for the crescendo of public expenditure to be expected in the fifth and sixth years of the administration. Above all, the economy should not go into its last years of high expenditure with the economy experiencing any serious inflationary pressures.

The Echeverría government's timing unfortunately went awry. Its first year in office, 1971, was one of economic recession rather than mere retrenchment, and it left memories not yet erased by 1972's satisfactory recovery. By 1973 events were getting somewhat out of control. The economy suddenly became overheated with a growth rate around 8 percent and shortages of raw materials and production capacity appearing in many sectors. The foreign trade deficit widened, and Mexico's traditional price stability disappeared.

In Echeverría's defense, many of the problems that developed in the end of 1973 were due more to bad luck than to bad judgment. Inflation in 1973, for instance, could hardly have been avoided any more than the series of natural disasters—first drought, then flooding, then earth-quakes—that hit Mexico all through 1973.

On the other hand, the administration had to take major responsibility for the country's other major economic problem, the decline in private investment. Although some private investment was obviously discouraged by the fact that the current world boom was reaching its end, with a slowdown likely in the U.S. economy, government action (and inaction) were certainly responsible for the private sector's general malaise. The government sanctioned wage increases much higher than productivity at the end of 1973. There was a good chance that a forty-hour working week (compared with the present norm of forty-two to forty-six hours) would be introduced into many sectors of industry. At the same time, the government was working on a formula and plan for the obligatory share of company profits that must be distributed among employees; the formula in force since 1963 normally meant sharing around 10-15 percent of profits. It was clear in 1973 that the new levels were certain to be higher. There was also talk of a new scheme of automatic wage increases linked to cost-of-living increases. Finally, foreign investors and profiteers of technology in Mexico were still awaiting the impact of the recent legislation regarding their operations.

6
The 1974-1975 Disequilibrium

What was not clear at the end of 1973, but what became clear later, was that an interplay had begun among three sets of forces, an interplay that would continue to have adverse effects on the economy through the remaining years of the Echeverría administration.

1. The first was a firm intention on the part of the authorities to increase public expenditures in response to what they regarded as social and economic imperatives.

2. The second was the private sector's evident disinclination to continue investing as much as in the past. In part, the private sector's attitude was attributable to economic causes—inflation was emerging, and the balance-of-payments situation after two years of relative improvement was becoming as precarious as in 1970. But psychosociological causes might have been equally important. After many years of privileges, the private sector found itself in a position of apparent, if not real, insecurity, facing a quickly growing public sector and mindful of the clearly less sympathetic attitude of the government toward its interests.

3. The third important change was that in the autumn of 1973 the world economy experienced the first of a series of shocks that were to disturb it in the next two years in a way it had not seen since the 1930s. Developments in the world economy had two major effects on Mexico. First, in 1973 Mexico was, because of lagging investment policy pursued by PEMEX, a net petroleum importer. Not only did the country lose an opportunity to take advantage of the oil boom, but it had to incur a greater deficit in the balance of payments. Second, because the changes in the world economy had a particularly severe impact on the United States, Mexico's imports—about two-thirds of which went to that country—were adversely affected.

Although it was not apparent at the time, 1973 was the shape of things to come. As it turned out, the forces of public sector expansion and the forces behind externally induced inflation proved to be much stronger than whatever forces were pushing in the direction of financial stability. The result was that Mexico found itself in a severe disequilibrium characterized not only by balance-of-payments problems but also by increased inflation and unemployment all through 1974 and 1975. The fall in private investment in these years compounded the economic crisis and contributed largely to the country's deteriorating economic performance.

Macroeconomic Overview

The trends in inflation, government borrowing, and the balance-of-payments deficit caused considerable official concern, and in mid-1973 the government and the monetary authorities began to take corrective action to stabilize the economy:

1. In July 1973 the government announced a general sixteen-point stabilization plan (discussed in detail below).
2. The monetary authorities tightened credit.
3. The central bank increased interest rates in an effort to mobilize additional domestic resources for the public sector.
4. Rates for electricity were increased by an average of almost 30 percent in October.
5. Oil and gas prices were increased by an average of 55 percent in December.
6. Similar price increases were granted for fertilizers and steel products at the beginning of 1974.
7. The federal budget for 1974 provided for only a modest increase in real expenditures over those in 1973.
8. The government planned to increase output as much as possible through the more intensive use of existing fixed investment, with new investment to be concentrated in the productive sectors.
9. In March and May 1974, the Bank of Mexico introduced further selective interest rate increases to attract deposits.[1]

Implicit in the government's stabilization strategy was a belief that these fiscal and monetary measures would have a positive effect in reducing inflation and in improving the balance of payments, as had been the case during previous periods (1965 and 1971) of economic difficulty.

The government recognized, however, that special factors were involved in the macroeconomic situation in 1973-1974, factors that were not present in 1964-1965 or 1970-1971. The rate of inflation, although lower than in 1973, was higher than in the past, thus making reduction to normal levels more difficult. Furthermore, increased inflation in world markets made a sharp decline in the value of imports extremely unlikely.

Given these conditions, the government aimed simply for an improvement in the balance of payments (accepting a large deficit) and an increased control over inflation so that policies aimed at higher growth could be pursued in 1975. The key to a sufficient degree of stability was given as the large volume of trade with the United States, and the desire of the Mexican government to maintain a stable value of the peso.

However 1974 was a year that would test the government's resolve and ability to carry through a major and complicated stabilization program. It was also a year that was critical in establishing the economic encouragement for the remaining years of the Echeverría administration.

Developments in 1974

Contrary to the government's pessimistic outlook, real GDP actually increased by almost 6 percent in 1973 (as compared with the 4.5 to 5 percent government forecast). Contrary to the statements made when the 1974 budget was presented to Congress and to the public, however, the finances of the public sector showed virtually no improvement during 1974.

In the government's original forecasts, one-third of the deficit was to have been financed from internal resources and two-thirds from external resources. The actual result was roughly half and half, with the absolute level of the internal borrowing quadrupling and the level of external borrowing doubling over what had been planned.

Even more disturbing was the deterioration in the balance of payments. The deficit of $US 2.9 billion (compared to the government forecast of $US 1.6 billion) meant that the current account deficit nearly doubled from 2.8 percent of GDP in 1973 to 4.4 percent in 1974. Poor performance in both exports and imports was responsible for the external account's rapid deterioration.

Although nominal exports rose by 31.8 percent—coupled with a 58.3 percent increase in nominal imports—real exports (1960 prices) increased by only 4.1 percent (as compared with an average rate of growth of more than 9 percent in 1971-1973). The biggest surprise was in the value of imports which (in 1960 prices) increased by nearly 27 percent, with imports of immediate and capital goods increasing by nearly 35 percent. Given the rate of GDP growth (5.9 percent), the country would normally not experience rates of growth in these imports of over 10 percent.[2] Three factors were responsible for the unusually large volume of imports.

1. the existence and development of full capacity in certain key sectors of the domestic economy, such as steel and cement, requiring large volumes of foreign supplies to assure that inflation could not increase.
2. the government's own investment program was import-intensive (Table 14).
3. firms in both the private and public sectors accumulated inventories in anticipation of further inflation.

TABLE 14

MEXICO'S PRIVATE AND PUBLIC SECTOR IMPORTS 1971-1975

	Private ($ billion)	Public ($ billion)	Total ($billion)	Public Sector Share of Total %
1971	1.80	.453	2.25	20
1972	2.07	.645	2.72	23
1973	2.59	1.22	3.81	32
1974	3.85	2.02	6.06	36
1975	4.08	2.50	6.58	38

Source: Banco de Mexico.

Although the government's fiscal and trade policies were dismal failures, monetary policy proved quite successful. The money supply increased by only 22 percent in 1974 (substantially smaller than the increase in nominal GDP of 31.2 percent), with domestic credit growing by 24.4 percent.

Because of the successful pursuit of tight money and credit policies, the rate of increase in consumer prices was 21 percent—slightly below the increase in 1973. The rate of growth of wholesale prices over the year was only 12.5 percent.[3]

Developments in 1975

In general, economic conditions (except for inflation) continued to deteriorate in 1975. The rate of growth of the gross domestic product rose, in real terms, by only 4 percent, compared with 5.9 percent in 1974 and 7.6 percent in 1973.

Among the negative factors most seriously affecting the economy during the year were: (1) the persistent (although declining) rate of inflation; (2) the fall in sales experienced by a large number of firms, necessitating large cutbacks in production; (3) an unprecedented increase in the country's foreign debt; (4) an increase in the trade deficit; and (5) a relative decline in private investment.

To pick up the slack in demand, the government (for the fourth consecutive year) increased its investment by 49.8 percent over that in 1974. Private investment increased by only 5.5 percent, as compared with an 8.1 percent increase the previous year. Total investment for the year (at current prices) was estimated at $182 million pesos, as compared with $111,968 million and $145,317 million pesos in 1973 and 1974, respectively. Private sector investment at constant 1960 prices therefore declined in absolute terms for the third year in a row. Private investment had accounted for 61.8 percent of gross domestic capital investment in 1970, but it had fallen to 46.7 percent by the end of 1975.

Inflation, though not as severe as in the two previous years, was still present. The wholesale price index increased by 10.5 percent, as compared with a 22.5 percent increase in 1974 (15.7 percent in 1973).

While the government's stabilization therefore began to take hold in 1975, efforts at monetary restraint were somewhat neutralized when the authorities officially approved price increases for a broad range of consumer and production goods.

Mexico's exports in 1975 were still not satisfactory despite the country's continuing efforts to find new markets and new products for export and the number of new export incentives initiated by the government. Exports in current prices rose by only 0.3 percent, as compared with 37.6 percent in 1974. More indicative of Mexico's plight was the fact that manufactured exports actually declined by 20.8 percent, falling to 41.8 percent of total exports. Imports, however, increased by only 8.6 percent, with the public sector exerting greater austerity in its purchases abroad.

Because of the country's continuing difficulties in reducing its deficit, the government initiated a new set of trade policies specifically designed to reduce the rate of growth of public and private sector imports, expand the pace of import replacement industrialization, and promote new exports abroad. The government's general strategy was one of expanding foreign exchange earnings while simultaneously limiting or at least controlling those activities that historically had depended on a high volume of imports.

During 1975 the Mexican public sector continued to depend very heavily on income generated by its decentralized agencies and enterprises and on foreign borrowing. Although tax revenues increased by 27.6 percent to $109,214 million pesos, they still represented only 31.3 percent of total government income for the year (the 1974 increase was 38.9 percent).

Several tax reforms were initiated in 1975 to increase the revenues at the disposal of the authorities and to combat inflation. These included (1) an increase in personal income taxes, with the maximum tax rate being increased from 42 percent to 50 percent; (2) the continuation of a 15 percent consumption tax, charged at all restaurants, hotels, and night clubs having a liquor license (for establishments without a liquor license, the old 4 percent tax continued in effect); (3) a sharp increase in tax rate on real estate, especially undeveloped property; (4) a 12 to 16 percent increase in the flat sales tax rate for Petroleos Mexicanos (PEMEX) (except for petrochemical products) and the legislation of a 50 percent ad valorem tax for all exports of crude oil; and (5) a new general structure for taxing Mexico's imports and exports.

Sources of Inflationary Pressure and Imbalance

During 1974 and 1975, therefore, there was slow economic growth with inflation and large balance-of-payments deficits. Several observers have attributed the economy's malaise to the fact that the government persisted in pursuing certain goals the achievement of which was made impossible by the country's existing productive structure. Others have argued that the government simply pursued poor policies within a favorable environment.

The issue is obviously complex and, in any case, not clear-cut. Any tentative conclusion as to the government's possible role in creating or perpetuating the inflation and balance-of-payments difficulties should be made only after an examination of: (1) the government's agricultural policies, particularly its price policies; (2) the adequacy of the measures adopted by the authorities to combat inflation; (3) the government's wage policy, particularly that of minimum wages; (4) the government's role in creating increased uncertainty in the private sector; and (5) the relationship between government expenditures and budget deficits.

Agricultural Policies

The Echeverría administration's agricultural policies, like those of its predecessors, tried to strike a workable balance between two partly competing long-term objectives: expansion of production and exports, and improvement in the economic well-being of the majority of the rural population.

In 1950-1970, production objectives had been pursued more effectively than welfare objectives.[4] The Echeverría administration oriented policy more toward welfare objectives. After 1970, production objectives were still considered vital, but much of the government's investment in this area was in social areas (health, sanitation, education) or in projects that would not be completed in time to increase output significantly until the late 1970s or early 1980s.

To achieve its objectives, particularly the creation of a more equal income distribution, the government's agricultural policies were directed toward: (1) the maintenance of high prices for agricultural commodities through price support programs, particularly of high prices for agricultural commodities maintained through purchases by the state agency CONASUPO; (2) subsidization of inputs, particularly credit; and (3) the development of roads and infrastructure in agriculture. Of these policies, the first was the most important and is of particular concern here. Support prices were announced for a number of agricultural commodities in 1963 and remained relatively constant until 1972.

Agricultural prices in Mexico are largely administered by CONASUPO, a semiautonomous price and marketing agency of the government. This agency has several social and economic objectives, including: (1) the promotion of increased purchasing power among low-income consumers and small farmers; (2) the promotion of greater efficiency in the marketing system, and (3) the stimulation of agricultural output.

During the 1960s, Mexican agricultural price policies as administered by CONASUPO had three main objectives: to encourage output increases and exports, to assure a minimum level of income for the poorer farmers, and to keep down the cost of living in Mexico City. The main instruments used to achieve these objectives were guaranteed prices for certain key commodities (e.g., wheat, corn, oilseeds, and sorghum), a very restrictive import policy for agricultural products, and ceilings on some major food prices.

Commercial farmers responded favorably to CONASUPO's price

supports, partly a result of relatively good collecting and storage facilities in the northern irrigated areas. The support price for wheat, together with expanding acreage under cultivation, was largely responsible for transforming Mexico from an importer of grains in the early 1960s to a net exporter of a number of crops by the end of the decade.

CONASUPO's prices, however, had several undesirable effects. The price structures established tended to promote the production of maize rather than wheat, even though wheat prices were higher in world markets. CONASUPO's prices were therefore causing an inefficient utilization of cropland, since Mexico was largely an exporter of maize and an importer of wheat.

By the early 1970s, a number of problems created by CONASUPO's price policies began to be felt. Agricultural production became stagnant, and in 1973 record price increases for agricultural goods and a spectacular rise in grain imports brought the agricultural sector into the center of public attention.

During 1972-1973, CONASUPO attempted to correct the shortage of basic commodities by increasing their support prices from Mex $940 to Mex $1,200 a ton for corn, from Mex $913 to Mex $1,200 a ton for wheat, and from Mex $1,750 to Mex $2,000 a ton for beans. The program failed, however, because private buyers bought up most of the domestic crop at prices noticeably higher than the support prices in order to resell them at even higher international prices. The result was a reduction of 50 percent (700,000 tons less) in CONASUPO's domestic purchases of corn. More importantly, CONASUPO was forced to change its traditional position—from that of an exporter to that of an importer. During 1973 alone, CONASUPO imported 1.4 million tons of basic commodities in order to stabilize its official domestic price. As a result of its price policies, CONASUPO ran a deficit of about a billion pesos (equivalent to 2 percent of the value of agricultural production). This deficit was financed by government subsidies, clearly an inflationary action, since the government itself was borrowing from the Central Bank to cover its deficit.

Admittedly, CONASUPO's policy of, for example, increasing support prices between 25 and 45 percent, had been shown to be effective in stimulating grain production. Yet the costs associated with this policy were substantial. The government had to raise consumer prices for such crops as maize, wheat, and sorghum by a large margin at the same time the authorities were attempting to achieve domestic price stability. The government's 1973 and 1975 anti-inflation programs were critically dependent on wage and salary restraint, both largely influenced by the price level of basic foodstuffs. Unfortunately, the government on several occasions had no alternative but to increase prices before summer harvests (since otherwise CONASUPO would have had to repurchase its sales). Moreover, the environment created by CONASUPO merchants often withheld stocks from the market in expectation of higher future prices. It is possible that these actions caused a reduction in supply large enough to force prices up even further.

There can be little doubt that the government's cereal policy was not responsible for much of the initial inflationary pressure experienced within the Mexican economy in the late 1960s. The rapid increases in agricultural output offset much of the inflationary pressure, and there were relatively small rates of price increases. Clearly, however, price increases after 1970 (Table 15), together with CONASUPO's financial deficits requiring government subsidies, have given Mexico's agricultural price policies a definite inflationary bias.

TABLE 15

CONASUPO'S FARM SUPPORT PRICES

Year	Corn	Wheat	Beans	Sorghum	Saffron	Barley
		Mexican Pesos per Metric Ton				
1963	940	800	1,750	--	--	--
1971	940	800	1,750	625	1,500	950
1972	940	870	1,750	625	1,500	950
1973	1,200	870	5,000	625	1,600	950
1974	1,500	1,500	6,000	1,330	3,000	1,200
		Percentage Change				
1972	--	8.8	--	--	--	--
1973	27.7	--	185.7	--	6.7	--
1974	25.0	72.4	20.0	112.8	87.5	26.3

Source: CONASUPO

In terms of production, the agricultural sector was the main focus of Echeverría's stepped-up investment program. Its share in total public expenditures grew from 8.8 percent in 1970 to 15.9 percent in 1975 without a commensurate increase in output. The absence of large year-to-year adjustments in the public investment program after 1971 clearly supports the argument that long-term social goals, rather than short-term production objectives, were a predominant concern of the government.

The government's agricultural policy, therefore, was clearly inflationary; it accelerated public expenditures greatly and expanded rural purchasing power without a commensurate (at least short-run) increase in output.

Measures to Combat Inflation

As noted above, the Echeverría government has initiated several anti-inflationary programs since 1971. Basically, these were: (1) stricter controls over prices; (2) redirection of public investments into short-term productive projects, especially into agriculture; (3) increasing foreign exchange by expanding exports and reducing imports; (4) a tighter grip on monetary policy, without causing a credit squeeze that might endanger investments and production; and (5) controlling the foreign debt by seeking the most convenient loans from the World Bank and the Inter-American Development Bank to finance technically sound and financially proved investment programs.

The orientation of the government's 1973 anti-inflationary programs stems largely from the official interpretation that the increase in domestic prices was due to:

1. higher prices for imports due to the general acceleration of worldwide inflation
2. the growth of internal demand at a more rapid pace than supply, caused in part by Mexico's strong economic recovery in the second half of 1972 aided by increased public sector expenditures
3. the failure of private investment to increase supplies of goods fast enough to satisfy the increased demand
4. the standstill in agricultural production
5. increased hoarding and speculation by many groups in anticipation of further price increases

On July 25, 1977, to combat these forces, the government outlined its sixteen-point program:[5]

1. readjustment of the public outlay among sectors and projects to the financing of strictly noninflationary activities
2. reinforcement of planning policies, particularly the timely payment for public sector purchases
3. restriction of the country's monetary expansion to the rate required by the increase in real output
4. greater financial support for short-term productive activities, principally in the agricultural sector
5. encouragement of greater use of industrial and agricultural capacity for a rapid increase of output
6. intensification of measures to stimulate private investment
7. strengthening of price controls
8. establishment of a consumer information and guidance campaign to make buyers aware of unusually high prices
9. achievement of a reasonable balance between the cost increases and price rise of mass consumption products
10. encouragement of rural, labor, and urban consumer cooperatives
11. promotion of supply and consumption centers set up by business associations
12. increased efficiency in the control of exports of food products, raw materials, and, in general, articles not produced in sufficient quantities to meet internal demand
13. import of cereals and other basic foodstuffs by the CONASUPO
14. increased imports of other products in short supply
15. selective price reductions
16. creation of a commission to assure proper balance between wage raises, increased productivity, and the cost of living

As these measures indicate, the administration's concern over inflation was real, but its chief objectives were still those of increased employment and social welfare. One leading official noted that under the program, expenditures would be revised with regard to size, sectoral structure, and finance in order to stimulate short-term productive activities and prevent inflationary bottlenecks. However, he made clear that the administration, in its fight against inflation, would not reduce its social investment or halt public works construction, since "the long deferment of social consumption in this country is an act of injustice that we cannot tolerate; we shall maintain our will to satisfy this need."[6]

Seen in this light, the government's measures to combat inflation were a halfhearted effort. Since strict control of the money supply was not emphasized, monetary policy was not effectively designed to put an immediate stop to price increases.

Increases in Minimum Wages

During the early 1970s, the prices of raw materials and foodstuffs increased more rapidly than did those of other goods and services, thus undoubtedly contributing to a number of severe inflationary pressures. The fall in urban real wages that accompanied the 1973 inflation eventually led to worker demands for an emergency increase in minimum and contractual wages. These demands were backed by more than 4,000 formal announcements of strike action and the threat in September 1973 of a general strike on October 1. As a consequence, the government granted an increase of 18 percent in the minimum wage in September and recommended a 20 percent increase in wages covered by union contracts. Public employees and military personnel received increases of 13-15 percent. Although they received less than they had asked for, the unions accepted this interim settlement, and only a very few of the strikes that had been announced actually took place, the longest lasting for only twelve days.

Over the fourteen-month period from October 1974 to December 31, 1975, however, minimum wages increased at an average rate of 22 percent, or approximately 6 percent higher than the increase in price levels: the consumer price index in Mexico City (MCCPI) had risen by 17.7 percent, and minimum wages there increased by 14 percent.

Uncertainty in the Private Sector

Whatever positive value the government's stabilization program may have had was almost certainly exemplified in the actions of the authorities vis-à-vis the private sector. An obvious solution to the problem of growing shortages, increased (inflationary-financed) government deficits, and balance-of-payments deficits would be (for a given level of aggregate demand) to increase the amount of goods and services available for immediate use—goods produced largely by the private sector. During the 1971-1976 period, however, private investment and production lagged far behind its potential.

The causes for this decline have been the subject of a great deal of comment and speculation. Because several objective and subjective government actions were influencing decisions in the private sector, it is impossible to discuss the topic in anything but very general terms. In terms of objective factors, the most important deterrent to private sector investment was probably the lack of credit. As noted in Chapter 5, the government in 1972 began in earnest to appropriate a larger and larger proportion of savings flowing from savers into the country's financial intermediaries. In addition, the reserve requirements of the commercial banks were also increased—ultimately to 100 percent on marginal deposits—as one of the central bank's anti-inflationary policies. The extent to which these actions deterred the private sector from investing is far from certain. The private sector did have alternative sources of credit: lines of credit from foreign banks were available, and many firms importing equipment automatically received supplier's credit to finance their purchases. These sources were not extensively tapped, however. External loans usually had interest rates higher than those charged by domestic banks. This and the obvious foreign exchange risk (as a peso devaluation became more likely) may have been enough to discourage private investors.

In terms of subjective factors, the most important deterrent to private sector investment seems to be that sector's increasing suspicion that the government was basically antibusiness and that the administration could not be counted on for support if an emergency arose.

Much of the uncertainty facing the private sector stemmed from the fact that officials in the administration had made contradictory statements about its role in business. President Echeverría often stated categorically in his annual state of the union messages that the future of Mexico did not lie in state socialism. Though he expressed his tolerance of all ideological systems, he often declared "Wherever socialism has been introduced up to now, it has generated dictatorship. For that reason, I am a confirmed advocate of freedom. Therefore, I am anti-socialist."[7] Despite this positive declaration, other officials in the administration raised many doubts. Some members of President Echeverría's team made statements that were frankly Marxist, displaying a conviction that the state transcended the individual, that private ownership of the means of production must end, and that private enterprise was not the best form of organization to solve Mexico's economic problems. Such statements, though running counter to the declared philosophy of the president, still went unchallenged and unrepudiated by him. The Mexican private sector and the outside world had, to a large extent, concluded that these statements carried weight and influence in government thinking. Added to these Marxist views were others, less ideologically oriented, springing from a sincere conviction that government officials could perform many business functions as well as or better than their private sector counterparts—a view of private enterprise that was implicit in the philosophy of President Echeverría.

Another subjective element was the "style" with which the

administration governed. Because the Echeverría administration prided itself on its "unprecedented" actions, the private sector always expected that additional fundamental social and economic changes were yet to come. The government's impatience to find solutions also pushed it into ill-advised policies, not only inconsistent with one another, but also involving encroachments on the private sector. Such uncontrolled fervor for reform undoubtedly frightened many investors sufficiently to cause them to postpone any long-term decisions until another administration was in office.

Subjective reasons would seem to underlie much of the private sector's disinclination to invest in the early to mid-1970s. There is no evidence that the government actually removed any of the subsidies or incentives that the private sector had grown accustomed to over the years.

International Factors

Developments in the world economy in 1974-1975 influenced domestic prices and Mexico's balance of payments. The Mexican authorities liked to blame most of the economy's balance-of-payments deficits and accelerated prices on the movements in the world economy, but they were as incorrect as those who blamed the 1974-1975 disequlibrium entirely on the policies pursued by the government.

Although the trend of domestic prices was closely linked to monetary expansion in 1972-1973, about 25 percent of the increases in the domestic price level was caused by changes in the prices of internationally traded goods. However, world inflation appears to have played a much smaller role in the price rise in 1974 and 1975 (Table 16). In addition to raising the price of imports in Mexico, the U.S. inflation indirectly influenced Mexican wage rates: that is, negotiated wage demands in Mexico are affected by the increase in wage differential between the two countries (Table 17).

Declining American tourism and the devaluation of the dollar in 1973 also weakened the purchasing power of the peso. President Nixon's 10 percent surcharge on imported goods hit Mexico especially hard.

The world economy had a more clear-cut impact on Mexico's balance of payments than inflation had. First, the drastic deterioration in Mexico's real exports in 1975 and to some extent in 1974 can be largely attributed to the world recession, particularly as it affected the United States. The U.S. recession appears to explain most—but not all—of the decline in real exports during 1974-1975. Prices and shifts in the structure of foreign demand for imports were responsible for the remaining proportion of the decline in exports. Second, the balance-of-payments current account grew not only because real (1960 prices)

TABLE 16

MEXICO: DOMESTIC COST PRESSURES INDUCED BY WORLD INFLATION, 1970-1975

	Change in Import Prices %	Share of Imports in Total Cost[a]	Cost Pressures Induced by Changes in Import Prices (percentage points)	Change in Domestic Price (percentage points)[b]	Cost Pressures Induced by Changes in Import Prices (% of total)
1970	7.1	0.15	1.1	5.0	22.0
1971	6.4	0.15	1.0	5.4	19.0
1972	9.6	0.15	1.4	5.0	28.0
1973	22.7	0.15	3.4	12.1	28.0
1974	24.6	0.15	3.7	23.7	16.0
1975	7.1	0.15	1.1	15.0	7.0

[a]Assumed to be 15 percent. The imports-to-GDP ratio's peak (including non-factor services) was 9.3 percent in 1973.

[b]Measured using the National Consumer Price Index.

TABLE 17

ECONOMIC CHANGES IN MEXICO AND THE UNITED STATES

1970 to 1975

	GDP(a)	Money Supply	WPI(b)	CPI(c)	IPD(d)	Wages(e)
	(billion pesos)			(indexes)		(pesos per day)
Mexico						
1970	418.7 (296.6)	49.0	174.1	108.7	141.2	26.99
1975	983.2 (390.1)	118.2	290.9	191.8	252.0	52.97 (64.62)(f)
5-year increase percent	135% (32%)	141%	67%	76%	96%	(139%)
United States						
5-year increase percent	53%(g) (10%)	33%	58%	39%	38%	37%(h)

Source: Computed from Banco de Mexico Informe Anual, various issues; United States Department of Commerce, Survey of Current Business, various issues.

Notes: (a) The figures in parentheses are real GDP in constant pesos of 1960.
(b) Wholesale price index Mexico City 1954=100.
(c) National index of consumer prices 1968=100.
(d) The implicit price deflator for GDP, with 1960 as base year.
(e) Arithmetic average of general minimum wage, weighted by economically active population in the 89 zones.
(f) The wage in force as of January 1, 1976, assuming that the weighted average increase was 22%, the same as in 1975.
(g) Gross national product.
(h) Average gross weekly earnings in private non-agricultural industries.

imports grew and real exports declined; it also grew to some degree because the terms of trade deteriorated—beginning in 1966, when the index was 95.7 (1960=100), and continuing to 1973-1975, when it fell to an average of 89.7.

In view of these figures, it would be misleading to suggest that the 1974-1975 disequilibrium could be entirely the result of inept government action—there is no doubt that the intervention of external forces greatly exacerbated the government's attempts at stabilization.

Government Expenditures and Budget Deficits

Although international events outside the government's control began to affect the economy adversely from 1973 on, Mexico's increasing internal and external disequilibrium in the latter years of the Echeverría administration was more a direct result of government action. In order to meet the Echeverría administration's goals—especially its social objectives—the role of the government in the economy had to increase dramatically. Unfortunately, the public sector, as inherited by the Echeverría administration in 1970, could not perform the task assigned it.

The extent of these changes, given the short time during which they took place, would undoubtedly cause temporary distortions and strains on any economy. But in Mexico, these problems were compounded by the fact that domestic savings, primarily public savings, grew relatively rapidly, but not rapidly enough to meet the steeply mounting rate of expenditure quickly. In addition to an expanded rate of domestic borrowing, therefore, the government's programs had to be financed by a rapid increase in foreign borrowing.

The inflation of the early to mid-1970s could probably not have been avoided—but it could have been attenuated through the curtailment of private sector demand. Although aggregate private sector demand (consumption plus investment expenditures) did decline from an average of 89 percent of GDP in 1966-1972 to an average of 86.5 percent of GDP in 1973-1975, the decline was mainly in investment; the level of private consumption remained constant.

To be consistent with its goals of equity and social justice, the government should have restructured the tax system to curtail the consumption of upper-income groups. But this was not done. The major deficiency of the government's economic strategy was its neglect of an obvious necessity; i.e., in order to implement its rather revolutionary institutional and investment decisions, which entailed a steep increase in public expenditures, it required an equally major effort to raise, through noninflationary channels, the necessary domestic revenues. Such a decision should have been made early in 1971, when the administration was preparing its economic program for the period through 1976. The result of the government's fiscal mismanagement was an unprecedented growth in the public deficit.

The government's stepped-up domestic borrowing, together with the decline in the growth of the private sector's voluntary financial savings (quasi money), was a major force behind the rapid monetary expansion of 23.1 percent per year from 1972-1973 compared with 15.1 percent from 1965-1975.

The government's increased borrowing had several major effects: (1) two-thirds of the growth of total bank credit was appropriated by the public sector during 1972-1975; (2) the severe credit restrictions on the private sector extended through 1976; (3) the public sector share of the financing of the current account deficit rose from 52 percent in 1972 to about 80 percent in 1975; and (4) the external public debt rose to about $10.5 billion, more than double the level at the end of 1972.

The government justified its actions by arguing that a decrease in public expenditures would not in itself eliminate the existing inflationary pressures and, on the contrary, might lead to stagnation similar to that prevailing in most of the developed countries during most of 1974 and 1975.

The big surge in government expenditures came just when agricultural production fell sharply in the early 1970s. Hence, whatever inflationary pressures would otherwise have been generated by the rapid increase in expenditures, they were intensified by lagging production in certain key sectors.

The fact that the percentage of GDP devoted to government resources was increasing is not in itself a sign of inflation. On the contrary, that can be expected and should be encouraged to grow. The rapidity with which it grew and the effect on the financing requirement, however, contained the seeds of inflation.

This fact was not conceded by the government, whose leading ministers argued up to the last days before the September 1976 devaluation of the peso that excessive spending could not have been the cause of inflation because the social and economic needs of Mexico were so great, and that spending for production to remove so-called bottlenecks was the only intelligent way of fighting inflation. The fallacy of the claim that any amount of spending is noninflationary so long as spending is on production should be obvious. If this were true, there would be no limit to the printing of money and the granting of credit to governments to increase national output. As for justifying the volume of government expenditure by relating it to Mexico's general needs or to its rate of population growth, this is a complete non sequitur, for neither the ability to spend nor the disaster from overspending has anything to do with national needs. It can only be concluded that financial policy in Mexico had a very unsound theoretical basis during the Echeverría administration.

Evaluation of Government Policies

Several criteria can be used to evaluate the economic policies of the Echeverría administration, particularly those initiated during the 1974-1975 period. These include an assessment of:

1. the magnitude of the changes being sought in the economy given the capacity of the economy to make the necessary adjustments
2. the appropriateness of the time frame for attempting to achieve the administration's major objectives
3. the consistency between the type of policies selected in light of the objectives they were intended to accomplish
4. the degree of preparation undertaken by the administration before initiating its policies

The Magnitude of Change

For the size of the government's actual expenditures to be appropriate for growth without inflation, the economy would have to have had a high degree of excess capacity, or the government, to avoid inflation, would have to have diverted a comparable degree of aggregate demand from the private sector. Although there are indications of high underemployment in Mexico, excess capacity in the strict economic sense was not widespread in the early 1970s, nor (as noted above) did the government effectively divert purchasing power from private consumption. The economy, therefore, did not have sufficient idle capacity that could be drawn upon to implement the government's social and economic goals, nor were sufficient resources shifted from the private sector to augment the government's programs.

The Appropriateness of the Time Frame

The reliance on foreign borrowing instead of on private savings to finance government expenditures clearly indicated a calculated decision on the part of the authorities to attempt to achieve a better distribution of income in the immediate future through mortgaging, simultaneously, future income by incurring higher debt.

It is clear that the government was trying to compress too much expenditure into too few years. It desired to accomplish as many of its goals as possible within its six-year term. However, because these goals largely involved correcting what the government considered to be long-standing social injustices, its time frame was far too short.

Realistically, the government should have settled for simply identifying these problems, bringing them to the attention of public opinion, and preparing the groundwork for resolving them. Given the many rigidities in the economy, especially in rural areas, many of the government's objectives could be permanently resolved only through gradual reallocation of resources. The government nevertheless acted as if it believed these rigidities were not present even in the short run. Thus, allocating for the fact that the external environment was not conducive to success, it can be tentatively concluded that the strucutral changes of 1974-1975 were bound to induce some disequilibrium—not so much because of their magnitude as because of the speed with which they were attempted.

Consistency of Policies and Objectives

As for the consistency between policies (actions) and objectives, it is clear that many of the government's projects were not as appropriate as they could have been. Several investments made in 1974-1975 could have been postponed without detriment to the essential goals of the government. The industrial parks projects of the Ministry of Public Works is a prime example: as inflationary pressures built up, it could have been delayed without sacrificing the government's major objectives.

Adequacy of Preparation

Finally, the government seemed ill prepared to undertake its socioeconomic programs. From an administrative standpoint, machinery was not established to monitor expenditures in order to keep them in line with allocations. In 1974 and again in 1975, budget overruns were common in nearly all areas of government. The government did not establish an effective system of budget preparation, control, and supervision before it began to implement its program.

In many instances, government agencies proceeded to spend, irrespective of the fact that the funds had not been authorized. This occurrence was widespread, with the Ministry of Public Works, the Ministry of Education, CONASUPO, and PEMEX the worst offenders.

Because of these deficiencies and reluctance or inability to initiate a major tax reform, the government entered 1974 with relatively few domestic resources to spend and no means of effectively controlling the utilization of the resources borrowed in foreign markets.

Conclusions

If the government had not attempted to meet its major objectives within too short a period of time, the disequilibrium of 1974-1975 would doubtlessly have been much less severe. Although developments in world markets would have caused large deficits in the balance of payments and inflationary pressures, the magnitude of disequilibrium would have been greatly reduced, particularly if the government had initiated a major tax reform in early 1970 or even 1971.

Apparently, the authorities hoped that by pressing ahead with the basic tasks, they could initiate the creation of a stronger, less vulnerable, more diversified, and more equitable economic and social structure. Obviously, this effort did not entirely succeed: in order to press ahead, Mexico had to incur a heavy external debt and accept a higher rate of inflation. As a result the country's income distribution worsened, rather than improved.

7
General Observations on the Echeverría Administration

The last few years, particularly since 1973, have shown the critical role of sound economic management in the attainment of Mexico's national goals. Such management is essential for improving the availability and use of domestic resources and for attracting the required amounts of supplemental capital from abroad. In this regard, the general approach and some of the specific measures the Echeverría government employed during the last few years of its regime to accelerate progress proved to be largely ineffective. In general, government action diverted rather than enlarged resources and also made it difficult for the private sector to obtain the capital required for future growth. In retrospect, it is clear that a number of policies introduced by the Echeverría administration, together with the change in world markets, has greatly weakened Mexico's ability to continue to grow at rates equal to those attained in the immediate postwar period. The forces of public sector expansion and the forces behind the world inflation proved to be much stronger than the policies the Echeverría administration adopted to achieve financial stability.

Throughout his administration, President Echeverría always appeared willing to sacrifice economic growth for the sake of political objectives at home and abroad. In early September 1976, with only three months left in office, he paid the price for the sacrifice: he gave in to international market forces and permitted the first devaluation of the Mexican peso in twenty-two years. The Bank of Mexico floated the peso, thereby permitting market forces to determine its true value. The peso immediately dropped 39 percent. By the end of October, it had declined in value by over 50 percent.[1]

Today (1977) it appears that the Echeverría administration's policies were a blind alley, failing to lead the Mexican people to greater prosperity. Instead, President Echeverría completed his six-year term in office with the country in near anarchy. The last several years of his administration saw few economic gains. Instead, Mexico began to experience increased class struggle, an unprecedented rate of inflation, and a rapid deterioration in the balance of payments.

Accomplishments under Echeverría

The Echeverría government, though falling short on most of its economic objectives, is probably to be most remembered for its decision, taken in 1973, to support a policy of responsible parenthood.[2] Progress toward a reduction in the population rate through reduced fertility will necessarily be measured in decades rather than in years, but the long-run significance of this decision cannot be overemphasized.[3]

The government also made some progress toward a more equitable social order, particularly in terms of institutional changes. Examples are the creation of INFONAVIT (The Workers Housing Fund), FONA-COT (the National Fund for Workers Consumption), and PIDER (the National Rural Development Program).[4] The government also introduced a new Water Law (1971) and a new Land Reform Law (1972) and made changes in the institutional framework governing the allocation of credit. In all of these the poor have at least begun to share in the benefits of Mexico's economic progress.

The National Water Plan (PNH), which has recently been completed, can be expected to lay the foundations for policies directed toward the efficient use of scarce and critical resources.[5] Several studies of regional development were made, and if they become bases for policy, they will represent a useful contribution toward dealing with problems arising from economic and demographic centralization. Finally, a nationwide study of natural resources (CETENAL), which was started in 1971 and is still under way, should provide a valuable tool for the preparation of a long-term economic strategy.[6]

One reason for the rather poor economic performance of the Echeverría administration was that many of the programs it initiated had very long gestation periods; i.e., they did not begin production until long after initial construction was begun. For example, many of the government's major projects to expand capacity in petroleum, petrochemicals, steel, fertilizers, and other branches of industry will not be completed until after 1976. When these projects come on-stream, mostly between 1977 and 1982, they will undoubtedly have a major impact on the sectors involved. Obviously, output should grow, but more significantly, increased output should reduce domestic inflationary pressures, and exports deriving from these projects should help improve the balance of payments.

In the case of agriculture, it is harder to be certain about the future consequences of recent investments and other social policies. But the growth of both current and capital public sector outlays—for extension and support services, on the one hand, and for new and rehabilitated agricultural infrastructure on the other—and changes in the allocation of credit should lead to an increase in crop production within the next few years. This expectation might be more realistic now than it has been in the recent past, when low agricultural support prices were a major cause of the decline in agricultural production. Support prices are now being fixed at levels comparable to those in international markets.

The continued expansion of transport infrastructure and the growth of installed power-generating capacity (the latter including the eventual completion of the large hydro schemes at La Angostura and Chiquasen) are also assets to the Echeverría government's economic strategy. With few exceptions, these projects should be completed well before the end of the López Portillo administration.

The implementation of these policies should strengthen the basis for long-run growth and could improve the economic conditions of the poor and reduce the disparities in incomes.

The Echeverría administration also made major strides toward increased public sector efficiency. In 1971 President Echeverría ordered the establishment of programming units in all spending agencies and ministries. Under his February 1971 Presidential Act,[7] working groups were set up in such public sectors as energy, transport, irrigation, and tourism to coordinate the government's overall investment program. The objective of the programming units is to prepare five-year investment plans, each containing a set of specific projects to be screened by the Ministry of the Presidency and the president himself. The plans include methods of project financing and recommendations on the rates and prices charged for public services. The new programming groups are a major breakthrough in Mexican economic management. If the system proves successful, three of the major shortcomings of Mexican planning will be overcome: (1) the inability of the agencies to identify a large number of profitable projects; (2) the short time goals of most agencies; and (3) the great uncertainty about the government's objectives and the role of the public agencies in Mexico's development effort.

Control and coordination measures continued to be strengthened under President Echeverría and are being expanded by his successor. In 1971 a public expenditure control commission was created—explicitly to screen public spending to achieve more economic use of public funds.

In practice, the commission arranges for bulk purchases of goods and is gradually opening more public contracts to competitive bidding. Its investment financing group also supervises internal and external borrowing operations of public sector agencies. In this regard, the committee is making a major attempt to contain the volume of public borrowing from foreign sources and to obtain funds from abroad on more favorable terms than in the past. Its strategy in this regard is to present a united front to international leaders, thus improving the government's bargaining position.

To a large extent, the government was able to obtain foreign funds on much more favorable terms; that is, it is now nearly impossible for lenders to approach several agencies in search of the one willing to pay the highest rate.

Conclusions

The period 1971-1976 may be considered a period of "destabilizing development" rather than a period of "shared development." The Echeverría administration inherited many problems from its predecessors, and it did not implement the fiscal and financial measures needed to achieve its objectives of more egalitarian and independent economic growth.

The economic record of the last three years of the Echeverría administration is thus one of gradual deterioration, which can be construed partly as a result of an adverse international environment and partly as a result of fiscal irresponsibility. The administration's critics have a somewhat different interpretation: namely, that Mexico's economic problems were a direct result of the government's implicit strategy to accept the consequences of additional inflation and additional debt as the price for moving toward meeting social and developmental objectives, through a more ample and more direct involvement of the public sector in the economy. A more accurate description of the government's actions probably lies somewhere between these two interpretations.

8

The 1976 Devaluation of the Peso

Currency devaluation is one of the most dramatic—even traumatic—measures of economic policy that a government can undertake. It always generates cries of outrage and calls for the responsible officials to resign. For these reasons alone, governments such as Mexico's are reluctant to devalue their currencies or even admit they are overvalued.[1] Because of the associated trauma, which arises because the many economic adjustments associated with devaluation are crowded into a relatively short period, governments have come to regard currency devaluation as a measure of last resort. Presumably, they are always prepared to stabilize the economy through monetary and fiscal policies in order to stave off a devaluation.

The Government's Stabilization Program

Stabilization programs are intended to eliminate the causes of inflation. Depending on the circumstances of each case, they may have to arrest inordinate wage increases, put an end to excessive credit expansion, or reduce budget deficits by cutting expenditures, by increasing direct or indirect taxes, by raising the tariffs of state enterprises, or by discontinuing subsidies previously granted. Furthermore, a stabilization effort should correct the distortions introduced by inflation. During 1975 and 1976, government attempts at stabilization were most effective in reducing credit expansion

Measures to Restrict Credit

A number of factors were also at work to restrict the expansion and availability of credit: (1) the international monetary and financial situation; (2) the relative decline of resource intake by the private banking system; (3) the deficit in the federal budget; (4) the compulsory bank reserve requirements; and (5) the anti-inflationary policy initiated by the government.

The international monetary and financial situation. During early 1976, the international capital markets were tight, causing available financial resources to become scarce and interest rates to increase. Thus, Mexico had to accept ever higher interest rate charges on foreign loans to domestic corporations and on funds deposited in the country by foreign investors.

The relative decline of resource intake by the private banking system. Due in part to the drain on foreign exchange reserves caused by speculation about possible devaluation of the peso and by disproportionately high spending because of inflationary pressures, private banks in the first eight months of 1976 attracted fewer resources than they had in the first eight months of 1975. That is, from December 1974 through August 1975, intake by private banks rose by $34,807 million pesos; in the comparable period ending in August 1976, the increase amounted to only $23,958 million. Through August 1976, the annual growth rate of intake registered a definite downward trend. Furthermore, most of the funds attracted were in dollars, with intake in pesos in constant decline. All this, of course, put a squeeze on credit and raised the cost of borrowing.

The deficit in the federal budget. From 1970 to 1976, federal revenues grew from $33,868 million pesos to $134,700 million, an increase of more than 295 percent. Meanwhile, the Mexican government's spending shot from $40,203 million pesos in 1970 to $192,000 million in 1976, a 377.5 percent rise. Thus, although in 1970 the budgetary deficit was $6,335 million pesos, in 1976 it was $57,300 million—more than eight times higher than six years before. Tax revenues helped finance this deficit— tax collections rose at an average yearly rate of 21.0 percent between 1970 and 1976—but they fell short of needs, forcing the government to resort to other revenue boosters, such as the expansion of money in circulation, increasing the foreign debt, and raising bank reserve deposits and the amount transferable to the public sector.

The compulsory bank reserve requirements. With respect to the last of the above points, the transfer of bank reserves for government use increased from $35,000 million pesos in 1970 to $120,000 million in 1976. The latter figure excludes direct loans made by private credit institutions to the central bank. At least in the case of the *financieras,* credit availabilities were reduced, since because of increased requirements there were less and less resources for private investment.

In 1973 these availabilities were set at 51.8 percent of surplus liabilities as of December 31. These were reduced to 36 percent the following year and to 25 percent in 1976. In other words, the *financieras* had to transfer 50 percent of their cash into the Bank of Mexico, 25 percent into financing development projects, and the rest into credits for all other financial activities.

The federal government's anti-inflation policy. Because of semireces-sionary conditions in the world economy and in Mexico starting in 1973, the federal expenditures and monetary resources increase was propor-tionately greater than the annual inflow of revenues. And although the government had to act with caution to avoid a slowdown in economic activity, this very program tightened the supply of money, thus causing the rate of inflation to decline to an annual rate of only 7 percent by mid-1976.

Despite the government's apparent reestablishment of control over inflation, fear of devaluation spurred the withdrawal of funds from domestic institutions or—when they remained—their dollarization. In the first eight months of 1976, total resource intake by private banking institutions rose only 8.5 percent from its December 1975 level, but intake in foreign currency, i.e., dollars, increased 102.5 percent in the same period (the increase in peso deposits was only 3.3 percent). The lack of peso resources had the effect of raising the effective cost of available loans. By mid-1976 banks faced a dim situation: low resource intake and compulsory use of what little money was available.

Measures to Strengthen the Balance of Payments

In order to shore up Mexico's balance of payments and thus strengthen the peso, the ministers of finance and industry and commerce announced in July 1975 the establishment of a new, aggressive economic and trade policy for the country. This effort, as noted in Chapter 7, was undertaken primarily to improve the country's external position. The major objectives of the new trade policy included: (1) optimum utilization of the country's purchasing power (in other words, a definite limitation on imports); (2) a full-fledged effort to develop the country's internal market in order to promote industrial development; and (3) improving export capacity.[2]

To achieve these objectives, a series of measures was put into effect simultaneously in three different areas: imports, import substitution, and exports. In essence, what the government hoped to accomplish was to promote activities that would generate foreign exchange earnings and at the same time limit those activities that might lead to a foreign exchange outflow. Clearly, the main thrust of the government's new effort was to check the continuing deterioration of the country's balance of trade. This deterioration threatened to put very strong pressures on the peso and its ability to maintain its traditional parity position with the U.S. dollar, particularly at a time when the dollar was gradually getting stronger.

Within the framework of the "new economic policy," the following measures were taken immediately with regard to imports. First, all nonessential imports were strictly limited through the establishment of strict quotas. In the case of nonessential items, import quotas were limited to the total volume imported in 1974. In many cases, however, quotas were adjusted so that imports were reduced by up to 50 percent. Some import quotas were increased, but only when the company involved promised to increase its exports by an amount equivalent to the increase in the quota. Second, the Ministry of Finance also increased tariffs on certain goods to complement the new quota system. Third, for certain nonessential products (i.e., materials not used directly in production), import permits were "temporarily" suspended. Fourth, imports were approved, when possible, only if they came from countries that purchased an "adequate" volume of Mexican products and that were not applying "unrealistic" import quotas to Mexican goods. Fifth, fines and other sanctions were levied against companies that ordered goods abroad before they received an import permit for those goods. Sixth, all public sector companies and agencies were required to present their import requirements at least one year in advance, so that national industries would have an opportunity to know what those requirements were, and private sector companies were asked to adopt the same policy with regard to new plant or expansion programs. Seventh, a more rational and consolidated purchasing policy by the public sector was implemented in order to obtain better prices abroad and to find markets for Mexican products. In other words, the purchasing power of the public sector was consolidated in order to be in a stronger bargaining position in negotiating imports. These were obtained under more favorable terms by offering in exchange products not easily sold in the world market.

In the area of import substitution, two major promotional measures were announced. Established import firms were required to start the substitution process through a series of measures that the Ministry of Industry and Commerce was to draw up at a later date, and a wide-ranging program was drawn up by the same ministry for promoting the domestic manufacturing of a broader scope of capital goods, such as equipment and parts, by both the private and public sectors.

Probably the most important government objectives were the following concerning export promotion: (1) a 75 percent import duty subsidy on machinery and equipment at least 60 percent of which is used in the production of goods for export; (2) an accelerated depreciation schedule for this machinery and equipment; (3) exemption from paying the federal sales tax on containers of any type made in Mexico and sold for use in export products; (4) a reduction in the degree of value added in Mexico required for an exporter of manufactured goods to be eligible for tax rebate certificates (CEDIS); (5) additional regulations on fiscal incentives for exporting companies and foreign trade consortiums; (6) elimination of all export taxes, except in cases where these are not applied for control purposes; (7) the probability that the government would reestablish the 100 percent subsidy in the 15 percent tax covering export sales of gold and silver; (8) a broadening of the activities and resources of specialized government export and industrial promotion funds such as FOMEX, FONEI, and FOGAIN; and (9) the establishment of sectoral export programs.

On the surface, these programs appeared successful: for the rest of the year following their initiation in July, the rate of growth of the country's trade deficit declined. A closer examination of the trade account reveals, however, that this decline was more the result of a decline in imports than a significant expansion of exports.

In early 1976 the Ministry of Industry and Commerce declared that the July 1975 import controls would continue indefinitely (they were originally to have been in effect until December 31, 1975). In a vaguely worded statement released in the first weeks of January, the ministry said that the controls must be continued in order to protect Mexico's foreign trade and to promote a much higher level of industrialization than previously through import-substitution schedules. Import permits, the statement declared, would be given only to "absolutely essential" production goods and foodstuffs. There was no immediate indication as to how long the control would remain in effect or if there were plans to change the controls under certain circumstances.

Impact of the Government's Policies

The government regarded the restriction of credit and the expansion of new exports as adequate to contain the trade deficit within limits compatible with a 12.5 peso. This optimistic outlook was supported by the trade figures for early 1976. In January and February 1976, Mexico's trade deficit decreased by 100 million dollars (14.4 percent) as compared with the same two months in 1975. The improvement was largely the result of expanded exports—imports did not continue their 1975 decline. The increase in exports was caused in large part by improved production of and increased foreign demand for agricultural products. In addition, in January 1976, tourism increased by 4.3 percent over January 1975.

In early 1976, therefore, Mexico's strategy appeared clear; i.e., simply holding on at the historic exchange rate while exports continued to expand. In this regard, the authorities were confident that exports of crude oil, refined products, and metals and mining products such as silver, zinc, copper, sulfur, and phosphoric rock would amount to about $US 1,500 million a year, thus reducing the trade deficit to manageable proportions within perhaps three years. They also counted on a much bigger dollar income—emanating from tourism and agricultural exports—and on a significant reduction in imports of petroleum by-products and food products. Meanwhile, the officials planned to keep up the rapid growth of the economy even if Mexico continued to incur big trade deficits. In fact, some Mexican bankers had argued that it was clever for a country such as Mexico to maintain an overvalued currency, because this made the importation of machinery and equipment necessary for modern industry relatively cheap. The overvalued peso also kept down the real cost of servicing the foreign debt. In any case, they argued, the wholesale price increases in the U.S. and Mexico had not diverged sufficiently to warrant the conclusion that the peso was sharply out of line with the dollar.

In short, many officials in Mexico who believed the peso was overvalued hesitated to support devaluation. They argued that the present (1975 to mid-1976) situation of Mexico was rare if not unique. The country had no foreign exchange control: the transfer of income and capital funds to other countries was free.

By mid-1976, however, Mexico encountered serious economic difficulties. Inflationary pressures, which had been building up in the country for some time, could not be diffused. Moreover, its balance-of-payments situation remained precarious, partly as a result of the progressive overvaluation of the peso and partly as a result of capital flight out of the country in anticipation of devaluation or the imposition of exchange controls.

Thus, although many of the government's policies to improve the balance of payments seemed to have good potential, the peso was devalued on August 31, 1976. On that date the government finally admitted that under pressures created by unrestricted maintenance of a fixed exchange rate, the country's exports of goods and services could not, in themselves, finance the imports required for economic development.[3]

Up to August 31, 1976, a large part of the foreign exchange earned from exports had been used to cover interest and dividends on previously acquired debts. In the words of the secretary of the treasury, who made the announcement of the floating of the peso, "It is not in the interest of the nation to increase the foreign debt because we persist in maintaining the present exchange rate."[4]

In his statement the secretary acknowledged for the first time the interrelationship in Mexico of inflation, devaluation, and exchange controls; i.e., the fact that if the rate of inflation in Mexico is greater than that of its main trading partner, the United States, the result will inevitably be a deficit in the Mexican balance of trade, which will finally result in a deficit in the country's balance of payments.[5] The secretary clearly saw that unless Mexico could maintain its recent high rates of international borrowing or offer high enough interest rates to attract short-term capital, consecutive deficits in the balance of payments would eventually cause a decrease in the central bank's foreign exchange reserves. A dangerously low level in foreign exchange reserves would in turn force the government to institute trade or exchange controls of one kind or another simply to maintain the value of the peso. Given the exchange structure of the Mexican economy, however, it was clear to the secretary and most officials that controls could not solve the country's economic problems but would only postpone the inevitable devaluation.

The government's strategy all through 1974 to mid-1976—direct controls, borrowing and export incentives to deal with the balance-of-payments deficits without resorting to devaluation—was obviously a stopgap solution. It was partly based on the correct assumption that devaluation alone (with no correction of the country's deeper economic problems, such as low productivity in agriculture, expanding population, and increasing unemployment) would not be a solution. Leading officials never denied the desirability of eventually adopting a more flexible, less protected economic system, where an adjustment in the parity of exchange would have a significant role to play. The so-called political decision not to devalue was supported by a number of thoughtful officials on the grounds that even if the peso was overvalued, devaluation would weaken the forces working for fiscal restraint. Their analysis was correct—given the strategy whereby the decision to maintain the rate of 12.5 pesos per dollar was made part of a government policy of delay, allowing the Treasury time to bring public sector expenditure under control. Failing that, to continue to a state of fundamental disequlibrium would mean simply waiting until pressures in the money and capital markets would build up to enforce a devaluation.

President Echeverría's Views on Stabilization

In his final state of the nation message on August 31, 1976, President Echeverría not only announced the devaluation but outlined what he felt would be Mexico's best economic and financial policies to accompany the floating of the peso.[6] Clearly, the degree to which these measures are implemented will ultimately determine Mexico's future monetary stability. Several policies were immediately put into effect. Given the fact, however, that he had only two months remaining in office, most of his proposals must be considered as suggestions for a stabilization policy rather than an irreversible program. They do indicate, however, official recognition of the seriousness of his failure in 1973 and again in 1975 to introduce a more comprehensive stabilization program. President Echeverría's six basic points for establishing a new economic policy consisted of:

1. *Preserving the international competitiveness of Mexico.* Ideally, Mexico should make every attempt to assure that prices and costs rise by less than the depreciation in the peso-dollar exchange rate. President Echeverría suggested three specific measures to implement this goal. (a) A tax on exports (in the form of a surcharge) would avoid diverting goods from the domestic market, thus preventing pressure on domestic price levels. (b) Although the certificates for the rebate of taxes on exports (CEDI) are no longer necessary owing to the devaluation, aid should be given to firms exporting. (c) There should be a selective reduction of tariffs and elimination of "unnecessary" import controls.

2. *Protecting the purchasing power of the people.* The implementation of this goal entails, according to President Echeverría, six specific measures. (a) Insofar as devaluation raises the prices of goods consumed by lower-income groups, these adverse effects must be avoided, mitigated, and compensated for. (b) The salaries and pensions of government employees and members of the armed forces should be raised to restore the purchasing power lost through devaluation, with the increase retroactive to September 1, 1976. As soon as possible, the same adjustments should be made in the wages of other workers to avoid depreciation of minimum wages and those of low-income and medium-income workers. (c) Strict and, if necessary, extended control over prices of essential consumer goods and raw materials should be maintained. Increases in prices should be permitted only if there is an authenticated rise in costs. (d) CONASUPO (National Company for Popular Subsistence) should not raise the prices of the products that it sells at retail. Its guaranteed prices to farmers, however, may have to be raised to compensate for increased costs. (e) The interest rate on small savings

accounts is to be increased, but the charge on bank loans to small borrowers is to stay the same. (f) Hoarding, speculation, and monopolistic practices in connection with essential commodities should be attacked by the government with all the legal faculties at its command.

3. *Avoiding unwarranted profits.* A bill will soon be sent to Congress proposing a tax on unusual or excess profits.

4. *Protecting the financial health of enterprises.* Special tax treatment should be given to private sector enterprises. Similarly, subsidies should be given to public sector enterprises to offset losses resulting from devaluation.

5. *Controlling the public deficit.* The public deficit should be reduced, but only insofar as necessary and without lowering the level of public investment in infrastructure, productive activity, and social assistance. The Echeverría administration did not state its intention clearly; it indicated only that the programming of expenditure should be undertaken to reduce the deficit to appropriate levels, adjusting it strictly to noninflationary limits.

6. *Regulating the growth of credit.* The last goal seems to be a corollary to the previous objective, i.e., to reduce the deficit. The president stressed that the new programs should require more precise instruments with a view to tailoring them to the country's needs, to priority activities, and to the small and medium-sized credit users. The Bank of Mexico should on this basis grant credit to the private sector through the establishment of a system of controlled growth, taking into account seasonal and annual fluctuations in their respective economic activities, their expansion needs, and the appropriate adjustment of the price levels of the country. The programming referred to above is to be complemented by a system regulating the credit extended to the public sector by the Bank of Mexico, with the application of quarterly financing rates strictly correlated to the management of the authorized budget, and with the corresponding financing machinery established by the treasury authorities. The public sector foreign debt should be managed in the same way.

The major economic contrast of President Echeverría's economic program was contained in his outline of the new exchange policy, which would hopefully result in:

1. the creation of new export opportunities
2. increases in tourism and the discouragement of excessive expenditures on the part of Mexicans traveling outside the country

3. the expansion of the domestic market and thus the creation of new investment opportunities in Mexico
4. the creation of new jobs (through greater investment activity and fuller use of installed capacity)
5. the improved competitiveness of in-bond industries
6. the repatriation of capital
7. the discouragement of contraband

The major reasons President Echeverría gave for dropping the fixed parity of the peso to the dollar included:

1. The persistent exodus of capital from Mexico. Capital outflows were forcing the country to borrow excessively in order to make up for the flight of foreign exchange. Capital outflows were also limiting the lending capacity of the banking system.
2. The substantial imbalance between Mexican exports and imports of goods and services. Mexico's balance of trade deteriorated because its major exports were losing their competitiveness in international markets. Similarly, he noted that Mexico's demand for imports increased as its inflation rate remained higher than that of its major trading partners, especially the United States.
3. The need to make rational use of installed capacity and new investment to facilitate the creation of additional jobs.

In discussing the decision to float the peso (in his Sixth State of the Union Message to Congress), President Echeverría pointed out that the former peso-dollar exchange rate had ceased to reflect differences between Mexican and international production costs. Mexico's over-valued currency had thus limited the scope of the country's productive activity and its ability to compete in world markets.

President Echeverría stated that if the peso-dollar rate had not been altered, the government's efforts to provide the working population with jobs would have become increasingly ineffective and public sector borrowing would have reached unjustifiable levels.

In establishing a criterion for the proper dollar-peso exchange rate, President Echeverría indicated that the new exchange rate of the peso must meet various basic requirements of economic policy. It must (1) promote the export of goods and services, making use of the country's existing capacity; (2) discourage expenditures on imported goods, including contraband, that compete with Mexican industrial products; (3) limit borrowing from foreign sources; (4) dissipate the distrust that has encouraged the flight of capital from

Mexico; and (5) keep domestic prices from rising excessively.

Appraisal of the New Strategy

The most obvious weakness of President Echeverría's program was the absence of any ringing declaration of a commitment to reduce the public deficit.[7] Similarly, the government's wage policy was too vague; it did not specifically set precise guidelines for restraining wage increases until price stability—the foundations of competitiveness, balance-of-payments equilibrium, and exchange rate stability—had been restored.

This is not surprising, because the president and some of his ministers had denied that Mexico's inflation was caused even in part by excessive (because inflationary-financed) government spending or by wage increases out of proportion to increases in productivity. In fact, they often denied that Mexican inflation was of domestic origin, asserting that it merely reflected financial disorder and inflation in the rest of the world.

It can be shown, however, that since imports amounted to only 6.2 percent of GDP in 1971 and 8.4 percent in 1975 and that since world price increases helped raise the prices of Mexican exports, outside influences played a relatively small part in determining Mexican inflation. If inflation in Mexico had been merely keeping in step with the rest of the world (for which the United States serves as a proxy, since 80 percent of Mexican international transactions are with it), all would have been well as far as the peso-dollar exchange rate is concerned, and equilibrium would not have been lost.

These two elements of policy are critical for the problem of monetary stability: if the public sector deficit continues to grow and if wage increases continue to be awarded to "restore purchasing power" regardless of labor productivity, the acceleration of inflation and the loss of international competitiveness again are assured. This is the tragedy of inflation in Mexico. Once monetary stability had been destroyed, it was an illusion to think that it could be restored within a relatively short period of time.

The decision of the authorities to devalue by no means reflected a decision to correct a "fundamental disequilibrium," i.e., structural balance-of-payments difficulties resulting from such factors as destruction or depletion of resources or a secular decline in world demand for Mexican exports (as opposed to the sudden falloff in demand caused by the U.S. recession). On the contrary, the Mexican economy had for some time been one of the most vigorous in the Western Hemisphere, with a rich resource base, a relatively diversified structure of production, and a political and social foundation conducive to economic and social advance. Pressures to devalue did not stem from long-run structural difficulties, but from a number of problems originating in the government's conduct of monetary and fiscal policy.

In addition to balance-of-payments problems brought on by the government's budget deficits and inflationary financing, Mexico at the time of the devaluation was experiencing increasing rates of urban unemployment and rural underemployment combined with a declining rate of growth of real output and a rather high rate of growth of the money supply (relative to the growth of the demand for money). The government's attempt through controls to maintain a stable peso-dollar exchange rate had distorted the structure of the economy.

Controls had led to a distortion of the economy in that it was producing goods that were not exported, but that were instead relatively intensive in their use of imports. Given that fact, there is sufficient theoretical justification to argue that the devaluation of the peso can be part of a policy package to create a more efficient economic structure. This latter structure should enable the country to achieve a higher growth rate and better balance-of-payments performance than during the 1973-1976 period.

Conclusions

In retrospect, President Echeverría had little choice but to devalue the peso. The rate of inflation in Mexico, though moderate by some Latin American standards, has for some time been well out of line with that of the United States. Such a situation was obviously dangerous for a country that relies as heavily as Mexico does on earnings from U.S. tourists and sends a very high proportion of its exports to that country. An adjustment in the exchange rate was thus inevitable.

The major consideration behind the decision by the Mexican authorities to devalue the peso was, however, the unwillingness of domestic and foreign investors (alarmed by gloomy forecasts about the country's economic and political future) to invest in the country or to hold peso-denominated assets. Most investors did not take very seriously the official assertions that the peso would not be devalued. They were correct. The Mexican government realized at an early date (probably as early as 1974) that it could not really maintain the 12.5 rate through imposition of exchange controls. With a comparatively unsophisticated civil service and a long, open frontier with the United States, it did not have the administrative machinery to police such control. Allowing the peso to find its own level on the exchanges was the only option left.

The collapse of the exchange rate in 1976 initiated a period of crisis, which President López Portillo inherited on December 1, 1976. The initial impact of the devaluation was to raise the relative price of high-import goods; i.e., goods consumed chiefly by the top third of Mexican households. This, plus the possible slowing the country's potential rate of growth and profits, should have a number of long-run impacts on the economy.

A decline in growth and private investment is not new to Mexico. A similar situation existed in the early 1960s. At that time, the favorable economic climate that had enabled the policies of the postwar years to yield high rates of growth was also dissipating, and the government apparently had an increasingly difficult task in satisfying the competing demands of business, bureaucratic, and trade union groups and at the same time sustaining the patina of populist measures needed to keep the support of the masses.

The outcome was a reversal by President López Mateos (1959-1964) of his modest shift back toward egalitarian reform in 1959-1961. This effort toward increased concern with social objectives had upset business and had caused a drop in private and foreign investment, forcing López Mateos to spend the last half of his presidency restoring the investment climate.

Foreign direct and portfolio investment poured in during the 1960s, putting off an anticipated balance-of-payments squeeze, and the growth rate revived as did income concentration. Recently, President Luis Echeverría also tried to tilt toward egalitarianism. Educational and other social expenditures were generously increased with a greater focus on the rural population, and sporadic efforts were made to tighten enforcement of the estate size limits set by the agrarian code.

Echeverría's reformist rhetoric exceeded his ability to deliver, however, and his tax reforms proved modest. As in the late 1950s and early 1960s, business responded with a drop in investment. The government felt impelled to finance much of its expanded physical and social investment program with foreign credits. This action increased Mexico's already sizable external debt and, through its inflationary impact, helped bring on the exchange collapse of 1976. Given Mexico's long tradition of governmental cooperation with the private sector, Echeverría clearly fitted policy too far to the left. It is not yet clear whether his successor, López Portillo, will veer back toward growthmanship-cum-inequality, and if so, whether he and the governing party can avoid the associated social unrest.

9
Problems Facing the López
Portillo Administration

When José López Portillo succeeded Echeverría as president of Mexico in December 1976, he inherited a country that was deeply divided politically and undergoing its worst economic recession since the early 1950s. The events of the previous three years under the Echeverría administration had made it clear to most observers that Mexico's legendary economic stability could no longer be taken for granted.

Condition of the Economy at the End of 1976

Few presidents have inherited such a political and financial crisis as López Portillo. By the time he was inaugurated, the peso had just lost half its value in a period of only six months, nearly $4 billion had fled the country, rumors of a coup d'etat were rife, and world banks were alarmed lest Mexico default on its foreign debts.

During President Echeverría's term, public foreign debt rose to more than $20 billion from less than $4 billion, thus making Mexico one of the world's major debtors. Real growth came to a halt, and inflation increased to nearly 40 percent. Mexico's problems were not helped by Echeverría's nationalistic antibusiness rhetoric, which only discouraged much of the private foreign investment the economy sorely needed.

Finally, in a striking display of political irresponsibility virtually on the eve of his retirement, President Echeverría expropriated 250,000 acres of the country's richest agricultural land and turned it over to a group of disorganized peasants.[1] The agrarian unrest unleashed by Echeverría interrupted agricultural production and investment at the worst possible time. The country had not grown enough food since 1971. Over the previous four years, it imported more than 11 million tons of grains and oilseeds, and any production loss was likely to expand the trade deficit, already over $2 billion, and further fuel the already disastrous rate of inflation.

Thus President López Portillo inherited a major financial crisis at his inauguration. He had the difficult task of trying to attract foreign investors without alienating the masses of the poor and without stirring up civil unrest. He had to find a way to balance public investment needed for new production and jobs (which business views as the certain road to further inflation and economic instability) with austerity in public spending (which leftists view as inhuman and dangerous).

One U.S. banker observed that Echeverría's most dangerous legacy was that he created a consensus of rising expectations among the poor—expectations that President López Portillo, not President Echeverría, will have to deal with.[2]

Echeverría's controversial performance over the previous months strengthened the determination of various interest groups in Mexico to press the new administration for favors. The conservative private sector, on the defensive for the past six years, will press the new administration to return to the economic policies that spurred growth during the 1960s.

The 23 percent wage increase that followed the devaluation of the peso on August 31, 1976, and the mass expropriation of private farms in northwest Mexico on the eve of López Portillo's inauguration, on the other hand, injected new militancy into the labor and peasant organizations.

The Tasks Facing President López Portillo

The interplay of the major influences on Mexican development over the next several years can be summarized tersely. The employment problem will create a political imperative for rapid economic growth, but there are two major constraints on using increased government spending for its alleviation: the need to moderate the recent acceleration of public expenditures and the external public debt, and the limitations on the country's ability to import, which are a result of the government's indebtedness. The key elements to the solution to this dilemna must involve a major recovery of private investment, particularly that investment oriented toward export markets and increased agricultural production. Improvement in the public sector's financial management would probably ease the considerable external financing task that Mexico will face during President López Portillo's administration.

Of the major problems faced by the president, that of stabilizing the economy was the most pressing, and the most difficult, particularly since the peso had just been devalued.

Events Following the Devaluation

The events following the two devaluations in the fall of 1976 are of interest in themselves.[3] More important, however, they point out the complex set of problems that President López Portillo would face immediately upon entering office.

Immediate Aftermath of the Devaluation

The first devaluation of the Mexican peso was sudden and unexpected. On Tuesday, August 31, 1976, the Mexican authorities had simply allowed the peso to float in the leading financial centers; i.e., the Bank of Mexico made no attempt to maintain the value of the peso by buying and selling dollars at the old rate of 12.5 pesos per dollar. By the end of the week (September 3), the bank adopted a policy of buying and selling dollars at the unprecedented rate of 20.6 pesos. Through this action, the peso was temporarily pegged at a rate giving an effective devaluation of 64.8 percent. Undoubtedly, this initial devaluation was too great. Part of the bank's strategy was to discourage speculation against the peso and to attract the foreign capital that began to be taken out of the country in the summer of 1976.

Within hours of the announcement of the devaluation, large stores in Mexico City began to increase their prices from 25 to 40 percent. Similarly, retailers of products (such as cars) whose price was under government control, refused to sell until prices were allowed to increase. The inability of the Ministry of Industry and Commerce to monitor and control price increases also gave the Mexican Labor Congress sufficient excuse to demand emergency wage increases of up to 65 percent. The private sector responded to these demands by offering just 10 percent. Obviously, after several years of inflation, expectations of an acceleration in the rate of price increase triggered a potential wage-price spiral. About two weeks after the devaluation, Mexico City had become the center of rumors ranging from the government's imminent freezing of bank accounts and the imposition of exchange controls to the nationalization of the banking sector. Clearly, the mood of the country was pessimistic, verging on panic.

The panic triggered by the peso drop only exacerbated the negative tendencies already present. The private banking system's total intake rose only 1.6 percent in September and only 2.3 percent in October. Intake of peso funds actually decreased 6.9 percent in the August-October period; during that time, foreign currency deposits increased by 110.1 percent.

The combination of sluggish resources intake and dollarization led to a critical situation for private borrowers. Continuation of the high reserve requirements also reduced the availability of credit. For awhile, peso loans were practically nonexistent. There were some dollar funds available, but—not surprisingly—hardly anybody was willing to risk dollar loans.

This all happened at a time when companies were most pressed in their cash flow and were in dire need of working capital. The lack of it, or its prohibitive cost, led some firms—particularly small and medium-sized ones—to close down either temporarily or permanently. On the other hand, the larger corporations were in most cases able to get the funds they needed.

Soon after the devaluation, the authorities decreed price increases of (1) 10 percent for all products subject to government controls (although some goods with high import content, such as motor vehicles, will eventually be allowed to increase their prices by 25 to 30 percent); (2) 15 percent for restaurants; and (3) 20 percent for hotels. Finally, by the end of the first month the government announced its own austerity-stabilization program. The major element in the government's program was a promise to cut expenditure to reduce the budget deficit—currently running at an annual rate of about $300 million.

These actions were at most simply holding measures, enabling President Echeverría to leave office with an economy that appeared to be over the worst of the impacts of the devaluation. The real belt tightening will take place in 1977 and 1978. Neither the IMF, U.S. Treasury, nor foreign bankers are ready to continue financing huge government deficits. Indications were that President López Portillo would have to introduce a new series of wage and price controls, tighten credit, reduce government expenditures, and, if the economy and politics permit, effect a major tax reform. Increases in the domestic price of oil and electricity, postponed by Echeverría, were also inevitable.

Confusion and Rumors, September-November 1976

The three months following the devaluation and the outline of President Echeverría's program of stabilization were a period of confusion and rumors. There was little confidence in the government's stabilization program and ability to restore financial and economic stability. After twenty-two years of a fixed exchange rate and statements by government officials that the peso would never be devalued, the public seemed in a state of shock.

Shortly after the devaluation, the government suggested guidelines for an emergency wage increase for organized labor. These guidelines called for increases of 23 percent. It was not clear, however, whether these wage increases were to be additional to, or inclusive of, any increases that had been obtained in collective bargaining sessions earlier in the year. For the most part, the 23 percent increase appears to have been viewed as additional. Minimum wages were also increased 23 percent, effective October 1. Simultaneously with the guidelines for wage increases, the government broadened the coverage of its price control program and issued a decree permitting a 10 percent increase in most prices subject to controls over prices prevailing on August 15.

The combination of wage and price increases led many to suspect that Mexico was entering a more vicious inflationary spiral than had prevailed and that further depreciation of the peso exchange rate was likely. In addition, and perhaps as a result of this, rumors began to circulate that bank accounts would be frozen, that foreign exchange controls would be imposed, that the government would nationalize the banks, and that a military coup was imminent.

These rumors circulated, died away, and were revived until the December 1 change in government. There were sizable transfers of capital into foreign exchange throughout this period. Part of these transfers remained on deposit with Mexican banks in the form of "Mex-dollars." Mexican banks pay higher interest rates on dollars than can be obtained elsewhere, making local dollar time deposits attractive.

The transfers out of pesos reached critical levels at least twice. On October 26, the Bank of Mexico announced that it would no longer buy and sell foreign exchange at the 19.7/19.9 rates, which had prevailed since September 13. On October 27, the buy/sell rates were 26.24 and 26.50, respectively. With banks operating at a one percent spread, the peso gradually appreciated until the week of November 15, when the rates leveled off at about 24.1 buying and 24.3 selling.

That week, the rumors of military coups, foreign exchange controls, etc., reached a peak, causing very large withdrawals from banks. The Bank of Mexico then decided to withdraw completely from the foreign exchange markets and ordered other credit institutions to do likewise. Brokerage houses took over the foreign exchange market. Although banks were technically excluded from the foreign exchange market, they continued to handle transactions that were technically registered on the books of brokerage houses. The foreign exchange controls were not introduced, nor were bank accounts, in dollars or pesos, affected.

Role of the International Monetary Fund

The role of the International Monetary Fund in the double devaluation decision is still far from clear, although it is known unofficially to have been important.[4] The fund had been consulting with Mexican government officials over the possible resort to devaluation for quite some time, but was fended off by Mexico's insistence on exhausting all other possible measures to deal with the situation.

Finally, after the step was taken, the IMF let it be known that it was ready to provide financial relief if "a reasonable line" was followed in dealing with inflation and federal spending.

At the end of October 1976, the Echeverría administration agreed with the IMF on a financial program to support an IMF "Extended Fund Facility" credit of FDR 518 million, or about $610 million. The authorities, who had steadfastly resisted the IMF and its views on stabilization, had to accept this program in order to be able to raise substantial support credits from the market, including a syndicated $800 million loan organized by the Bank of America in November 1976.

The IMF program recognized that Mexico had very limited financial room for maneuvering and that, therefore, urgent measures were needed, particularly on the fiscal side. Unlike normal standby arrangements, which last for only one year, the IMF program will last for a period of three years, with specific targets that have to be met each quarter of the first year in order for Mexico to progressively draw down the credit, and with more general objectives for the following two years.

The targets are the normal ones in such cases, including a ceiling on total monetary expansion, targets for international reserves, and a limitation on net external borrowing from all sources, short-term or long-term, of $3 billion in the first year of the program. This figure assumes about $5 billion of gross borrowing and $2 billion of debt amortization. The underlying assumption behind the very strict borrowing limit is that Mexico will take stringent tax and expenditure measures in short order, since otherwise there is no prospect of being able to limit external borrowing to a figure as small as targeted.

Beyond the current year, the program envisages that the public sector deficit will be reduced from a projected 6 percent of GDP in 1977 to 4 percent and 2.5 percent, respectively, in 1978 and 1979. These are undoubtedly very ambitious objectives, especially if they are seen against the hope (but not the operational target) of achieving a significant increase in private investment under the same period, from about 14 percent of GDP in 1976 to 18 percent in 1979.

The action of the authorities so far suggests that it will be very difficult to achieve the final objective for the first year, at the end of which new quarterly targets have to be negotiated for the following year. So far the only meaningful measures have been increases in telephone and electricity rates and some increases in motor vehicle taxation. The income tax changes are of marginal fiscal importance, and some increases in luxury consumption taxes are unlikely to yield very much if the authorities are successful in holding back import-dependent consumption.

Problems Facing López Portillo Stemming from the Devaluations

The devaluations' impact on the economy and their ultimate success or failure in improving the Mexican balance of payments will depend of course on what policies the new administration adopts.

The immediate problem facing the administration was that of dealing with the side effects of the devaluations. Obviously, a devaluation of this magnitude favors the future and penalizes the past. That is, past investments were encouraged by an undervaluation of foreign exchange and heavy protection. These past investments represent present interests that are hurt by the change, and the individuals who gained most are putting great pressure on the government for "emergency" relief. In contrast, the new rate will encourage the things that have yet to be done; hence, the administration cannot count on existing interests to speak for it. From an economist's standpoint, this is the way it ought to be: no one should be rewarded for resting on past accomplishments; the rewards should go instead to those who seize the new opportunities. But the Mexican political process has another rationale, that of accommodating existing interests. Accordingly, all of the pressures of supplementary measures to accompany the devaluation will come from those who want to be shielded from its effects. And these measures, if implemented fully, would greatly vitiate the favorable effects of the devaluation.

First, the administration will have to deal with pressures to allow certain essential imports to enter the country at an official parity instead of the free-market rate. These range from basic foodstuffs to intermediate inputs into "distressed" industries. They are, of course, products whose production in Mexico has long been artificially discouraged by the country's system of protection. The effect of importing them at a preferential rate would be simply to prolong this artificial discouragment.

Second, the new administration will have to consider a more vigorous implementation of price controls than was initiated under President Echeverría as a means of keeping the prices of basic essentials from rising. If effectively implemented, this too would artificially discourage the production of essential goods.

Third, the administration will have to deal with pressures for a more rapid rise in the legal minimum wage than in past years. This pressure will come mainly from organized labor in the modern sector. In Mexico, roughly 75 percent of the labor force does not come under the minimum wage legislation, and it is in this group that the majority of poor Mexican workers are found. A rapid rise in the legal minimum wage for an already favored minority will hurt the majority of workers in two ways. Not only will the cost of living respond to the wage increase; but also, and more importantly, it will slow down the rate of increase of jobs in the modern sectors, both by reducing the competitiveness of Mexican products in world markets and by encouraging substitution of capital for labor.

Finally, the new administration will have to deal with the issue of an ad valorem tax to increase government revenues and prevent the income distribution from worsening—through the increase in exporters' profits. The effect would only be to discourage many new exports with good earnings potential.

Significantly, the Echeverría administration reduced the export tax one month after the August 31 devaluation. It is doubtful that the new administration should tax exports at all, particularly primary products, since the tariff system already imposes a tax on all exports as high, perhaps, as could be justified for terms of trade reasons. There is merit to the argument, since the protection system tends to discourage such processing of primary products. Moreover, labor-intensive processing is further discouraged by unrealistically high market wage rates.

On the other hand, the existence of the present structure of unrealistic wage and interest rates means that it might be uneconomic capital-intensive processing that is encouraged. A general reform of the tariff system and policies to bring the prices of labor and capital into line with their social opportunity costs would be a superior means of encouraging processing in Mexico. A tax on the export of crude materials is only a second-best remedy. And insofar as the tax is extended to semiprocessed and processed products, it will limit the favorable effect of the devaluation in promoting new exports without any compensating benefits.

Conclusions

Pressures for measures to counter the effects of the devaluation may tend significantly to reduce its beneficial effects. If the López Portillo administration can resist these pressures and limit the extent of the countermeasures, the rest of the 1970s and 1980s could witness significantly higher inflows of private foreign capital—because of the increase in profitability of investment and thus a significantly higher rate of growth for the Mexican economy, led by a second phase of import replacement in basic manufacturing and a vigorous expansion of industrial exports.

The decade ahead offers Mexico both an opportunity and a challenge. The opportunity lies in the fundamental strength of the country's economy, which enables Mexico to forge more rapidly ahead in the development and diversification of the economy and in building a more effective defense against possible external economic pressures. The challenge lies in the extent to which monetary and fiscal policies can be further adapted to the objective of reestablishing a stable economic environment and restoring the strength of the peso. If maximum advantage can be taken of the opportunities the current expansion of the U.S. economy affords and if the challenges inherent in the rising level of economic activity can be effectively dealt with, Mexico will go far in solving its basic problem of reconciling rapid economic development with monetary and exchange rate stability—both of which are fundamental to balanced growth.

10
The Economic Policies of the López Portillo Administration

Until he became president on December 1, 1976, López Portillo did not articulate the broad nature of his economic programs, but as a former finance minister, he was fully aware of the gravity of Mexico's economic crisis.[1] On a number of occasions since his inauguration, he has given brief sketches of his economic policies, but he has still (summer 1977) failed to produce a comprehensive document outlining in detail his solutions to the country's economic problems.[2]

Off the record, he has indicated that a period of austerity would be necessary, during which time the lower income groups would inevitably suffer the most severely, but he feels that by 1979 the economy should be progressing along sound lines. He considers two major variables to be vital in determining the success of his policies: (1) restoring the confidence of the private sector and the U.S. government in the long-run potential of the economy; and (2) his ability to control inflation and the highly explosive political forces unleashed by President Echeverría.[3]

In practice, President López Portillo has not had a real choice in forming his economic policies. He took over an economy suffering its worst crisis in almost four decades, with inflation at an annual rate of 45 percent, the GDP expanding by just 2 percent, unemployment growing rapidly, and the currency sinking in response to the panic flight of capital out of the country.

With or without the IMF agreement, which was drawn up in exchange for $1.2 billion of credit over three years, the new president had certain priorities forced on him: he had to stabilize the peso but allow it to float to avoid overvaluation; he had to lower inflation by limiting wage increases and controlling the government deficit; and he had to stimulate domestic investment to create much-needed jobs by gaining the cooperation of the private sector.

The most important documents reflecting López Portillo's thinking are his inaugural speech, which indicates the need for an alliance for production, and the federal budget, presented to the parliament in December 1976.[4]

The Alliance for Production

On taking office, President López Portillo proposed "a program by which we can govern events together." The country, which "has been demanding a change in procedures and attributes . . . must organize to produce, to distribute and consume in accordance with our own system. . . . We shall thus surmount our economic problems and strengthen our mixed economy, showing neither hostility nor preferences but rather patriotic, nationalist firmness."

"Such must be the popular, national and democratic alliance for production; it means offering everyone viable alternatives which permit us to conciliate national objectives of development and social justice with the specific demands of the several factors of our economy."

The Alliance for Production was designed to combat inflation, reestablish external imbalance, raise the economic growth rate, and lower unemployment levels.

The state has pledged itself to handle public expenditure with efficiency and austerity; it has already begun restructuring public administration, and its economic and fiscal policies are designed to give impetus to alliance objectives. Private enterprise is supposed to invest in socially and nationally essential branches, step up production to lower costs, and create more jobs. It is further committed to cut prices on ninety commodities. Labor, for its part, has curbed wage demands so as not to intensify inflationary pressures. The Alliance for Production is thus a pact among the state, the private sector, and labor, a pact that forms the basis of a far-reaching commitment among these groups. The pact was signed in January 1977.

This is a step in the right direction, but the Alliance for Production is really nothing more than a series of general statements of intention by the signatories. The private sector is not bound to its pledges. Similarly, the government's incentives to industry are not explained in detail and do not bind the authorities to introduce any specific legislation. Nevertheless, the pact is indicative that relations between the president and the private sector, in sharp contrast to the previous administration, will be cordial.

The pact, though not obligatory, is of interest. It consists of two parts: a six-year program involving 140 companies in ten major branches of industry, and a plan under which the Confederation of Chambers of Industry promises to invest 250 billion pesos over the next two years (1977-1978).

The Alliance for Production appears to be a first step toward the French or "indicative" method of development planning; that is, it seeks to improve the informational basis on which public, and especially private, decisions are made. Certain assumptions of sectoral growth over the next six years were made, thus giving firms in these areas assurance that their investments were likely to be profitable. The alliance thus works to reduce the uncertainty that has in the past been a major element in the lower levels of private investment and therefore in growth itself.

Investment by Industry

The six-year program covering the ten sectors involves:

1. *Petrochemicals.* In return for official pledges that PEMEX (the state oil company) will ensure that adequate supplies of feedstocks are available, firms in the secondary petrochemicals sector will invest $1 billion over the next six years. It is freely admitted, however, that this area will not create a significant number of new jobs.

2. *Capital goods.* Around $840 million will be invested over the period. In contrast to petrochemicals, it is anticipated that this area will be one of expanded employment, with more than 20,000 new jobs created during that time. The administration also promises to give: (1) advance information on state sector requirements for machinery and equipment; (2) assurances of satisfactory payment terms from official buyers; (3) encouragement to "buy Mexican"; and (4) efforts to obtain new trade agreements with those countries with which Mexico is economically integrated.

3. *Mining.* Mining companies will spend about $4 billion, aimed at doubling output over the next six years. It is estimated that 80,000 new jobs would thereby be created. Investment incentives and changes in mining legislation and taxation are promised by the government if the $4 billion target is met.

4. *Cement.* On the assumption that tax credits on exports and improved prices are forthcoming, $832 million of capital spending is committed by the private sector.

5. *Vegetable oils and fats.* The government's goal in this sector is to improve the system of procurement from farmers. Prices are to be guaranteed and supply quotas established. The authorities' most important undertaking will be to set up a fund to provide credits for crop purchases.

6. *Automotive industries.* The government wants to continue its long-standing aim of raising the percentage of domestic value added created in the industry. For instance, incentives are promised to parts producers who invest in increased capacity. Presumably, the official promise "to modify existing legislation that might restrict development" will mean in practice that there will be further limits imposed on the use of imported components by Mexico's assembly industry. That industry has agreed to encourage the development of local manufacture of parts and to raise exports.

7. *Tourism.* The government target for this sector is 5.5 million foreign tourists and 27 million domestic tourists by 1982. To reach this goal, nearly $1 billion needs to be invested over the next six years. It is estimated that this investment can create 97,000 new hotel rooms and 100,000 new jobs. Official support will include promotion, national tourism offices, and improvements to the infrastructure.[5]

Few details are available at this time (August 1977) about the 250 million pesos that the Confederation of Chambers of Industry will spend over the 1977-1978 period—other than that 800,000 new jobs will, it is hoped, be created (this compares with an estimated 750,000 new jobs required each year to contain unemployment at, in the present maximum context, acceptable levels).

The Short-Term Program

The Mexican government's budget is more than a mere balance sheet of anticipated government income and expenditures. It is a graphic description of projected government activities for the ensuing fiscal year. By its very nature the process of preparing, adopting, and executing a budget involves a set of complex decisions made by the leading agencies of government.

It would be naïve, however, to consider the budget-making process in Mexico simply in terms of the formal relationship between the legislative and executive branches, that is, in isolation from the political environment in which they both act. This is especially true because the president is preeminent in all phases of political action. In Mexico his power is particularly evidenced in the budget process. In actual practice, presidential power extends even further, for the chief executive dominates the political party (PRI) that has virtually absolute control over both houses of Congress, where the few and ineffectual opposition legislators are in no position to challenge presidential leadership in fiscal affairs.

The budget for 1977 was sent to the Chamber of Deputies on December

15, 1976. President López Portillo, in his message to the Congress, called it "a budget of transition, which splices together the labors of the outgoing and incoming administrations." Since the last such budget of transition, that of 1971, Mexico has had five budgets with large deficits, with the consequent need to borrow to supplement the resources from revenue. As noted in previous chapters, the nature of the borrowing in these years was largely responsible for the inflationary pressures now plaguing the economy.

The budget for 1977, though labeled "noninflationary and nonrecessionary," nevertheless calls for a record volume of government spending.[6] It represents an increase of 59 percent over the announced budget for 1976 and is 38.9 percent higher than the amount actually spent in 1976. The private sector awaited the budget with considerable interest, since the level of government spending will be a key factor in the development process of the national economy, particularly because of the problems posed by devaluation and because it was the new administration's first budget.

To demonstrate the administration's acknowledgment that the government should have a firmer control of the economy, President López Portillo, before submitting the budget, requested passage of the following legislation: (1) the Organic Law of the Federal Public Administration, aimed at fully regulating both those government departments under the direct control of the executive branch and the so-called decentralized agencies and state-owned companies; (2) the Federal Budgeting Accounting and Public Spending Law, to link executive branch programs with basic decisions on public spending and also to streamline the handling of the federal budget by removing the old 1935 Budget Expenditures Law from the books; (3) amendments to the Treasury Accounting Law to strengthen the checking function of Congress; and (4) the Public Debt Law, for closer supervision and control of both the domestic and foreign debt.

With these and other changes in fiscal and monetary legislation, all of which the Congress approved in January 1977, the new administration is apparently bent on modernizing the government apparatus. Undoubtedly, this legislation was passed because of widespread feeling in Mexico that many of the country's economic problems stem from the government's ill-conceived and ill-structured efforts in fiscal and monetary management.

The 1977 Budget: Overview

The 1977 budget was drawn up to function within the new

organizational framework of the federal government. The budget itself is highly controversial, with most of the discussion centering around the possible inflationary impact the budget may have on the economy.[7] It shows a very large deficiency in revenue compared with planned expenditure. Its proposals, in continuing old and introducing new projects, take into account the "requirements for economy arising out of our present economic situation, and though it must lead to the utmost strictness in foregoing nonessential spending, to which we must conform so long as our country has acute social deficiencies, it has likewise compelled us to postpone many necessary and beneficial expenditures."

This statement of the president is quoted in full here because it is his only explicit recognition—in the expenditure part of his message—of the need to cut back on public sector spending, even on the most desirable of objectives, if scarce economic resources available to the government have already been preempted by needs of higher priority.

In terms of the distributional changes, the 1977 budget shows decidedly (relative to the 1976 budget) less concentration on transport and communications and a diminished relative share of resources allocated to agriculture. Industry is the beneficiary of the changed emphasis, both in current and capital expenditure. Social development probably received a slightly diminished share in the total, although its share in investment increased. The constant share of tourism in the total, although its percentage of investment declined, may indicate a decision to rely largely on the private sector for the growth of this industry. The rapid growth of the share of administration in total expenditure may have been retarded, despite the continued increase in its share in investment expenditure.

Impact on the Economy

The impact of the government's fiscal activity on the economy has been increasing during the postwar years. Not only is a significant and increasing share of national income disposed of through the government budget, but also, and more important, is the increased tendency of the Mexican authorities to manipulate the budget with a view toward regulating employment, income, and prices. Clearly, the intelligent use of the budget for this purpose—or even the restriction of the budget to a neutral role—requires accurate knowledge of the budget's net effects on the economy. The size of the budget surplus or deficit provides a first indication of these effects.

A rough picture of the budget's impact on the economy may be gleaned from the pattern that has emerged over the last five or six years. During the 1972-1976 period, actual public sector expenditures were greater than the budgeted amounts by 19.5, 17.3, 19.7, 15.6, and 20.6 percent for the years 1972-1976, respectively. Except in 1972, the state entities were more responsible for creating these excesses than the federal government was. For the public sector as a whole, the actual amount financed by borrowing exceeded the budgeted amount by 35.9, 24.4, 33.3, 58.5, and 34.5 percent, respectively, in these same five years. The state entities were again the main culprits. In the last four years (1973-1976), their excesses of actual overbudgeted borrowings were 66.3, 65.5, 106.2, and 93.8 percent.

In 1977 the federal government will probably finance its deficit by borrowing 135.4 billion pesos. This is 38.7 percent of the 349.8 billion pesos of total spending. The state entities will probably borrow 85.6 billion pesos, or 26.1 percent of their 327.6 billion pesos of total spending (Table 18). Of course, the accuracy of these estimates of borrowing requirements depends not only on spending but also on revenue received.

On the basis of past performance, the forecasts of expected revenues have been similar to forecasts of expenditures. Actual revenues have always exceeded those budgeted, notwithstanding the fact that the percentage of total revenue actually received from borrowing was always greater than the percentage budgeted. These patterns undoubtedly underlie the government's decision to borrow slightly more of the total in 1977 (32.6 percent) than was borrowed in 1976 (32.0 percent). The absolute revenue budgeted in 1977—677.4 billion pesos—is 37.7 percent greater than the estimated actual amount in 1976 (and 54.1 percent greater than the 1976 budget); and the 221.0 billion pesos to be borrowed in 1977 is 40.4 percent above the actual amount of 157.4 billion pesos budgeted in 1976.

The accuracy of the forecast of the financing requirements for 1977 depends of course on the accuracy of the revenue figures. As indicated, the budgeted amounts have always been exceeded in the past. Inflation and the general uncertainty over the government's wage and price policies make forecasts in this area difficult, especially for revenues, which, of course, vary directly with changes in the price level. The revenue from the income tax is particularly vulnerable to fluctuations in prices and real growth, yet it is expected that over 30 percent (76.6 billion pesos) of the federal government's nonborrowed revenue of 251 billion pesos will be raised by income taxes paid by individuals and companies. This estimate will have to be reduced if measures to control inflation significantly reduce the level of production. Two of the large tax levies—

TABLE 18

MEXICO: PUBLIC EXPENDITURE AND BORROWING, 1972-1977

(Billion pesos)

Year	Federal Government			State Entities			Total Public Sector		
	Total Expenditure	Borrowing	% Borrowed	Total Expenditure	Borrowing	% Borrowed	Total Expenditure	Borrowing	% Borrowed
1972									
Budget	54.7	15.1	27.6	68.6	12.5	18.2	123.3	27.6	22.4
Actual	77.2	22.3	28.9	70.1	15.2	21.7	142.3	37.5	25.5
Increase Actual over Budget	41.1%	-	-	2.2%	21.6%	-	19.5%	35.9%	-
1973									
Budget	89.4	32.9	36.8	84.5	17.2	20.4	173.9	50.1	28.8
Actual	102.2	53.7	33.0	101.8	28.6	28.1	204.0	62.3	30.5
Increase Actual over Budget	14.3%	2.4%	-	20.5%	66.3%	-	17.3%	24.4%	-
1974									
Budget	114.1	37.4	32.8	116.8	20.0	17.1	231.0	57.4	24.8
Actual	135.9	47.0	34.6	140.7	33.1	25.5	276.5	76.5	27.7
Increase Actual over Budget	19.1%	25.7%	-	20.5%	65.5%	-	19.7%	33.3%	-
1975									
Budget	186.1	54.2	29.1	160.6	32.3	20.1	346.7	86.5	24.9
Actual	200.5	70.5	35.2	200.2	66.6	33.3	400.7	137.1	34.2
Increase Actual over Budget	7.7%	30.1%	-	24.7%	106.2%	-	15.6%	58.5%	-
1976									
Budget	238.0	83.2	35.0	201.6	33.8	16.8	439.6	117.0	26.6
Actual	259.2	91.9	35.5	271.0	65.5	24.2	530.2	157.4	29.7
Increase Actual over Budget	8.9%	10.5%	-	34.4%	93.8%	-	20.6%	34.5%	-
1977									
Budget	349.8	135.4	38.7	327.6	85.6	26.1	677.4	221.0	32.6

Source: Constructed from tables in Anexos Estadisticos of the December budget measures 1973-1976.

on industry (42.9 pesos) and on commercial receipts (40.6 billion pesos)—which account for 33 percent of federal government nonborrowed revenue, are also quite vulnerable to a fall in the level of business activity.

Another conflict between revenues and stabilization stems from the fact that the public sector depends so heavily on the decentralized agencies and enterprises (see Chapter 4). These companies were originated (or absorbed) by the government primarily to promote economic development. Yet because the public sector depends on them so heavily for its revenues, the prices charged for the goods and services produced and sold by these companies must be economically sound (with very few exceptions, such as the National Railways System and CONASUPO); i.e., they must cover costs and expenses. Price increases for many of these enterprises may be necessary to improve the government's financial position, yet because many of the products of the public enterprises enter into the production of private sector goods, firms will want to raise their price in order to absorb the additional costs. Clearly, the government's revenue position, dependent as it is on funds from the public enterprises, places severe constraints on its stabilization program.

More important, inflation-caused uncertainties and difficulties in planning are particularly serious at this time. Doubts about the accuracy of the budget estimates, on both the revenue and the expenditure side, are bound to diminish the general confidence in the ability and will of the authorities to stop inflation.

Inflationary Aspects of the Budget

A government budget is either neutral, inflationary, or deflationary. The terms *inflationary* and *deflationary* are used here to indicate increases to or subtractions from the amount of money expenditure, i.e., the flow of purchasing power. Under conditions of full employment in Mexico, changes of this kind are accompanied by corresponding price changes; under other conditions, the accompanying changes in production are likely to be more important. The inflationary or deflationary effects of government income and expenditure thus defined can be approximately measured by ascertaining the net budget deficit or surplus.

Although the percentage of GDP devoted to government resources is expected to grow in 1977, this fact in and of itself is not a sign of inflation. On the contrary, this percentage can be expected and should be encouraged to grow. However, the rapidity with which it is expected to grow and its effect on the financing requirement contain the seeds of inflation. Given the budget's prospective gross financing requirement of 221 billion pesos in 1977 and the fact that the government is encountering grave difficulties in drawing further on foreign sources of finance, one can only conclude that the 1977 budget is inflationary.

On the last day of 1976, in meeting with members of the Congress, however, the president is reported to have said that the budget is not inflationary because the expenditure is directed to production, and that expenditure oriented to production will never be excessive because only production "will remove us from the risks of inflation, as the most intelligent way of fighting inflation."

This is an echo of two arguments used by ministers in the last weeks of the previous administration: that excessive government spending could not have been the cause of inflation because the social and economic needs of Mexico are so great; and that spending for production to remove so-called bottlenecks was the only intelligent way of fighting inflation.

As noted in Chapter 6, the claim that any amount of spending is noninflationary so long as it is on production is clearly fallacious, since it does not take into account the fact that inflation at any given time is caused by aggregate demand exceeding aggregate supply. There is certainly no reason to believe that just because output is oriented more toward production, aggregate demand and supply will balance at a stable price level. Justifying the volume of government expenditure by relating it to Mexico's general needs or to its rate of population growth is a complete non sequitur, for neither the ability to spend nor the disaster from overspending has anything to do with national needs. Clearly, the government will have to demonstrate that its financial policy has a sounder theoretical basis than in the past few years if Mexico is to attract the private foreign capital it so desperately needs.

Conclusions

The López Portillo administration has demonstrated with its 1977 budget that the slump in the economy was a source of greater concern than was fiscal and monetary imbalance. The government's spending program provides heavy government investments to inject new life into the economy despite the risk of greater inflation and financial disruption, both key factors in the country's current economic crisis.

And even though the government declared that the need to avoid a full-scale recession more than justified high-level expenditures for the year, the large increase in government expenditures casts doubt on the administration's ability to sidestep the problems into which the economy was drawn in the last six-year presidential period and to which the devaluation of the peso was largely attributable.

The question is how such an ambitious spending program can be financed. If domestic financial resources become scarcer than they were at the end of 1976, the liquidity of the financial system will have become so restricted as to make private investment impossible. The decline in private investment would occur at a time when most observers feel that such investments are vitally needed to support government efforts in restoring a high rate of noninflationary growth.

According to President López Portillo, the budget is flexible and can be reviewed and changed in accordance with changing circumstances. In all likelihood, however, the government will not have the degree of freedom it wishes. The authorities are currently under pressure from the IMF to reduce the budget deficit from 11.5 percent of GNP in 1976 to 6.5 in 1977 and to only 2.5 percent by 1979. Further constraining the government's freedom to spend is the IMF-imposed limit of $3 billion on the net increase permitted in 1977 for Mexico's public foreign debt. This new credit must cover the country's balance-of-payments and budget deficits as well as finance investment to increase oil production and exports.

For most political and economic problems facing President López Portillo, the point of reference remains the events of 1976. In all likelihood, in fact, this government's policies for its six years in office will be dominated by its attempts to cope with the legacy of 1976—a year in which López Portillo was the official presidential candidate, but had little influence over decisions.

11
Patterns of Development, 1976-1990

By the late 1960s, it looked as if Mexico had entered on the road to sustained growth. For nearly fifteen years, its national product per capita had increased steadily by over 3 percent, and aggregate output had increased by about 6 percent per year. The level of investments and the expansion of education and health services gave good promise that the economy would be able to continue at this rate of growth. Inflationary pressures and large balance-of-payments deficits were beginning to develop, however, and during the early 1970s only piecemeal measures and palliatives were undertaken to correct these problems. The failure to stabilize the economy ultimately led to economic crisis and devaluation in 1976. Firm demand management, responsible wage policies, and better investment planning probably could have gradually redressed the balance of payments without retarding growth. Indeed, it is quite likely such measures could even have accelerated growth.

Whether Mexico will soon be able to return to a path of sustained growth, what efforts will have to be taken for that purpose, how much growth can be expected, and what factors will govern and limit the rate of growth—all are obviously highly speculative matters. The issue is surrounded by many political uncertainties, and any attempt to answer these questions must be conditioned by assumptions that may never come true. The ideal policies must be structured so that President López Portillo and his successors will be able to implement them within the constraints of the country's basic institutions and known natural and human resources. It is also natural to assume that a country with independence as a cornerstone of its national credo and with nonalignment becoming an important element in its foreign policy should prefer to base its economic development mainly

145

on its own resources and effort.

Evaluation of Mexico's Macro Alternatives

A major obstacle in developing realistic forecasts of the Mexican economy is the absence of a tableau of the economy indicating all of the relevant relationships. Because an economic and social entity such as Mexico is very complex, it is impossible to build models capable of reflecting all the interactions of the social and economic matrix. One is left, therefore, with two choices. They are (1) to build models that are approximations of reality, or (2) to analyze each situation on a partial equilibrium (all other things being equal) basis. The advantage of the former method is that it enables one to trace what effects a change in one or more variables has on all the other variables. It provides a simultaneous solution on a general equilibrium basis. The advantage of the latter method is that the level of reality approximation can be raised to a point where differences are almost insignificant from the point of view of the problem being analyzed.

For purposes of analyzing the country's growth alternatives and likely development patterns, it was thought best to choose the first method and build an econometric model capable of projecting, through computerization and common sense, all the key macroeconomic variables over the period to 1990. The model was constructed to enable the various choices facing the government to be evaluated and to provide a framework for discussion about the constraints and limitations likely to be imposed upon the country's growth.

Description of the Macroeconomic Model of Mexico

The model developed in the Appendix was designed to quantify as many relationships as possible that were discussed in qualitative terms in the main text. Thus, it is intended to provide further insights into the mechanisms at work in the Mexican economy. The relationships in this model should be viewed primarily as a conceptual device; i.e., given our best forecasts about such variables as the growth of exports, the level and composition of government expenditures, and so on, the model indicates the likely state of affairs over 1976-1990 for different aspects of the economy (private investment, public investment, public and private consumption, balance of payments, etc.).

The model has two uses: it is intended to outline a simple and generally applicable procedure for making a first reconnaissance of the growth alternatives confronting the Mexican economy, and it provides some criteria for choosing among these alternatives.

Assumptions Used in the Models

The projections below entail a large number of assumptions.[1] Our approach in this respect has incorporated the following characteristics. (1) In general, we have made optimistic assumptions about the future. This affects not only our implicit assumptions about such factors as the growth of the United States economy but also elements such as the ability of the government to control domestic inflation through the proper use and timing of such tools as wage policy and fiscal restraint. (2) Although there are indications that the Mexican economy may be going through a turning point, and although behavioral relationships are shifting in a way that may make growth increasingly difficult, we have made optimistic assumptions that the past behavior patterns will hold for the future. (3) We have assumed that the government will continue to play an increasing role in the economy. Hence, we have projected both government consumption and investment to increase somewhat faster than GNP.

Given these assumptions, the model is designed to examine whether the economy can actually achieve the main objectives of the country. These are:

1. the highest rate of growth permitted by existing resources and by the pressing immediate needs of the population
2. the safeguarding of relative price stability within the limits set by the country's institutional constraints and price movements abroad
3. the maintenance of a reasonably small deficit in the balance of payments

Briefly, the model worked as follows. First, it assumed two rates of real GNP growth—6 percent (1960 prices) and 8 percent. It then projected the requirements—imports, investments, savings—needed to achieve the associated levels of income. Second, the U.S. economy was assumed to grow at 3 percent in real terms, which, given the degree of overvaluation of the peso and available imports in the previous year, determined the likely growth of exports. Third, given the rate of growth of GNP, exports, and the exchange rate, the model produces a foreign trade or external gap difference between exports and imports. Fourth, at each rate of GNP growth, another disequilibrium, the domestic gap, occurs between the amounts of domestic income saved and invested. At both 6 and 8 percent rates of growth, the level of investment needed to achieve that expansion was higher than the desired or potential (ex ante) savings at that level of income. Domestic savings do not appear to be adequate to finance these rates of growth, indicating that public savings, for example, are limited by the inflexibility of the tax system and that private savings may be directed into investments overseas owing to higher rates of return there than in Mexico. Fifth, the two gaps must adjust to equality to comply with the conventions used in computing national income accounts. Finally, the process that takes place when the two gaps become equal (ex post) is assumed to be under government control and is based on a realistic assessment of alternatives.[2]

As emphasized before, the forecasts merely work out the implications of various assumptions about the economy and an econometric analysis of its key components. Obviously, Mexico's prospects could change if such variables as the level of exports are changed.

Results of the Simulations

A number of assumptions (see the Appendix for complete details) are implicit in the simulations (Tables 19, 20, and 21). Most important, rates of real GNP growth of 6 and 8 percent were assumed each year over the 1976-1990 period. A growth of 12 percent in current prices was compatible with each in the sense that the size of the external gap did not exceed 6 percent of GNP (the actual 1975 figure being slightly less than 5 percent).

The external gap was felt to be controlling, since it must be filled with foreign resources (borrowing, foreign private capital, short-term portfolio capital), and after the devaluation and general economic disruptions in 1976, it was felt that these sources of funds might not be as available to Mexico as in the past.

In terms of borrowing, it is of course difficult to define a precise point at which increasing external debt might create a creditworthiness problem for Mexico. However, there are several ways of looking at the problem that suggest its seriousness. The best way for the problem examined here is to compare the current account resource balance, plus debt servicing payments, with the imports of investment goods. It seems reasonable to assume that except for some temporary short-term loans, regular foreign capital inflows are by and large used to finance imports of investment goods. Since the ex ante domestic gap was higher than the external gap for both 6 and 8 percent GNP growth rates, it would probably not be prudent for Mexico to pursue a policy of allowing the trade gap to widen so that, ex post, it would equal the savings gap. Instead, the savings gap was adjusted downward to, ex post, equal the trade gap. Thus import of investment goods imposes an upper limit on the gross receipts of foreign capital. When borrowing requirements

TABLE 19

MEXICO: EX ANTE MACROECONOMIC FORECAST, 1975-1982

(Billions of Pesos)

	1975	1976	1977	1978	1979	1980	1981	1982	Average Annual Rate of Growth 1975-1982
Gross National Product	954.7	1069.3	1197.6	1341.3	1502.2	1682.5	1884.4	2110.5	12.0
Gross Domestic Product	972.2	1088.9	1219.5	1365.8	1529.7	1713.3	1918.9	2149.1	12.0
Private Consumption	703.7	784.9	836.6	914.3	1000.2	1094.2	1196.5	1307.4	9.3
Government Consumption	80.7	101.5	123.7	148.7	177.6	211.6	252.0	300.0	20.6
Total Consumption	784.4	886.4	960.3	1063.0	1177.8	1305.8	1448.5	1607.4	10.8
Private Investment	129.8	154.1	179.7	214.3	254.4	301.5	357.3	423.6	18.4
Government Investment	87.4	110.0	134.0	161.1	192.4	229.3	272.9	324.9	20.6
Total Investment	217.2	246.1	313.7	375.4	446.8	530.8	630.2	748.5	19.3
Savings	170.3	182.9	237.3	278.3	324.4	326.7	435.9	503.1	16.7
Domestic Gap	-46.9	-63.2	-76.4	-97.1	-122.4	-154.1	-194.3	-245.4	26.7
Exports	79.8	93.6	104.5	117.6	132.6	149.5	168.6	190.0	13.2
Imports	108.1	122.9	141.1	162.2	186.5	214.0	245.2	280.4	14.6
External Gap	-23.8	-29.3	-36.6	-46.6	-53.9	-64.5	-76.6	-90.4	21.0

Source: Computed by author.

Note: Assumes real rate of GNP growth of 6.0%.

TABLE 20

MEXICO: EX ANTE MACROECONOMIC FORECAST, 1983-1990

(Billions of Pesos)	1983	1984	1985	1986	1987	1988	1989	1990	Average Annual Rate of Growth 1983-1990
Gross National Product	2363.8	2647.5	2965.2	3320.9	3719.5	4165.8	4665.7	5225.6	12.0
Gross Domestic Product	2407.1	2695.9	3019.5	3381.7	3787.6	4242.0	4751.1	5321.2	12.0
Private Consumption	1427.1	1556.6	1692.8	1838.4	1992.3	2153.4	2320.6	2492.1	8.3
Government Consumption	357.1	425.3	506.7	603.8	719.8	858.3	1023.8	1221.5	19.2
Total Consumption	1784.2	1980.9	2199.5	2442.2	2712.1	3011.7	3344.4	3713.6	11.0
Private Investment	502.1	596.6	708.8	842.6	1002.4	1193.1	1420.8	1692.9	18.9
Government Investment	386.9	460.7	548.8	654.1	779.8	929.8	1109.1	1323.3	19.2
Total Investment	888.9	1057.3	1257.6	1496.7	1782.1	2122.9	2529.9	3016.2	19.1
Savings	597.6	666.6	765.7	878.7	1007.4	1154.1	1321.3	1512.0	14.2
Domestic Gap	-309.3	-390.7	-491.9	-618.0	-774.7	-968.8	-1208.6	-1504.2	25.4
Exports	214.0	240.9	271.1	305.0	343.2	386.1	434.4	488.8	12.5
Imports	320.2	365.2	416.0	473.6	538.6	612.2	695.3	789.3	13.8
External Gap	-106.2	-124.3	-144.9	-168.5	-195.4	-226.1	-260.9	-300.5	16.0

Source: Computed by author.

Note: Assumes real rate of GNP growth of 6.0%.

TABLE 21

MEXICO: EX POST MACROECONOMIC FORECAST, 1976-1982

(Billions Pesos)

	1975	1976	1977	1978	1979	1980	1981	1982	Average Annual Rate of Growth 1975-1982
Real Rate of GNP = 6.0%									
Gross National Product	954.7	1069.3	1197.6	1341.3	1502.2	1682.5	1884.4	2110.5	12.0
Private Consumption	703.7	751.0	796.8	863.8	931.7	1004.6	1078.8	1152.4	7.3
Government Consumption	80.7	101.5	123.7	148.7	177.6	211.6	252.0	300.0	20.6
Total Consumption	784.4	852.5	920.5	1012.5	1109.3	1216.2	1330.8	1452.4	9.2
Private Investment	129.8	154.1	179.7	214.3	254.4	301.5	357.3	423.6	18.4
Government Investment	87.4	110.0	134.0	161.1	192.4	229.3	272.9	324.9	20.6
Total Investment	212.2	246.1	313.7	375.4	446.8	530.8	630.2	748.5	19.7
Savings	188.4	216.8	277.1	328.8	392.9	466.3	553.6	658.1	19.6
Domestic Gap = External Gap	-23.8	-29.3	-36.6	-46.6	-53.9	-64.5	-76.6	-90.4	21.0
Real Rate of GNP = 8.0%									
Private Consumption	703.7	751.0	796.8	863.8	931.7	1004.6	1078.8	1152.4	7.3
Government Consumption	80.7	80.9	100.6	123.4	149.8	181.2	218.6	263.4	18.4
Total Consumption	784.4	831.9	897.4	987.2	1081.5	1185.8	1297.4	1415.8	8.8
Private Investment	129.8	156.7	202.8	239.6	282.2	331.9	390.7	460.2	19.8
Government Investment	87.4	110.0	134.0	161.1	192.4	229.3	272.9	324.9	20.6
Total Investment	212.2	266.7	336.8	400.7	474.6	561.2	663.6	785.1	20.6
Savings	188.4	237.4	300.2	354.1	420.7	496.7	587.0	694.7	20.5

Source: Computed by author.

exceed this limit, it could be regarded as a danger signal. Whatever temporary respite it affords, increased foreign borrowing on hard terms cannot solve the problem of Mexico's external disequilibrium (which in 1975 was already reaching serious proportions).

The adjustment of the ex ante domestic gap to that of the external gap was made in two steps. First at 6 percent GNP growth, private consumption was reduced, thus generating a higher savings rate. In policy terms, a major tax reform would be implied. Since the external gap did not exceed 6 percent of GNP for any of the years, a rate of 8 percent GNP growth rate was reflected, and government consumption was then reduced to bring the larger domestic gap into equality with the external gap. At 8 percent real and 12 percent nominal rates of growth, the rate of government consumption was still excessive—over 20 percent per annum. The best alternative at this point would probably be to transfer some tax revenue back to the private sector not only to maintain morale but also to assume adequate purchasing power for the expanding industrial sector.

Needless to say, the projections of the trade (exports-imports) and resources (savings-investment) gaps are not necessarily estimates of external resource requirements. The trade gap may be considered as approximating the upper bound of the requirement of foreign capital. The size of the gap may be regarded as an indication of the magnitude and nature of policy adjustments required if the assumed growth rate of GDP is to be realized. The greater the adjustment through export-import policies and the efficiency of capital investment, the smaller the requirement for foreign exchange and the less underutilization of potential domestic savings.

Results of Macroeconomic Forecasts: General Considerations

Given the results of the simulations and the policy options open to the Mexican government, several very general observations about the movement of the economy up to 1990 are possible.

1. A general compatibility among all the economic policy measures exists in the sense that the available policy instruments appear capable of eliminating any potential contradictions between Mexico's different socioeconomic objectives. Furthermore, economic policy, as is unfolding under the López Portillo administration, is potentially consistent in the sense that the policy tools, if used correctly, would exert a favorable impact on the government's goals in the direction desired.

2. A rate of economic growth higher than 8 is possible through heavier investment by the federal government, but there must be simultaneously an expansion of the private sector and promotion of

exports.

3. An increase in employment over and above past trends is possible if the economy expands rapidly and if growth is reoriented toward strongly labor-intensive activities, such as agriculture and tourism services.

4. More equitable income distribution is feasible if federal spending continues to concentrate on the lowest income groups and if this expenditure is financed to a greater extent by taxes from the highest income groups. On the other hand, reorientation of the economy toward the agricultural sector will generate more jobs for the poorest groups (unemployed and underemployed) and thus directly benefit the lower-income segments of the population.

5. The balance-of-payments current account and the service rate on external debt should improve even though the economy expands at a rate faster than in the past owing to oil exports (discussed below). In addition to oil exports, if the government prevents the peso from becoming as overvalued as in the past (a 10 percent overvaluation was used in the simulations) and because the federal government has recently stepped up its aid to the agricultural sector, Mexico should not be constrained by foreign exchange as in the past. The chief constraint on the economy in recent years has been foreign exchange, but the government should now take steps needed to increase domestic savings and thereby reduce the external savings required to finance total investment levels.

If for some reason the domestic and trade gaps cannot be constrained in the range forecast, the authorities can always reduce the rate of growth of income. A 5 percent level of GNP growth, for instance, would still be a reasonable growth rate by comparison with many developing countries: it would also considerably reduce the two gaps over the next decade and a half. For a country with Mexico's potential and successful past performance, however, decelerating the rate of income growth is not an acceptable alternative. In particular, the rate of growth of employment would also be slowed down. Worse yet, those likely to be made unemployed or underemployed by the reduction of income growth would be the poorer segments in the economy.

An alternative might be to impose increased quotas, tariffs, or other import controls in order to reduce the demand for imports. Although these policies might work in the short run, they should not be regarded as a viable solution. The macroeconomic model indicates that import controls could lower the external gap. However, a reduction in imports would lower the total availability of resources and thus accentuate the internal (savings-investment) resource gap; i.e., a reduction of imports would lead to higher domestic prices and thus increase the ex ante import demand. The extent to which domestic prices would rise depends of course on the extent of trade controls and the monetary and fiscal policies concurrently initiated by the government. If foreign demand were curtailed and investment financed through foreign borrowing (rather than tax increases), the inflationary pressure might be quite severe. Trade restrictions, therefore, cannot be considered acceptable long-run policy tools to be used in achieving high rates of domestic growth.

The implications of these projections for Mexico's monetary, fiscal, and planning policies are extensive, with several points standing out.

1. Although high rates of capital formation are necessary to sustain Mexican economic growth, consumption is also necessary to maintain a level of demand that assures full utilization of productive capacity, present and potential. Thus, a policy of restraining consumption will be self-defeating unless nonoil export proceeds grow rapidly. The reduction of consumption made necessary by the size of the domestic gap may create excess capacity. Investment would thus tend to decline, thus reducing the country's rate of growth. A policy of encouraging additional fixed capital formation over the levels forecast would lead to larger imports, however, and unless exports grow more rapidly, the external gap would lie outside the feasible range.

2. There is of course a link between the trade gap and the exchange rate. To the extent that the exchange rate is not in equilibrium, greater economic efficiency could be achieved by adjusting it. More precisely, as will likely be the case in Mexico with a 12 percent nominal GNP rate of growth, the peso will soon become overvalued again in terms of the rate that would clear the markets for foreign exchange. Under these conditions, devaluation would probably raise export earnings, particularly through its favorable impact on exports of manufactures, lower import demand, and hence reduce the current account balance-of-payments deficit (the trade gap).

3. Import controls through tariffs or quantitative restrictions would also raise the domestic prices of imports. But as noted above, they would create further distortions in the economy. Devaluation is superior in reducing imports, since it would raise the prices (in terms of local currency) of both exportables and importables in relation to domestic prices and wages, thus restricting imports and at the same time encouraging exports. If import controls or devaluation are to succeed in reducing the deficit in the balance of payments and thus the foreign capital inflow, it is necessary to restrict domestic consumption even further by raising taxes in order to expand domestic savings (to offset the

reduced level of foreign borrowing). The increased taxation needed to increase domestic savings, however, is likely to weaken investment, and thus additional investment incentives will be needed to counteract this effect. For that purpose, a reduction in profits taxation would be desirable.

Based on the forecasts, the following additional short-term economic policy guidelines are recommended.

1. Sharp changes in government expenditures should be avoided and a stable growth sustained so that real GDP will increase at 8 percent, a rate that, historically, is not necessarily associated with excessive price pressure. If the average annual rate of 8 percent is attempted through short spurts over 8 percent, to compensate for periods of recession, a high rate of inflation may develop.

2. Sharp changes in the growth of the money stock should be avoided. Even if recommendation 1 is not met, this would be possible as long as government expenditure increases are offset by increases in taxes.

Conclusions

The forecasts indicate that real rates of 8 percent income growth are feasible for Mexico over the 1976-1990 period. For a number of reasons, particularly employment, the authorities should strive for this goal. However, several elements may modify the forecasts.

On the optimistic side, high growth may be easier to attain than indicated, and the Mexican authorities need not place total emphasis on taxes or reduced government consumption to equalize the gaps at the 8 percent rate of growth.

Any of the other components of national income could (under normal circumstances) be treated as variables bringing the two gaps together. It is likely that a broader approach of this sort would result in more savings and exports and thus a higher level of national welfare than would be the case if the government concentrated on only one variable.

On the other hand, foreign capital requirements could be reduced by adopting policies that encourage import replacement or export promotion or both.

In short, if the authorities attempt to borrow at the level indicated by the ex post gaps, there might be an upward bias in the amount of domestic or foreign savings that would be needed over time to achieve the 8 percent GNP growth. Several alternative measures can enable the government to reduce the size of the resource gaps and thus the level of borrowing. Price changes, particularly increases in consumer prices vis-à-vis the overall price level, can play an important role in the adjustment process.

On the pessimistic side, several constraints not considered implicitly in the model may make an 8 percent rate of growth very difficult to attain. These include the problems posed by the rapid increase in population, water shortages, and increased difficulties in attracting foreign capital.

12
Potential Obstacles
to Accelerated Growth

The projections of 8 percent annual increase in real GNP made in the previous chapter are based on fragile assumptions. Unfortunately, there is little chance that things will turn out to be more favorable in Mexico than were assumed in this forecast. Major oil finds were already taken into account. Other mineral discoveries and perhaps a more liberal policy by the United States toward Mexican exports and immigrants are the only circumstances that might brighten the outlook significantly.[1]

Natural Conditions for Growth

The 8 percent growth rate is, therefore, a reasonably optimistic basis for the projections. To justify this choice, an examinatin of Mexico's natural conditions, international relations, and other factors is necessary.

The first problem is to determine whether the physical capacity or potential of the country can generate this rate of growth, i.e., can the economy increase employment, improve the quality of labor, expand the stock of real capital, and employ better and more suitable technologies and still maintain an 8 percent real growth rate.

Clearly, Mexico cannot grow faster than its physical capacity permits. But it certainly can grow more slowly, depending partly on its ability to take advantage of its physical possibilities and partly on its ability to finance growth expenditures such as real investments, education, and health expenditures. It is not easy to identify the upper limit of the country's growth rate, and perhaps strictly speaking, no rigid upper limit can be determined, particularly if one is not willing to specify what conditions should be present at the end of the projection period. Yet it is obvious that the physical conditions for growth will be an important factor in determining whether Mexico will ultimately join the ranks of the developed economies.

A survey of a country's unused resources may give a rough idea of the growth potential—unused resources being interpreted broadly to include unused technical knowledge. Mexico has few known natural resources that are not already utilized. The practical possibilities of expanding cultivated areas under irrigation at reasonable cost have been largely exhausted. Certain minerals are, however, available in sufficient quantities to serve as the basis for further expansion of modern industry. Otherwise, oil is the only resource of major importance. In 1974 major discoveries of petroleum in the states of Chiapas and Tabasco, together with new wells at Cotaxtla in Veracruz, assure Mexico a place as one of the world's leading oil producers.[2]

Thus nature has not endowed Mexico with an abundance of wealth; the country will have to follow the long, narrow road of building up the productive capacity of the people through increasing their skills and equipment.

Mexico has the same advantage that all other underdeveloped countries have: the opportunity to achieve rapid growth through simple imitation. It might be argued that the relative abundance of engineers and other educated workers in production and administration would help Mexico catch up relatively quickly. But rapid catch-up is probably conditioned by the existence of relevant skills in the lower echelons, and here Mexico has no particular advantage over many other underdeveloped countries. Similar arguments apply to the existence of unused capacity in industry; unused capacity may be a symptom of underdevelopment itself and is not necessarily a source of easy progress, even temporarily. In summary, it is difficult to point to any particular physical circumstances other than oil that should make it easy for Mexico to accelerate its rate of growth to 8 percent.

Major Obstacles to Accelerated Growth

Although under existing conditions Mexico may have a difficult time in achieving an 8 percent growth rate, a number of factors could actually tip the scale in the other direction and at worst make the picture grim, indeed.

In the first place, rapid population growth—in addition to making it difficult for the economy to achieve the high rates of savings required for 8 percent growth—will increase the scarcity of land and natural resources and thereby might make growth increasingly difficult to overcome through capital investments.[3]

Second, shortages of water will begin to limit further expansion of several of Mexico's major industrial and agricultural centers, thus necessitating the costly development of new sources of water, or relocating some activities, or both.

A third area of possible concern is foreign capital. In the attempt to find an upper limit to the growth capacity, it was assumed that the yearly inflow of external funds would not increase much beyond 5 percent of GNP. This is probably a very realistic assumption in terms of the maximum level of foreign resources. But even less foreign capital may be available. Because of the devaluation controls imposed by the International Monetary Fund and the foreign banks' disinclination to increase their exposure in Mexico, foreign resources will surely become more limited, and loans will be made on less advantageous terms than in the past. The availability of loans and private investment will presumably depend on the outcome of the current stabilization program and on the bankers' subjective evaluation of the ability of the economy to return to a pattern of high stable growth.

The influence of these three factors on growth cannot be determined in more than very approximate terms. Other constraints (which cannot be identified) may become important, but these three constraints are already beginning to influence Mexico's growth pattern.

Problems Posed by the Expansion of Population

Mexico's population is currently growing at a rate of 3.5 percent per year, and migrating at a rate to make the urban-rural ratio 60 to 40 with urban areas growing at 5.6 percent yearly compared with only 1.6 percent for rural areas. It is also a very youthful population, with nearly half its members under fifteen years of age.

These factors contribute to a potentially critical situation. Food resources should increase in proportion to needs, but it is by no means certain that they will be able to. The country's arable and pasture lands are nearly saturated. Increased production can come only from increased yields. Sufficiently high yields, however, may require a level of investment greater than the country can afford. Then too, the concentration of a majority of people in the money economy of the cities will require an increase in their purchasing power in order to pay the higher prices the farmer must get if inequalities in income distribution are not to deteriorate any further. Such a rise in income is contingent upon the availability of jobs in the industrial sections of the cities, since the rural areas no longer are able to attract or provide sufficient livelihood for the younger generations. Increased opportunity for employment is, in turn, contingent upon increased industrial production at a time when many skills and new markets are not readily available. Moreover, the increased population will create pollution problems, which the country is completely unprepared to handle.[4]

On the basis of fairly realistic assumptions about the fall in death rates and a slight fall in fertility, it can be predicted that Mexico's population will roughly double—from 50 million in 1970 to 100 million in 1990. Similar increases in the numbers of those expecting jobs can be projected. The capital requirements for creating these jobs are staggering, with estimates running around $5 billion annually, or about 20 percent of GDP. This amount of investment is unlikely, if past trends are any indication. The unemployment problem in all its aspects will be with Mexico for a long time.

Rapid population growth in Mexico will unquestionably be a major problem, but the means for dealing with it in ways consistent with humane values appear to be more extensive than is usually assumed. Population growth per se is not an unsurmountable barrier to economic growth in Mexico. The opposite appears more nearly correct: only if there is a major failure in development need population growth lead to human tragedy. There is one problem, not two—and that problem is solvable. The solution is not automatic; it requires a special effort. Failure to mount an effective development effort will be doubly costly: it will not only postpone progress but also make it harder to come by.

If the solutions to the problems arising from rapid labor force growth lie in accelerated economic growth, it is fairly clear that faster growth is conditional on new economic policies. Since the most important parameter influencing the projected 8 percent growth rate is the availability of savings, these policies would therefore have to introduce a new tax reform and develop more effective ways of mobilizing voluntary domestic savings. Since the López Portillo administration has recently moved in these directions, it can be said that its policies are, in this respect, fully consistent with the country's long-run needs.

Water Shortage as a Constraint on Growth

Although population may not directly act to limit growth in Mexico, its growth may indirectly hinder the country's advance. Increased personal consumption of water will reduce that available for industry and agriculture—which may have serious consequences. Mexico is among the water-poorest countries of its economic size in the world. Its water supply is not only limited in overall terms, but moreover is not readily available in some major areas.

Five of the country's major rivers (the Papaloapán, Coatzacoalcos, Tonata, Grijalva, and Usumacinta) account for over 50 percent of the mean discharge of all major Mexican rivers. Unfortunately for meeting the country's major water requirements, their combined drainage area covers at most 10 percent of the country's surface. In addition, these rivers are all located in the underpopulated tropics of southeastern Mexico. Furthermore, Mexico's water problems have been made difficult by the fact that 52 percent of the country's land area is located in zones that receive fewer than twenty inches of rainfall a year, and another 11 percent of the surface area receives between twenty and thirty inches a year. More than 75 percent of the country is arid or semiarid. Moreover, more than 85 percent of the total known water resources are located in areas below 500 meters, but 70 percent of the population and 80 percent of the country's industrial activity are located at altitudes above 500 meters.

Mexico's water resource problem, therefore, has two aspects.[5] First, water resources are limited in supply. Second, the location of supplies does not coincide with that of demand. Clearly, the water supply may become a constraint to growth or an arbiter of change in terms of the future geographic structure of the country's economic activity.

Estimates of the demand for an availability of natural resources through the year 1990 are certainly subject to wide margins of error. They may, however, be useful in pointing out that water shortages may begin to constrain urban and agricultural growth. They also help identify the potential magnitude of the problem and determine if government action is warranted and if so at what cost. Scarcity has the general connotation that solutions to resource problems can always be found if sufficient funds are available. Projections to 1990 are, therefore, primarily useful in focusing more sharply on minimum cost solutions.

On the basis of simple extrapolation techniques, a recent study has shown that Mexico will encounter severe problems in this regard from the 1980s onward. Although water scarcity will not completely inhibit the country's economic expansion, it will almost certainly impose certain locational changes in the economy.

Urban-Industrial Water Shortages

Industrial and domestic users together account for about one-fourth, and agriculture for three-fourths, of Mexico's total water requirements. In 1965 industrial and domestic demand was below one percent of Mexico's surface water runoff.

By 1990, however, total domestic and industrial water demand will probably increase by seven times. Although even a tenfold increase in demand would not present severe problems on a national scale, water supply bottlenecks are very likely to develop in some regions. The magnitude will depend on many variables, including (1) population size; (2) the success of the government's industrial decentralization policy; (3) political decisions resolving the competing claims of industry and agriculture; (4) the cost of basin water transfers; and (5) the efficiency of water use and the development of water-saving methods, waste water treatment, and waste reuse.

The Valle de México, with close to ten million inhabitants in 1970, faces imminent and severe water problems. Demand is expected to surpass supply within the next five to ten years, depending on how much water can be withdrawn from storage in the valley sediments without jeopardizing buildings and other urban structures. To meet demand thereafter will require the development of larger supply systems than now exist in the world. Because the Valle de México is an intermountain basin, water will have to be pumped over a vertical head of 1,000 to 1,500 meters and for a distance of more than 200 kilometers. The required volume may range between 65 cubic meters per second (m^3/sec) and 110 m^3/sec, depending on the expansion of the metropolitan area after 1980, and the implied energy requirements for pumping would vary from 0.7×10^7 MWh/year to 1.2×10^7 MWh/year. This in turn would necessitate power plants of between 800 MW and 1,370 MW (11 and 19 percent, respectively, of total national installed capacity in 1970), if capacity were used exclusively for round-the-clock pumping.[6]

The Lerma Basin is another area of possible water shortage. This basin drains an area of about 53,000 square kilometers between Mexico City and Guadalajara, to which it currently exports about 20 m^3/sec of water. The basin has a population of approximately 7 million people, with Querétaro and Toluca two of the fastest growing cities in the country. To the extent it diverts water to its own needs, the continued growth of both Mexico City and Guadalajara might be hindered. Peak levels of water demand in Guadalajara already tax the capacity of the existing water system, and most of its underground water resources appear to have been exploited.

Water recycling is not yet a common practice in Mexico, but it could go far toward mitigating the problem of water scarcity. Water contamination is likely to become a more pressing problem with continued industrial growth. Contamination, expressed in biochemical oxygen demand compared with available water resources, is most noticeable in the Valle de México, the Bravo region, and the Lerma and Papaloapan basins. Wastewater treatment devices may become mandatory in these regions, which would affect the existing pattern of regional advantage and disadvantage in terms of industrial location.

Despite these problems, there appears to be enough water in Mexico to meet aggregate urban-industrial demand through 1990. The real issue is obviously the cost of transferring water from surplus areas to high demand areas.

Agricultural Water Use

Agriculture is by far the most important source of demand for water in Mexico. It is likely to become increasingly dependent on water availability and control. Mexico appears to have sufficient water resources to sustain the projected level of agricultural growth, provided sufficient financial resources are allocated to their development, but regional constraints will probably change the spatial structure of agricultural production.[7] Since the water resources of the northern coastal areas are likely to be fully developed within a few years, these areas will lose their present dominance unless expensive interbasin water transfers are carried out. The central region (State of México, Hidalgo, Puebla, and Tlaxcala), which contained a fourth of the agricultural labor force in 1970, has only limited potential for agricultural expansion. There is little additional land, water resources are fully exploited, and most farms are already too small to maintain a family with the present cropping pattern. Unless there is a shift to intensive horticulture, this region will not be able to support any population increase without a decline in the average income level.

Some of the constraints that are caused by regional differences in supply and demand for water may turn out to be less severe than implied by an extrapolation of geographic trends. The regional water problem is, and will remain, more serious than the national problem. And whether directly (by forcing a new spatial structure on the economy which might be less conducive to growth than that which would emerge if water were not scarce) or indirectly, regional water scarcities could definitely pose a constraint to the country's long-run economic growth.

The costs to growth could, however, be reduced by devoting human and financial resources to research designed to find ways and means of economizing on water use. Any research leading to increased efficiency in water use, to national water pricing, to efficient interbasin transfers, and to efficient desalination may help limit the severity of the constraint water will impose on growth.

Energy Shortage as a Constraint on Growth

Until several years ago, it appeared that increased scarcities of energy would impose a severe constraint on Mexico's growth. The country is not well endowed with hydropower or coal resources, and nuclear power is unlikely to become a significant source of energy for several decades. The country's oil deposits also appeared to be on the verge of depletion.

Mexico's energy picture was dramatically altered in December 1976, when PEMEX increased its figure for proven reserves from 6.3 billion to 11 billion barrels. Later that year, the director-general of PEMEX announced that 60 billion barrels of recoverable oil is a low estimate. This figure has been substantiated by several foreign experts.

Those increases are largely the result of the discovery of new fields. The area where oil was first struck in May 1972 was at Reforma, on the borders of the southeastern states of Chiapas and Tabasco, west of the city of Villahermosa. Since then discoveries have been made in the Gulf of Mexico, near Cotaxtla in the state of Veracruz, and near the Guatemalan border.[8] The geological formations are similar in all these areas, and there is growing confidence that these structures form one huge hydrocarbon basin, which may well stretch across the entire Yucatán Peninsula as well.

In addition, PEMEX is embarking on exploration of potential oil-bearing structures in the northern states of Baja California and Tamaulipas—where commercial quantities of natural gas have been found and—in Coahuila, Chihuahua, Sonora, and Durango.

Given the limited resources of PEMEX, the emphasis of the López Portillo administration during its six years will be on exploring and exploiting the southeastern deposits. The Chiapas-Tabasco area is already producing 60 percent of Mexico's daily output of 1 million barrels—the balance comes from the traditional drilling area of Poza Rica—and should account for the expected increase to 2.2 million barrels per day (b/d) by 1982. Domestic demand permitting, half of it should be available for export and, at 1977 prices, would fetch $4.5 billion a year. With foreign sales averaging 150,000 b/d, oil will already be Mexico's principal export in 1977. By 1982 it will account for more than half the country's foreign exchange income and will dwarf tourism.

The 1982 target of 2.2 million b/d of production depends on the completion of four complex and expensive development programs involving capital investment of $15.5 billion. Unlike finds in the North Sea or Alaska's North Slope, the new oil finds in Mexico pose no major technical problems.

Mexico's prospects as an oil exporter are unavoidably linked to those of the United States as an importer. At present, and for the foreseeable future, all but a symbolic trickle of Mexican oil exports are destined for the United States, which is as anxious to provide a market as PEMEX is to secure one. According to most projections, the United States is unlikely to reduce its oil import needs during the 1980s, when Mexico will come on-stream as an exporter comparable to Venezuela today.

The impact of Mexico's new oil discoveries will in fact mainly be felt domestically. The current recession has posed severe social problems, but oil exports should enable Mexico to resume rapid growth by 1979. Although some of its ambitious, capital-intensive petrochemical projects may be postponed by a year or two, the government's basic strategy of using crude exports to pay for an industrial capacity to transform crude oil is sound. Needless to say, energy no longer seems a limiting factor to growth.

Constraints Associated with Increased Difficulty in Attracting Foreign Capital

The Mexican economy has not been able to generate sufficient savings internally to achieve its major goals of high growth and increased opportunities, both of which are necessary for continued social and political stability.

Two major factors are involved. (1) A large volume of investment is required to finance vitally needed social overhead projects such as rural schools, roads, and so on. These projects are very slow in maturing and thus not attractive to most Mexican investors. (2) Domestic savings are in any case not sufficient (owing to the low levels of taxation) to finance Mexico's capital requirements.

Three foreign sources have provided the bulk of capital needed to supplement the country's domestic savings: official international financial institutions, foreign private institutions (mainly commercial banks) and bond markets, and foreign businesses in direct investments in Mexico. The official institutions—the World Bank and the Inter-American Development Bank—have been major providers of capital in the past, but they are unlikely to do so in the future. First, their resources are small in relation to the needs of developing countries or as a share of international capital supplies. Second, there is great pressure on these institutions to place more of their funds in the poorer developing countries—countries much more in need of capital than Mexico.

Unfortunately, Mexico's prospects for attracting large volumes of capital from foreign private capital markets and businesses are not as promising as in the past.

Sources of Foreign Private Capital

There are three primary types of financing available to Mexico from private foreign lenders: trade credit, loans and credits from banks and other financial institutions, and bond issues. Trade credit is typically of short duration, nonrenewable, and, therefore, not a good source for the country's major long-run capital requirements. More important is the access of Mexican borrowers—both public and private—to private foreign capital in the form of loans and bond issues.

The international markets for private loans and bonds have changed dramatically in recent years. Although recent trends in the international flow of private loan capital from these sources have been very favorable for Mexico, the availability of such funds during the next ten years is much more uncertain. The criteria used by lenders in evaluating the creditworthiness of potential borrowers, given the state of the Mexican economy, will mean that the country will have a difficult time in obtaining capital on the same scale and terms as in the past few years.

Foreign Capital Flows to Non-OPEC Developing Countries

During 1973-1975 roughly one-half of the total foreign capital for the non-OPEC developing countries came from official sources such as government-to-government loans and loans from international agencies such as the World Bank and the IMF. Of the half from private sources, most originated in bank credits, and a very small amount was raised through bond issues. Direct investments and trade credits each provided about 10 percent of the requirements of these countries.

Clearly (as seen from a comparison of Tables 22, 23, and 24) the major trend in international financial markets in the last several years is the increase in non-OPEC borrowing. This is particularly evident in the case of Eurocurrency credits, where their share rose from around one-third of the total in 1972 to over half in 1975. By contrast, these countries have not participated in the recent growth in the international bond market. Bond issues of non-OPEC developing countries actually declined from 1973 to 1975, but total international issues increased by 140 percent.

Borrowing in the Euromarkets by non-OPEC developing countries has been highly concentrated among a small number of countries. Mexico and Brazil each received about one-quarter of the total credits flowing to this group of countries during the 1973-1975 period, although their share has fluctuated sharply from year to year (Table 24). Argentina, Peru, the Philippines, and South Korea have also been major borrowers, accounting for another 15 percent of the total. Most of the rest went to

TABLE 22

PRIVATE FOREIGN LOANS AND BOND ISSUES

(Billions of U.S. Dollars)

	1973	1974	1975
Eurobonds	$ 4.2	$ 2.1	$ 8.6
Foreign bonds outside the United States	2.6	1.4	4.0
Foreign bonds in the United States	1.0	3.3	6.2
Total bonds	$ 7.8	$ 6.8	$18.8
Eurocurrency bank credits	21.9	29.3	21.0
U.S. bank credits to foreigners	0.9	1.2	2.5
Other bank credits to foreigners	2.0	3.0	4.0
Total bank credits	$24.8	$33.5	$27.5
Total bonds and bank credits	$32.6	$40.3	$46.3

Source: <u>World Financial Markets</u>, June 1976, Morgan Guaranty Trust Company of New York.

other higher-income or mineral-rich developing nations, although many other countries have also participated in the market to a minor extent. In 1974 and 1975 a total of forty-three developing countries received at least one Eurocurrency credit.

For private bank credits, interest rates in the Euromarkets are typically established as a fixed premium above the London Inter-Bank Offer Rate (LIBOR) for short-term borrowings between international banks participating in the Eurocurrency market. During the late 1960s and early 1970s, interest rates for loans to countries such as Mexico were typically higher than for loans to industrialized countries, although the difference was not always that great. During 1974 and 1975, lower-income countries paid on the average about 10 basis points (100 basis points are equivalent to 1 percent) more than higher-income developing countries including Mexico. Mexico and other semiindustrialized countries with a good record of repayment often paid about 25 basis points more than the more developed countries. These spreads were much smaller than in the 1960s, when the differential between the

TABLE 23

SOURCES OF FOREIGN CAPITAL, NON-OPEC LDCs

(Billions of U.S. Dollars)

	1973	1974	1975
Official bilateral	$11.5	$15.1	$16.3
Official multilateral	3.6	6.1	7.5
Total official	$15.1	$21.2	$23.8
Direct investment (net)	3.6	3.6	3.5
Trade credit	2.2	5.8	3.9
International bond issues	0.6	0.2	0.3
Bank credits	7.5	10.5	15.3
Total private	$13.9	$20.1	$23.0
Total	$29.0	$41.3	$46.8

Source: World Financial Markets, June 1976, Morgan Guaranty Trust Company of New York.

developing countries and industrialized nations was often several hundred basis points. In the early 1970s, Mexico was an anomaly among developing countries, that is, it was able to borrow at rates very close to those prevailing for industrialized countries.

Outlook for Private Foreign Loans

The dramatic expansion in the volume of international bank credits during the past three years, particularly in loans to Mexico and other developing countries, is largely attributable to the simultaneous occurrence of four extraordinary events.

1. The threefold increase in international oil prices instituted by OPEC in late 1973 and 1974 created a massive flow of funds into the oil-exporting countries. Large volumes of surplus oil payments, particularly from the Gulf States, were placed by the oil-exporting countries in the Euromarkets, greatly increasing the pool of international short-term and medium-term loan capital.

2. At about the same time, the system of fixed exchange rates among major countries disintegrated, and currency values began fluctuating

TABLE 24

EUROCURRENCY BORROWING

(Percent of Total)

	1972	1973	1974	1975	1976 (first half)
Developed countries	60%	63%	71%	34%	34%
LDCs	36	33	24	53	53
OPEC	(10)	(13)	(3)	(14)	(16)
Mexico	(3)	(7)	(3)	(11)	(6)
Brazil	(8)	(3)	(6)	(11)	(8)
Other	(15)	(10)	(12)	(17)	(23)
Communist countries	4	4	5	13	13
Total	100%	100%	100%	100%	100%
(Millions of US$)	$6,857	$21,851	$29,263	$20,992	$12,709

Source: World Financial Markets, June 1976. Morgan Guaranty Trust Company of New York.

freely. The consequent uncertainty over future currency values produced a substantial decline in the volume of international bond issues. Capital that would normally have flowed into longer-term bonds and loans was directed to the shorter-term bank credit market, thus expanding this pool even further.

3. In light of the increased availability of funds, a number of developing countries began to expand their borrowings in the Euromarkets, usually to finance their higher oil import bills, but also, as in the case of Mexico, to expand their domestic development efforts.

4. The raw material price boom of 1973 and 1974 made such large-scale borrowings appear to be sound investments, at least for those developing countries such as Mexico possessing significant mineral wealth and relatively low levels of indebtedness.[9]

Although these markets thus grew rapidly in the early to mid-1970s, the conditions under which they grew and made loans cannot be expected to arise again. This change in conditions will have two adverse effects for Mexico. First, the country will face greater competition for available funds, and second, lenders will be more hesitant in extending loans. In other words, there is a high chance that restricted availability of capital in the industrialized countries in the next decade will constrain the willingness of private lenders to extend credit to Mexico. Considerable evidence indicates that capital investment requirements in the developed countries will absorb a significantly higher percentage of the savings generated in those countries than has been the case in the past, leaving less available for foreign lending.[10]

In nearly all of the industrialized countries, but particularly the United States, capital investment needs, when expressed as a percentage of gross national product (GNP), will be greater than past levels. In many industries, unit capital costs have increased substantially more rapidly than the general level of prices, thus necessitating greater financial commitments to achieve a given level of capacity expansion. In addition, a host of other economic and social objectives, not present before the 1970s, will have to be met; each will require considerable volumes of investment. These objectives include (1) the development of domestic energy sources as an alternative to imported oil; (2) the development of pollution abatement devices; and (3) the investment of enormous sums for improved public transportation and, particularly in the United States, rehabilitation of the central areas of several major cities.

Although the demand for capital in the developed countries is expected to accelerate, the supply, again expressed as a percentage of GNP, is likely to be reduced. Since the late 1960s and early 1970s, business savings in the United States and Western European countries have been in a steady, even precipitous, decline. Simultaneously, government savings—the surplus of revenues over current expenses— have become highly negative in these countries. Up to 1975, however, aggregate savings in most advanced countries remained relatively steady as a percentage of GNP because of steadily increasing savings rates by households. Household savings cannot be expected to be as high in the future, since they expanded largely as a result of the growing economic uncertainty in the first half of the 1970s, caused by accelerating inflation and the energy crisis and culminating in the most severe recession in the developed countries in thirty years—events that are not likely to be factors in the near future.

Although business savings are expected to recover and government deficits will be smaller in most countries, it is still improbable—given the generally negative climate for business profits and the steadily increasing demand for government-provided social services—that business and government savings will return to the levels typical of the 1960s. If so, and if household savings rates, as is likely, return to more historically normal levels, the supply of capital will most likely be substantially tighter in the future than in the past several years.

Under such circumstances, Mexico will find more and more competition for available funds.[11] Major lenders will probably give preference to their more established private customers or the foreign governments of developed countries. A considerable premium will probably be placed on creditworthiness, and if Mexico's credit rating declines as a result of the 1976 devaluation, that rating will imply a very much reduced access to funds, rather than merely higher interest costs. International lenders are also likely to turn increasingly from countries such as Mexico to private borrowers. Lending to private businesses is more profitable than to national governments and is also the more traditional avenue of international loan capital flows. Only recently have governments such as Mexico's become major foreign borrowers, and then only because the major international financial institutions had excess deposits. Lending to governments has always been considered a marginal activity by commercial banks.[12] These loans will, therefore, suffer disproportionately as the competition for funds increases.

The general shift of commercial banks away from loans to developing countries is likely to be reinforced in the case of Mexico. Many of the larger and more venturesome international banks have already increased their holdings of Mexican debt to their desired limit of exposure. Even under the best of conditions, these banks are not likely to expand their loans to Mexico more rapidly than the future growth in their (the banks') total assets, capital, and surplus, or other standards used in evaluating country-risk exposure.

The Outlook for International Loans: Summary

During the next decade and a half, Mexico will be faced with growing foreign borrowing needs. At the same time, it must expect, as world economic conditions improve, much greater competition for available capital funds from primary clients of banks—industrial corporations, government entities, and other borrowers in industrially advanced countries. World capital supplies in relation to demand should become even tighter over the next decade than in the past. Because loans to governments of developing countries are on the low end of bank lending priorities during periods of tight credit, supply conditions may be expected to shift interest away from lending to governments of developing countries.

In terms of Mexico's ability to achieve an 8 percent rate of growth through 1990, the constraint imposed by tightening credit is perhaps the greatest.

Foreign Direct Investment

Attainment of an 8 percent real growth rate, within an environment consistent with Mexico's commitment to a mixed economy and modernization of its labor force and technology, will require, given developments in the international capital markets, that a substantial proportion of foreign capital be in the form of foreign direct investment.

In comparison with other Latin American countries, Mexico has been more successful than Argentina in increasing foreign direct investment in recent years, but less successful than Brazil (Table 25), where foreign direct investment increased from $US 169 million in 1971 to $US 977 million in 1973.

Direct investments by U.S. firms in Mexico grew from $US 1.2 billion in 1965 to $US 2.8 billion in 1974, but was close to 2.4 percent of total foreign direct investment by U.S. firms throughout the period.

The return on U.S. investments in Mexico has increased from 8.1 percent to 12.6 percent from 1965 to 1974, but has lagged behind the world average return, which grew from 11.1 percent to 21.2 percent over the same period.

Foreign direct investment in Mexico increased rapidly from 1972 to 1974, but suffered a check in 1975 and even a reduction in real terms if the inflation in the United States (and thus the reduction in the purchasing power of the dollar) is taken into account. Preliminary data indicated that direct private investment suffered a more severe decline in 1976.

In addition to the general reduction in the amount of funds available from the industrialized countries, a number of factors concerning investors' uncertainty over economic conditions in Mexico were involved: (1) uncertainty in the minds of foreign investors, particularly up to September 1976, about whether the peso would be devalued; (2) uncertainty about whether the Mexican authorities could or would bring the country's inflation under control; (3) uncertainty over the frequency of labor disputes and whether these disputes would become increasingly disruptive; (4) uncertainty over the implications of the growing distrust of foreign investment by Mexican business, society, and politicians; (5) uncertainty about whether foreign investment will be able to earn a reasonable return in the future.[13]

The general air of uncertainty within the private sector (both domestic

Table 25

FOREIGN DIRECT INVESTMENT COMPARED WITH GNP
FOR SELECTED COUNTRIES

	Foreign Investment End 1973 (US$ millions)	GNP, 1973 (US$ millions)	Foreign Investment as Percent of GNP
Argentina	$ 2,450	$ 34,410	7.1%
Brazil	7,450	73,020	10.2
Indonesia	1,700	10,620	16.0
Iran	1,150	21,510	5.3
Mexico	3,085	45,690	6.7
Philippines	920	11,580	7.1
Spain	2,990	47,900	6.2
Turkey	420	19,840	2.1
Canada	39,167	118,961	32.9

Sources: OECD, Development Cooperation: 1975 Review. Statistical
Annex Tables 32, 46, 48;
Statistics Canada, The Canadian Balance of International
Payments, 1975,Table 1;
Government of Canada. Foreign Direct Investment in Canada.
Ottawa, 1972, p. 15.

and foreign) has arisen not so much as a result of particular pieces of legislation or acts of government, but as a result of Mexico's deteriorating economy. A number of policies and practices have undoubtedly discouraged direct private investment in particular sectors of the economy.[14] These sectors could contribute more effectively to employment, output, and improvement in the foreign exchange balance than in recent years if present policies and practices are changed or modified.

Needless to say, success in attracting foreign direct investment and technology in the amounts required, and on terms consistent with national economic independence, can be achieved only by an array of policies and measures that together create a climate of mutual confidence and understanding between the government and people of Mexico, and the foreign investors participating in the development of their country. Without such a favorable investment climate, it is very difficult indeed to see how the country will be able to achieve an 8 percent growth rate through 1990.

This is particularly true in light of the relationship between international borrowing and foreign direct investment. Officials in Mexico have given the impression that international borrowing is an alternative to, or a way of reducing the need for, foreign direct investment. This is not entirely true, because it does not take into account the way international bankers have traditionally exercised their function. For most banks, international lending arises out of, and subsequent to, foreign direct investment in a country. Banks generally have been more cautious about risk and less informed about conditions abroad than major corporations. Only after a good many of their most important domestic clients acquire a substantial, long-term interest in doing business in a foreign country, such as Mexico, do banks develop the confidence, knowledge, and capabilities of keeping well informed about the country, which in turn enables them to extend financing there to other borrowers. Their large domestic customers operating in the foreign market usually remain their most important clients in the market in terms of the bank's long-term financial interests. Moreover, their clients' opinions about conditions in the country continue to be a major influence on the banks' assessments of lending conditions. As banks acquire detailed knowledge and extended experience in a foreign market, they become capable of and interested in financing local companies. They then become one of the most important channels to induce and assist less internationally experienced companies to undertake business in the foreign market. Thus, international lending and foreign direct investment in a country are closely interacting and reinforcing activities that tend to rise and fall together.

The recent large flows of international lending to governments in a number of developing countries, particularly Mexico, are in many respects exceptions to the above pattern. As indicated earlier, however, these flows of capital were the result of exceptional and temporary circumstances. Nevertheless, most foreign banks that can keep well informed on Mexican conditions and that are now active in lending to the government of Mexico may be expected to seek to enlarge their activities to identify creditworthy opportunities. However, restrictions on foreign banking operations that limit their presence to agency offices substantially retard the expansion of their activities. Such restrictions keep banks from acquiring an intimate knowledge of the market from daily activities. A more rapid expansion of foreign lending, particularly to Mexican companies, and a more liberal expansion of credit to Mexican government entities during times of credit restraint or uncertainty could be obtained. To do so, foreign-financed institutions, like other foreign investors, would need to be permitted and encouraged to broaden their bases of operation in Mexico.

Conclusions

The stable growth experienced by Mexico during the 1955-1970 period can be duplicated and perhaps improved upon during the late 1970s and through the 1980s. In order to do so, however, a number of institutions and time-honored traditions must be changed.

The constraining effects on economic growth of such factors as water scarcities cannot be quantified with great precision. Much will depend on whether the problem of water scarcity is anticipated on a sectoral and regional level with adequate foresight to allow necessary adjustments to be made.

The population problem will demand imaginative and innovative solutions. There is no precedent in world history for the increasingly severe pressure of human resources on natural resources that will inevitably emerge in Mexico over the next two and a half decades. No other country with 50 million people has ever had a rate of population increase of 3.5 percent. Moreover, Mexico itself has never experienced population growth at this rate.

Demographically, Mexico's case is unique. External migration might conceivably relieve some of the pressures on the labor market that could arise from population growth during the next twenty-five years, and external cooperation may be a major factor in financing the economic growth that would have the same effect. But the major effort will have to be an internal one.

Sustained and rapid growth will ultimately depend on whether the inflow of large amounts of external capital, for both the private and public sectors, is adequate. Before foreign capital can be obtained in sufficient volumes, the government must initiate a number of reforms. This should not give rise to undue concern. There is no reason to suppose that Mexico could not or indeed should not break new ground in respect to external financing in order to confront the problems associated with accelerated growth.

13
A Long-Term Development
Strategy for Mexico

The Need for Immediate Reforms

Continued political stability and pragmatic leadership will be vital to Mexico's future development. Sufficient flexibility combined with proper discipline in economic planning and nondogmatic resilience of the economy will also be vital.[1] The Mexican political economy has so far stayed relatively clear of doctrinaire ideologies—of either the West or the East. The economic system has been a mixture of private enterprise and public guidance with predetermined roles for both the public and private sectors. A continuation of this independent national policy is crucial to the success of future development efforts.

Also of crucial significance is the continuation of a favorable climate for growth and progress. Mexico's spectacular economic advances in the past were the result of farsighted political leadership and a unique combination of several diverse, but interrelated, factors such as (1) a growing U.S. market; (2) internal social harmony; (3) individual adaptability to industrial discipline; (4) foreign technical and financial assistance; and (5) a commitment to economic growth by the state. These factors must continue to exert their influence if high rates of economic growth such as the 8 percent forecast in Chapter 11 are to be attained.

From all indications the López Portillo administration has reestablished this propitious atmosphere.[2] Clearly, however, new measures will have to be taken to find fresh sources of foreign capital and to increase domestic savings and investment rates. Many other socioeconomic problems will have to be resolved in order to assure sustained economic growth. Success will depend on the ability of the administration to solve problems as fast as they are created by solutions already at hand. Economic development is a race between answers found and new questions raised. To avoid another economic crisis like the 1976 debacle, the Mexican leadership should immediately initiate a series of reforms to deal with current problems.

In this regard, the following recommendations are made.

1. Measures ensuring a rapid rise in exports will be essential to prevent a rapid rise in the debt-service ratio resulting from the devaluation and declining willingness of banks to renew or expand their loans to Mexico.[3] A comprehensive set of measures will be required, including all or most of the following: (a) strong fiscal and monetary measures to reduce inflation; (b) maintenance of an equilibrium peso/dollar rate of exchange; (c) temporary special credit and other assistance measures enabling seriously affected enterprises to adjust to new market conditions; (d) direct measures to ensure maximum export of petroleum and natural gas; (e) strong encouragement to direct investments in Mexico, particularly in export industries.

2. Loan periods on new borrowings should be lengthened to the extent possible by accepting moderately higher interest charges and other measures.

3. Access to new and longer-term sources of funds should be enlarged by a concerted effort to reestablish Mexico's creditworthiness in international bond markets.

4. Major government utilities and industrial enterprises should be established and operated on a basis that will enable them to market their own issues in international bond markets. This procedure will help reduce the constraints on government borrowing arising from single borrower exposure limitations on United States bonds.

5. New approaches to cofinancing arrangements between international official institutions and private banks should be explored and developed to overcome the existing limitations both types of institutions currently face in their abilities to meet Mexico's credit needs.

6. Strong measures to attract direct investments by foreign corporations and financial institutions will be useful not only in bringing in an important source of capital and technology, but also in creating an environment favorable to expansion of Mexico's borrowing abroad.

The Need for a Long-Term Development Strategy

There is no law of development guaranteeing that once an 8 percent growth rate is established, it will continue indefinitely—the assumptions underlying the projections upon which this rate was selected indicate that economic growth at this rate will be neither easy nor automatic. Reasonable degrees of effort and sacrifice, of wisdom and luck, will be needed. In particular, the government will have to adopt measures to guide the economy along this path.

Together these policies comprise what is referred to here as a long-run development strategy. In addition to the immediate measures mentioned above, the macroeconomic model implies that the government must concentrate its efforts in two major areas: long-term demand management and the attraction of foreign capital.

Long-Term Demand Management

The quantitative dimensions of the task of the government's overall demand management depend primarily on: (1) the control of the share of private income in total national income; (2) the automatic increase in tax revenues with the rise in private disposable income; and (3) increases in the rate of private savings.

The central core of the government's policies over the 1975-1990 period must center around making domestic savings, both private and public, sufficiently large to cover the investments required for the 8 percent target rate of growth. In large part, the macroeconomic model developed in the Appendix indicates this is a question of keeping down private consumption and such public consumption as does not bear on the growth of production. The government's financing problem, therefore, will be largely to keep private consumption down sufficiently to make room for both public and private investment. The increased private consumption must still be considered an important element in the country's growth pattern, not only because a rising standard of living is a major object of economic policy, but also because the political feasibility of a particular economic policy depends much on consumers' reactions to it.[4]

Control of Private Consumption

The macroeconomic model developed for Mexico indicates that without the initiation of special measures, private consumption may tend to increase roughly in proportion to national income. Since monetary policies in Mexico appear to have little effect on private consumption patterns, the major burden of overall demand management must be borne by discretionary tax increases. The quantitative task of the tax policy will be to reduce the rate of increase of real disposable income from around 6.5 percent (presuming the rate of increase of real GNP is 8 percent) to 4.5 percent. In principle this can be done equally well by direct (income) or indirect (commodity) taxes. As the examination of CONASUPO's policies in Chapter 6 indicates, substantial relative price increases for food and other agricultural consumer goods are necessary and could be accomplished by gradually eliminating present substantial food subsidies and thereafter levying taxes on food at rates that increase each year.

The size of this annual increase will depend on the income and cross elasticities of nonfood consumption in relation to food prices. The annual increase in food taxes will have to be high, assuming the price elasticity for food to be relatively low. It is even conceivable that the food taxes alone may prevent total per capita consumption from increasing by more than 1 percent per annum and thus total consumption in the country by no more than the permitted 4.5 percent. Otherwise, general taxes will have to be imposed in order to reduce disposable income sufficiently. An obvious candidate here is the income tax.

The main long-term issues that will confront the Mexican monetary authorities arise from the fact that: (1) credit requirements are likely to increase rapidly as overall development achieves and maintains a high momentum; (2) there are still definite limits to the economy's ability to adjust to volatile changes in international capital markets, and therefore inflows and outflows of short-term capital cannot be precisely regulated; and (3) given the low level of taxation, financing of government deficits through the banking system will be inflationary unless the liabilities of the banking system increase at a sufficiently rapid rate.[5]

Issues for Monetary Policy

The monetary authorities will have an important role to play in demand management, both through creating an environment conducive to increased domestic savings and through controlling inflationary pressures.

As noted in Chapter 3, the authorities have taken several steps to modify these problems. First, they have made efforts to extend the maturity structure of financial instruments. The creation a few years ago of financial certificates with fixed maturities and the issuance of promissory notes with longer-term maturities are steps in that direction. There is a need for further measures along this line, however, to reduce the heavy reliance on virtually all short-term savings instruments to finance long-term investment.

Clearly, the success of these measures will depend on the confidence investors have in the economy's long-term economic outlook. Furthermore, the government's ability to activate a genuine fixed-interest securities market will be constrained by the savers' current preference for liquidity (as opposed to high yields). The authorities can overcome this problem, however, by trading fixed-interest claims without discount if sold before due date. In the long run, the development of a fixed-interest securities market is particularly desirable, since it would establish a firm basis enabling private industry to float bonds.

A closely related field, the expansion of the stock market, also deserves attention. In Mexico, stock market transactions amount to only about 5 percent of the financial institutions' transactions in fixed securities. Most business firms in Mexico are opposed to disclosure of financial statements in order to trade their paper, and this hesitancy over scrutiny of their records has hindered the development of the market. There are ways by which the government could appease some of the prevailing apprehensions of the country's leading industrialists. It could, for example, consider tax incentives for issuers and buyers of shares. Institutional investors could be encouraged to place a share of their resources into the stock market.[6]

The Need to Establish Greater Independence
for the Monetary Authorities

As earlier chapters have indicated, the early 1970s found the government in a position where it had to seek foreign funds both to maintain the exchange rate and to finance the public debt. Increased foreign borrowing added dramatically to the stock of high-powered money, but allowed the central bank to avoid greater increases in domestic credit in its funding of government deficits.

The necessity for external borrowing to finance the current account deficit of the balance of payments without losing reserves, however, gradually imposed restrictions on the central bank's control of the money supply and thus reduced its flexibility in conducting monetary policy.

The environment in which the central bank had to conduct policy was such that: (1) Mexican interest rates were at equilibrium with world rates, with the higher Mexican rate existing to compensate for risk and liquidity premiums—therefore, the central bank could not independently set the nominal rate of interest in Mexico above this equilibrium rate; (2) monetary policy could be used to divert savings from the private to the public sector; (3) the central bank could not, however, independently control the money supply of Mexico; (4) the central bank could influence domestic credit creation and the money multiplier; but (5) the bank could not independently control foreign reserve levels, and therefore had little ability to control the money supply; and (6) the central bank could in association with the private or public sector choose the avenues of domestic credit creation through (a) direct loans to the public and private sectors, (b) the private and public banking community, and/or (c) the federal goverment.[7]

During the 1970s monetary policy was increasingly constrained by the government's fiscal policy. As the public sector's financial requirements increased (mainly because of its incapacity to increase tax revenues at the same rates as public expenditures) and as the balance of payments deficits increased, the Bank of Mexico had to tolerate greater increases in the national money supply than it would have wished.

The central bank—in responding to increased government demands for financing—raised marginal reserve requirements. The money multiplier was not significantly reduced, however, since these requirements were met with new issues of government bonds. The bonds simply constituted a transfer through the banking system from the private to the public sector, and thus the new marginal reserve rates on the money supply were minimal. Indeed, the money supply continued to grow rapidly. A vicious cycle was established: as the money supply expanded, so did prices.

The resulting inflation affected the amount of savings in real terms captured by the banking system. This in turn limited the ability of the country's banking system to finance the public deficits, making it necessary for the government to turn to primary financing from the Bank of Mexico. In order to avoid the increase in the national money supply, the bank made several attempts to capture savings at pre-1972 rates by increasing domestic interest rates. Further increases in interest rates were necessary to compensate investors for keeping their money in Mexico despite increased foreign exchange risk. These savings offered only a temporary solution, however, and therefore an unstable one.[8]

The existing limitations on monetary policy, when coupled with the deterioration of the rate of savings captured by the banking community and the increased interest rates in both real and nominal terms, should be grounds alone for initiating a significant increase in taxes to enable the government to finance its own deficits. It is clear that the present inflexibility in the tax structure—with its effect on the monetary sector—creates a situation incompatible with an 8 percent rate of growth. Because of the need to maintain high levels of government expenditure while simultaneously keeping the external gap in bounds, the government must initiate tax reforms to give monetary policy more flexibility in dealing with the balance of payments.

Measures to Attract Foreign Direct Investment

In assessing policies and measures that are best suited to expand the inflow of foreign direct investment and foreign technology into Mexico, the government must first identify the factors mainly responsible for the recent decline in this source of foreign capital. It can then identify the measures that are best suited to attract foreign investment and technology to sectors or activities for which it is particularly needed.

Historically, government policies in Mexico have created a climate within which foreign investment has been both impressive and fragile. It is impressive because it has been achieved, against a background of revolution, as part of a process of self-determination that has led to nationalization (with fair, and by some standards generous, compensation) of the oil industry and public utilities, the reservation of natural resources to Mexican ownership, and the adoption of agrarian, labor, and social policies regarded by important investment interests as inconsistent with a prosperous and enterprising private sector. It is fragile because the confidence built up over many years can be dissipated—as the last few years have witnessed—in a few short months by policies or pronouncements believed, whether rightly or wrongly, to herald a changing investment climate.

Private Direct Investment

Several recent surveys have indicated that in addition to the general atmosphere of uncertainty over the direction of government policies and the ability of the authorities to stabilize the economy, foreign investors are particularly concerned because (1) they are unable to manufacture efficiently because of uncertainty in the supply of domestically produced components; and (2) the relatively high costs of some components prevent goods produced in Mexico from competing effectively in export markets.[9]

Obviously, the government must make a major effort to attract foreign investors who can contribute most to the development of an efficient manufacturing sector in Mexico; in this regard, there should be more flexible management of import controls. The unreliability or high cost of domestic supplies should not be permitted to discourage the establishment of potentially efficient and low-cost enterprises.

As a first step in this direction, a system should be devised whereby manufacturers are automatically granted import licenses when local suppliers fail to meet cost and delivery specifications. Not only would this policy enable new or expanded enterprises to eliminate costly delays caused by unmet delivery schedules, but it would also provide incentives for suppliers to make deliveries on time and according to specification. Furthermore, it would serve notice of the government's determination to establish a competitive industrial environment.

As a second step, import controls should be eliminated. As measures are taken to improve the balance of payments, it should be possible to relax import controls and gradually permit the entry of competing foreign goods over appropriate tariff barriers. This would reduce costs far more effectively than measures such as price controls.

As a third step, most price controls should be eliminated. Because much industry has grown up behind import controls and also is forced to use high-cost domestic inputs, the dismantling of the existing price control system will have to go hand in hand with the dismantling of import controls. Nevertheless, it should be possible through screening processes to identify products that could be withdrawn from price control at an early date.

The fact that Mexico must act quickly to restore the confidence of foreign investors to achieve its development goals has several implications for tax reform. The government should:

1. continue to improve the administration of the existing tax system
2. confine changes in legislation and rates to the purpose of improving administration, encouraging new investment, supporting dispersion of industry, and extending coverage to government corporations
3. undertake serious investigations into ways of making long-term improvements in the tax system

The first two measures, if included in public statements, should provide the kind of reassurance that foreign investors need if they are going to contribute significantly to the future economic growth of Mexico. Among the changes that should be considered are the granting of tax incentives to all new investment, even though it may not be 51 percent Mexican-owned, and the extension of import duties to government corporations.

With regard to the third suggestion, the increases in taxes recommended in the previous sections will have to be structural so as to provide, on the one hand, for the incentives needed to encourage industrial investment and the dispersion of industry and, on the other hand, for the infrastructure and services at the state and local levels that will be needed to support such investments.

Other policies and measures to reestablish substantial inflows of private direct investment should be designed to deal with the following problems.

1. The most important influence on the decisions of foreign investors will be the general economic policy statements made,

documents published, and actions taken by the new administration. These should include:

   a. an explicit statement of the role seen for foreign direct investment in the attainment of national goals
 • b. a clear statement on the future value of the peso, supported by measures that show that it can be sustained
 • c. strong action to reduce inflation
 • d. announcement of policies for industrial labor, industrial costs and prices, industrial dispersion, and taxation consistent with rapid progress toward national goals

2. Recent legislation on control and ownership of industry and on government participation in industry, has led some foreign investors to doubt whether there is a future for them in Mexico. The government should make plain the following commitments:

 • a. to continue to interpret the new legislation in a way that recognizes the reasonable concerns of foreign investors
 • b. to follow policies for government participation in industry that not only encourage foreign investment in the private sector, but also allow for association of foreign direct investment and government agencies where needed and appropriate

3. Other measures that would encourage both national and foreign capital to invest in important sectors include:

 • a. greater emphasis on national planning
 • b. a more effective and more goal-oriented set of investment incentives
 • c. export incentives focused more on export market development than on tax rebates
 • d. an industrial promotion organization and capability that can provide investors with comprehensive, well-qualified, and readily available assistance at all stages of getting projects from identification to operation

Foreign Loans and Bond Issues

In addition to the obvious need of establishing good financial and economic management to keep its balance-of-payments current deficit at an acceptable level, the government should pursue several policies to strengthen its position in the international capital market.

1. *Debt maturities.* The greatest problem in debt servicing is to refinance maturing debt. Difficulties in this regard are especially acute when access to new sources of capital is constrained. A longer maturity structure than now exists in Mexico's foreign debt would obviously facilitate the implementation of a long-term economic strategy, free from interruptions caused by periods of temporary financial difficulties. It would seem prudent, then, to seek foreign loans of longer maturity than have been typical in recent years. The growing willingness of foreign commercial banks to provide longer-term loans as the world financial uncertainties of 1973 and 1974 recede should assist such efforts. In the case of Mexico, the additional security provided by longer-term borrowing would be worth the higher interest rate that would probably be required (given the fact that most commercial banks prefer to reduce the maturity period of loans to countries with balance-of-payments problems).

2. *Use of bond issues.* Because of the nature of most commercial banks' resources, there are limits to the length of maturity on loans from this source (which in 1976 accounted for over 40 percent of Mexico's public indebtedness). Although bond markets frequently provide funds for periods of ten to twenty-five years, developing countries have generally been kept out of the bond market by the reluctance of lenders to make long-term commitments to what they consider to be high-risk borrowers.

Mexico is going through a difficult period now, but its favorable longer-term economic prospects are well known; and despite the economy's current problems, it was successful in floating several bond issues in 1975 and 1976.

An increased effort to issue bonds would be beneficial for two reasons. Mexico would receive the advantages of lengthened debt maturities, and, more importantly, it would gain access to a very large pool of funds not tapped through the use of bank credit. Many institutions such as insurance companies, as well as private individuals, are major bond investors, especially in the United States. Given the anticipated shortage of foreign loan capital in the future, Mexico could greatly expand its borrowing potential by making greater efforts in the bond markets.

The efforts might include an attempt at decentralizing government borrowing in the bond market. This need not be incompatible with continued close coordination of total public foreign borrowing. A large and growing source of loan capital from the United States is in the form of bonds issued by foreign, national, and local governments and public enterprises such as electric utilities. About 75 percent of the foreign bond issued floated in the United States in the past three years have been of this nature; the vast majority were Canadian, with municipal bonds predominating. Mexico has successfully marketed bond issues through PEMEX, and it should be possible to extend the practice to other federal government agencies. With the development and strengthening of state and local government administration and finance, the possibility of their issuing bonds might be explored.

3. *Bond ratings.* An essential prerequisite to the expansion of borrowing in the U.S. bond markets is to obtain a rating from one of the major bond rating services. The $75 million bond issue of the United Mexican States in 1975 was unrated, but it is unlikely that many more such issues, especially by government agencies or municipalities, could be floated without a rating. In fact, the Mexican issue was the only foreign bond issued in the United States in the past two years that was not rated.

A bond rating serves two purposes.[10] First, it conveys information about the investment quality of the borrower. Most individual investors, who comprise a significant part of the bond market, and many smaller institutional investors do not have the means independently to evaluate bond issues. They rely on the rating of the bond for information essential to making a purchase decision. The absence of a rating leaves them with no basis on which to make an investment decision and thus almost automatically excludes them as potential buyers.

The second function of a bond rating in the United States is to qualify legally a bond for purchase by certain institutions. Pension funds, savings banks, and other fiduciary agencies supervised by state and federal regulatory authorities are in most cases permitted to purchase only securities that meet legal investment standards set by the relevant authority. This generally means that the securities must be rated by one or more of the three rating services and must achieve one of the higher rating grades.

Conclusions

It has been argued that under favorable external conditions and with good domestic economic policies, Mexico should be able to grow at a rate of 8 percent in real terms through 1990. This is a respectable rate of growth and by 1990 should raise the country's economy on a per capita basis to a level comparable to that of a country like Spain today. There is no need to inquire as to what level Spain may have reached by that time.

What matters for the Mexican people is that their country will begin to approach the status of what we today call an economically developed state, where extreme poverty need no longer be tolerated and a relatively decent standard of life can be secured for everybody.

Another key to sustained growth lies in the success of some of the educational and administrative reforms now under way. Mexico's political philosophy of state assistance and guidance to the private sector as well as significant direct involvement in basic industries calls for a bureaucracy of better-than-average competence and efficiency. A state that wishes to do much must be able to do it well.

The authorities must particularly see to it that the country's administrative bureaus and academic circles train and prepare Mexico's growing middle classes to serve their country faithfully and diligently. These energetic and intelligent men and women are now, after the Echeverría years, more than ever before keenly aware of their growing politico-economic rights and power. The task ahead is to teach them to be equally aware of their duties and responsibilities in the service of their country.

Appendix:
A Macroeconomic Forecast
of the Mexican Economy

A first step in forecasting the Mexican economy was the development of a framework that accurately depicts the recent interactions among the major economic forces at work in the country. A second step is to draw on these relationships in order to construct an empirical model that quantitatively depicts these relationships. The explicit purpose is to provide a relatively simple national income account model that will forecast the behavior of key macroeconomic variables in Mexico to 1990 and that will also show the effects of monetary and fiscal policy on these variables.

A Monetarist Model of Income Adjustment in Mexico

Before the final forecasting model was developed, several tests were made to ascertain the importance of money in determining the level of economic activity in Mexico.

This analysis was intended to throw light on two issues crucial in determining the scope of monetary policy available to the Mexican authorities. If in fact the quantity theory of monetary approach is accurate in explaining changes in the economy's money income,[1] then since a large percentage of Mexico's GNP is in the foreign sector, Mexico may not be able to pursue an independent monetary policy and simultaneously maintain a fixed exchange rate.

The analysis used to examine these issues is based on a Prais-Polack monetary model adapted for the Mexican economy.[2] This model was chosen because one of its central features is a money supply function that explicitly includes foreign trade.

The Prais model is essentially a classical one. It assumes substantially full employment of resources and that the major cause of changes in money income is changes in the stock of money. It is a short-run model in which the capital stock is assumed to be fixed and is specified as follows:

(1) $\bar{L} = KY$

(2) $\dfrac{\Delta L}{\Delta t} = X - M$

(3) $E = Y + a(L-\bar{L})$

(4) $M = mY$

(5) $X = X(t)$

(6) $Y = E + X - M$

where

$\bar{L}$ = desired liquidity
L = actual liquidity
E = expenditure
M = imports
X = exports
Y = income
a = liquidity reaction parameter
K = proportion of income in liquid form
m = propensity to import .

As can be seen from equation (1), a constant velocity of money ($K = 1/V$) is assumed. The two unique aspects of the model are: first, that changes in liquidity—roughly speaking, the money supply—are determined by conditions in the balance of trade as seen in equation (2); and second, that domestic expenditures are equal to income but are suppressed by any excess of desired liquidity over actual liquidity—the larger the liquidity reaction parameter a, the faster the adjustment to disequilibriums in the money market.

In this model, since the velocity of money is assumed to be constant, the most crucial variable becomes the marginal propensity to import, because the adjustment to any exogenous disturbance occurs in the foreign sector.

Before the Prais model can be tested to see how well it can predict movements in major macroeconomic variables in Mexico, it must be reformulated for empirical testing. Regressions were run on a model of the form:

(1) $\Delta M_d = a_{11} + a_{12}\Delta Y$

(2) $\Delta M_s = a_{21} + a_{22}D + a_{23}B + a_{24}L$

(3) $\Delta M_d = \Delta M_s$

(4) $B = X - IM$

(5) $IM = a_{51} + a_{52}Y$

(6) $X = X(t)$

(7) $L = 1(t)$

(8) $\Delta DC = d(t)$

where

ΔM_d = change in money demand

ΔM_s = change in money supply

ΔY = change in income

X = exports

IM = imports

ΔDC = net claims of banking system on the government

L = long-term capital movements

B = trade balance .

The estimates for the parameters for the period 1956-1974 are:

(1') $\Delta M_d = 689.5 + 0.1022\Delta Y$ $r^2 = 0.8603$
(10.23) $F = 104.7$

(2') $\Delta M_s = 1487.4 + 0.2147B$
(21.1) $r^2 = 0.9712$
$+ 0.5285L + 221.7170\Delta DC$ $F = 168.7$
(6.7) (4.3)

(3') $IM = -3.3 + 0.1252Y$ $r^2 = 0.9521$
(18.4) $F = 337.9$.

By combining equations (1') and (2'), it is possible to obtain the money multipliers of external variables on money national income.

From the equilibrium condition (3)

$$\Delta M_d = \Delta M_s$$

we have

$$689.5 + 0.1022 \Delta Y = 1487.4 + 0.2147B$$
$$+ 0.5285L + 221.7170 \Delta DC ,$$

or

$$\Delta Y = 7807.2 + 2.1008B + 5.1712L$$
$$+ 2169.3 \Delta DC .$$

Next, the data were directly estimated in this (3′) reduced form of the model, yielding

$$(4') \quad \Delta Y = 7359.4 + 2.8671B$$
$$(21.1) \qquad r^2 = 0.9712$$
$$+ 2.6225L + 1715.08 \Delta DC \qquad F = 168.75 .$$
$$(6.6) \qquad (4.3)$$

The hypothesis of a significant difference between the coefficient estimates of (3′) and (4′) could not be accepted in any case at the 95 percent confidence level.

Thus by use of a simple quantity theory model that explicitly includes the foreign sector in the money supply function, we are able to explain approximately 97 percent of the variation in Mexican money income.

Simple Keynesian and Simple Quantity Theory Models of the Economy

For comparison, two extreme alternative models (Tables 26 through 29) of the economy were developed—a simple Keynesian model (in 1960 constant prices) and a simple monetary (quantity theory) model (current prices). Statistically, there is little to choose between the two models. The t ratios are significant in both and the r^2 quite high. Both models were estimated with a two-stage least-squares procedure. In the Keynesian fiscal policy model, the importance of taxes in stimulating government expenditure is again illustrated, but in the monetary model increased government investment has a strong deterring effect.

TABLE 26

MEXICO: SIMPLE KEYNESIAN INCOME DETERMINATION MODEL, 1960-1974

(Billions 1960 Pesos)

(TWO-STAGE ESTIMATION)

Private Consumption

(1) $PC = 1.149 + 0.118PC(L) + 0.656PC(L)$ $r^2 = 0.999; F = 4,984.10$
              (99.7)   (6.1)

Private Investment

(2) $PI = -52.440 + 0.436Z(L) + 1.906X(L)$ $r^2 = 0.904; F = 56.3$
                   (6.1)   (8.7)

Government Expenditure

(3) $GE = 6.445 + 0.834GAPD(L) + 1.614T(L)$ $r^2 = 0.942; F = 96.75$
                  (13.14)   (4.57)

Taxes

(4) $T = 6.902 + 0.102Y$ $r^2 = 0.947; F = 252.7$
                 (15.9)

Imports

(5) $IM = -3.373 + 0.103 PC + 0.598GI$ $r^2 = 0.958; F = 149.8$
                   (17.1)   (2.9)

Government Investment

(6) $GI = 7.924 + 0.302T + 0.795LTC$ $r^2 = 0.914; F = 63.8$
                  (9.3)   (3.2)

Source: Computed by author.
Note: PC = private consumption; Y = gross national product; PI = private investment; Z = terms of trade; X = exports;
GE = government expenditure; GAPD = the domestic resource gap; T = federal government tax revenues; IM = imports;
GI = government investment; and LTC = long term capital inflows. (L) indicates variable was lagged one year.

TABLE 27

MEXICO: IMPACT MATRIX OF SIMPLE KEYNESIAN MODEL

	PC(L)	Y	Z(L)	X(L)	GAPD(L)	T(L)	LTC
PC	1.195	6.549	0.000	0.000	0.000	0.000	0.000
PI	0.000	0.000	3.455	19.058	0.000	0.000	0.000
GE	0.000	0.000	0.000	0.000	8.292	16.190	0.000
T	0.000	1.031	0.000	0.000	0.000	0.000	0.000
IM	0.124	1.054	0.000	0.000	0.000	0.000	2.377
GI	0.000	0.641	0.000	0.000	0.000	0.000	4.073

Source: Computed by author.

Note: PC = private consumption; Y = gross domestic product; PI = private investment; Z = terms of trade; X = exports; GE = government expenditure; GAPD = the domestic resource gap; T = federal government tax revenues; IM = imports; GI = government investment; and LTC = long term capital inflows. (L) indicates variable was lagged one year.

Note: Derived by increasing each exogenous variable by one billion pesos; i.e., a one billion peso increase of GDP(Y) increases imports (IM) by 1.054 billion pesos.

TABLE 28

MEXICO: SIMPLE MONETARY MODEL (1960-1975)

(TWO-STAGE LEAST SQUARES ESTIMATES)

(Billions Pesos)

Taxes

(1) $T = -5.240 + 0.091Y$
$ (29.3)$
$ r^2 = 0.979;\ F = 855.37$

Private Consumption

(2) $PC = 82.652 - 19.355T + 19.339\ CG + 0.568\ PC(L)$
$ (3.9) (4.3)$
$ r^2 = 0.997;\ F = 1690.39$

Private Investment

(3) $PI = 0.002 - 2.231\ ICOR(L) + 0.233\ PC(L)$
$ (2.1) (25.6)$
$ r^2 = 0.975;\ F = 535.00$

Imports

(4) $IM = -3.031 + 0.126Y$
$ (13.0)$
$ r^2 = 0.972;\ F = 625.03$

Money Demanded

(5) $\triangle M = 463.551 + 1.113\triangle Y$
$ (13.0)$
$ r^2 = 0.904;\ F = 168.88$

Source: Compiled by author.

Note: Where T = federal government tax revenues; Y = gross domestic product; CG = government consumption;
ICOR = incremental capital output ratio; PC = private consumption; PI = private investment; and IM = imports.
(L) indicates variable was lagged one year.

TABLE 29

IMPACT MATRIX FOR SIMPLE MONETARY MODEL

	CP(L)	CG(L)	ICOR(L)	Δ GDP	IG	E
Tax	0.2525	6.4158	-0.7037	0.0000	0.3154	0.3154
PC	0.7904	69.212	13.6200	0.0000	-6.1051	-6.1051
PI	2.3270	0.0000	-22.3080	0.0000	0.0000	0.0000
IM	0.3488	8.8639	-0.9722	0.0000	0.4358	0.4358
M	0.0000	0.0000	0.0000	1.1133	0.0000	0.0000
Y	2.7686	70.3481	-7.7158	0.0000	3.4590	3.4590

Source: Computed by author.

Note: Computed by increasing each exogenous variable CP(L), CG(L), ICOR(L), Δ GDP, IG, and E by an inventory of 10.

Because there was little statistical difference in the Keynesian and quantity theory models,[3] it was concluded that both could yield useful insights into the workings of the economy and that they should be considered complementary, rather than diametrically opposed, approaches in examining the Mexican economy. The forecasting model developed below, therefore, though primarily a monetary model, incorporates a number of Keynesian (constant price) elements.[4]

Implications of the Models

Since the monetary or quantity theory model seems to fit the Mexican economy, it has several important implications for policy. In our model an increase in the money stock, indicative of an expansionary monetary policy, will lead to either a subsequent decrease in international reserves and the money supply when all adjustments in the foreign sector have been completed, or if adjustments do not take place in the foreign sector, a continuous balance-of-payments problem, assuming a fixed exchange rate. In either case, the expansive monetary policy cannot be sustained; in the first case it is simply self-defeating, and in the second case, either devaluation or a reduction of liquidity are needed to correct the trade balance.

These results illustrate the importance of the foreign sector, or the degree of openness of the economy, in making internal independent monetary policy impossible if the authorities wish to maintain a fixed exchange rate. Suppose, for instance, that the monetary authorities attempt an expansionary monetary policy. Actual liquidity is now greater than desired liquidity, and as expenditures rise (as seen from equation [3]), subsequent increases in money income and imports then occur (from equations [4] and [6]). The increase in imports leads to reduction in international reserves and liquidity (equation [2]). If equlibrium in the balance of payments is to be restored, given a fixed exchange rate, then imports and income must fall. The intended expansionary policy is thus frustrated.

A Forecasting Model of the Mexican Economy

The following macroeconomic model attempts to analyze a number of questions facing the Mexican authorities. Two of the most important are: (1) how do changes in the domestic component of the money supply affect aggregate demand; and (2) how do changes in aggregate demand affect domestic income, the balance of payments, and thereby the level of reserves.

The model specified is a linear one and has been estimated on an annual basis for the period 1956-1975. The fact that data on key economic variables, such as gross domestic product, are not available for intervals smaller than one year precluded the construction of a quarterly model. Because the model was specified in linear terms, it leads directly to tractable solutions without too great a sacrifice in realism. Generally, the true test of a model (in this particular case, the only test) is its ability to predict the behavior of certain variables. Two types of projections were made: a simulation of the values of income and the balance of payments over the period 1956-1975, and a forecast of the values of all endogenous variables for 1976-1980.

Value of Imports

The demand for nominal imports is specified as a linear function of private expenditure in current prices, the price of imports, and private expenditure in the previous year.

$$(9) \quad IM = a + b_1 PE + b_2 PIM + b_3 IM(L) \, ,$$

where IM is the value of nominal imports in period t_1; PE is aggregate private expenditure in period t; and $IM(L)$ is an index of the price of imports in period t.

The rationale of this formulation is that a rise in domestic demand for all goods, including foreign, should lead to an increase in the demand for imports, and that a rise in import prices would result in a decrease in demand. Some measure of domestic prices should be used to capture the effect of any substitution between foreign and domestic goods.

Since actual imports may adjust to demand with a lag, an adjustment is specified to the effect that imports change in period t according to the difference between demand for imports in period t and the actual value of imports in the previous period. This effect is determined by the $b_3 IM(L)$ term in equation (1).

Several formulations of (1) were estimated:

(9A) $IM = -43.779 + 41.880 \left(\dfrac{PIM}{PW}\right)$
                  (21.8)

          $+ \; 0.547 IM(L) + 0.056 PE$
            (11.5)   (2.1)

$F = 203.9$
$r^2 = 0.9745$

(9B) $IM = -22.113 + 21.10 \left(\dfrac{PIM}{PE}\right)$
                  (12.5)

          $+ \; 0.319 IM(L) + 0.0940 PE$
            (20.7)   (3.9)

$F = 199.18$
$r^2 = 0.9739$

(9C) $IM = 2.3760 - 2.729 \left(\dfrac{PW}{PIM}\right) \cdot (OV)$
                  (18.3)

          $+ \; 0.0782 PE + 0.438 IM(L)$
            (14.5)   (2.1)

$F = 183.4$
$r^2 = 0.9717$

(9D) $= -45.058 + 0.026 PE$
                  (45.4)

          $- \; 0.117 IM(L) + 0.6368 PW$
            (3.7)   (6.7)

$F = 707.8$
$r^2 = 0.9925$

where the price indexes used were

PIM = import price index (1960 = 100.0)
PW = wholesale price index (1960 = 100.0)
OV = degree of peso overvaluation (percent 1955 = 0.0) .

The results indicate that imports are not price sensitive, perhaps because by the 1960s import controls had greatly reduced the amount of nonessential imports.

Private Domestic Expenditure

In the standard Keynesian model of a closed economy, aggregate private expenditure (consumption plus investment expenditure) depends on the level of income and the rate of interest (on long-term bonds). Monetary policy in this context affects expenditure by changing the interest rate and thereby affecting investment expenditure.

Rather than introducing a single interest rate that represents the yield on only one asset, it is undoubtedly more appropriate in analyzing the Mexican economy to include all liquid assets as a determinant of private expenditure.

Since the public has a desired stock of liquid assets (which in Mexico would be represented by one of the measures of the stock of money), a change in money supply would create an excess demand or supply of this stock of money, and this in turn would cause changes in expenditures as the public attempted to restore or get rid of cash balances to reestablish its desired position.

The income relevant for this calculation is permanent income or permanent nominal gross domestic product in current prices, since several studies have shown that individuals base their expenditures on a longer-term concept of income than current year gross domestic product.

Estimation of permanent income for Mexico is admittedly arbitrary. The series developed here attempts to capture the lag in the response of expenditure to the inflation in the 1970s.

The series was thus calculated using the formula:

$$YE = aGDP + (1-a)(1 + g)YE(L).$$

The value for g was set at 9.362—the average rate of GDP growth between 1955 and 1970. Various values of a were used to determine when the standard error was minimized. The value of a that achieved this was 0.1. The series used was therefore:

$$YE = 0.1GDP + (0.9)(1.0936)YE(L).$$

Because of the inelasticity in the tax system, the government must borrow from the banking system. Hence the public sector may preempt funds that might have been utilized by the private sector. To test for this effect, GE, government expenditure, is included in the regression:

$$(10) \quad PE = a + b_1 GE + b_2 YE + b_3 M ,$$

where PE = private expenditure (in current prices) in time period t; YE is expected gross domestic product (also in current prices) in period t; M is the stock of cash in period t, and GE is government expenditures.

The results are as predicted with:

(10A) $PE = 3.920 - 0.9896E$
                    (60.5)
                                                $F = 1258.4$
          $+ 0.0258YE + 8.3245M$ $r^2 = 0.9958$
              (9.4)   (5.4)

The money series used was M_1. Other definitions of money (M_2 and M_3) gave significantly poorer results.

Government Expenditure

A large proportion of government funds for expenditure in Mexico are obtained from the Bank of Mexico. These funds make up for the usual shortfall in taxes. There is undoubtedly a lag between desired and actual government expenditures:

$$(11)   \quad GE = a + b_1 BMCG + b_2 T + b_3 GE(L) \ ,$$

where *BMCG* is Bank of Mexico's claims on the government; T is the government's tax revenues, and $GE(L)$ is government expenditure in the previous year. The result is:

(11A) $GE = 2.002 + 0.158BMCG$
                      (41.1)
                                              $F = 604.5$
          $+ 0.814T + 0.555GE(L)$ $r^2 = 0.9913$.
              (10.9)   (2.5)

The Supply of Money

The supply of money is specified basically as a behavioral function of the monetary base (MB). It is assumed that the supply of money is a linear function of the money base in period t, period t-1, period t-2, and so on. Or the supply of money has the following pattern:

$$(12)   \quad M = a + x_1 (RM + zRM(L) + z^2 RM(L2) + \ldots) \ .$$

By applying a Koyck transformation to (4), an estimating equation can be obtained:

$$M = a(1 - z) + x_1 MB + zM(L) \ .$$

The variable x is the money multiplier and is really a function of variables such as income and the rate of interest.

In the estimation of (4), it is implicitly assumed that x is constant. On an annual basis, this multiplier was not strictly constant (Table 30) over the 1955-1975 period but was stable enough so that it is not too unrealistic to assume its constancy for purposes of this analysis.

Regressions were made with these definitions of money: (1), $M1$, which is basically currency and coins plus demand deposits; (2) $M2$, which consists of $M1$ plus *bonos financieras* (private and public), *bonos hipotecarios* (private and public), *cedulas hipotecarias, titulos financieras, depositos de ahorro, otros depositos a la vista, certificados de participacion Nafinsa, bonos generales, bonos de ahorro,* and *bonos del ahorro nacional;* and (3) $M3$ is a comprehensive measure of total liquidity.

The results indicate that all these measures of money are very stable functions of the money base:

$$(12A) \quad M1 = -1.003 + 0.379MB$$
$$(89.3)$$
$$+ 0.849M1(L)$$
$$(9.1)$$

$$r^2 = 0.9979$$
$$F = 4030.8 \; .$$

$$(12B) \quad M2 = -0.562 + 0.0941MB$$
$$(93.4)$$
$$+ 1.1223M2(L)$$
$$(18.8)$$

$$r^2 = 0.9981$$
$$F = 4537.6 \; .$$

$$(12C) \quad M3 = -0.888 + 0.5683MB$$
$$(51.4)$$
$$+ 0.9985M3(L)$$
$$(8.7)$$

$$r^2 = 0.9938$$
$$F = 1356.0 \; .$$

When the money base was defined as high-powered money H (Table 30), the results were similar; only that for $M1$ is given here.

$$(12D) \quad M1 = -1.072 + 0.6737H$$
$$(115.8)$$
$$+ 0.9721M1(L)$$
$$(6.8)$$

$$r^2 = 0.9987$$
$$F = 6728.0 \; .$$

Demand for Money

The aggregate demand for money balances is generally specified as a function of income and the cost of holding money. This cost is not a

TABLE 30

MEXICO: MONEY MULTIPLIER 1955-1975

(Billions of Pesos)

	Money Base	Money in Supply	Multiplier
1955	7.89	10.52	1.333
1956	8.81	11.69	1.327
1957	9.38	12.49	1.332
1958	9.66	13.39	1.386
1959	11.56	15.43	1.335
1960	12.31	16.89	1.372
1961	13.47	18.01	1.337
1962	15.35	20.27	1.305
1963	17.81	23.68	1.330
1964	21.23	27.64	1.302
1965	22.26	29.58	1.329
1966	24.63	32.75	1.330
1967	27.01	35.39	1.310
1968	31.34	39.99	1.276
1969	33.35	44.34	1.330
1970	35.57	49.01	1.378
1971	38.89	53.06	1.364
1972	46.66	64.33	1.379
1973	62.84	79.87	1.271
1974	81.31	97.47	1.199
1975	97.69	118.27	1.211

Source: Computed from data in Banco de Mexico, Informe Anual, various issues.

direct cost but an opportunity cost. It represents the income that an individual has to give up when he chooses to hold money rather than to hold an interest-yielding asset.

As such this cost can be represented by the interest rate. Data on Mexican interest rates are not completely satisfactory for this purpose. Their values do not vary often, and it is not completely clear as to which interest rate is the most satisfactory measure of the true opportunity cost of holding money as balances rather than investing it in interest-bearing assets. Because of these problems, a more simple measure of the opportunity cost of holding balances—expected inflation—was used.

The other variable in the demand-for-money function was permanent income as defined in (1) above:

$$\text{(13)} \quad MD = a + b_1 PEI + b_2 YE ,$$

where *PEI* is the expected rate of inflation (using the *GDP* deflator). *YE* is the measure of permanent income as above. The results were:

(13A) $M1D = -9.625 + 1.509PEI$
$\qquad\qquad\quad (40.2)$
$\qquad\qquad\qquad + 0.134YE$
$\qquad\qquad\qquad\quad (39.3)$

$r^2 = 0.9947$
$F = 1581.8$

(13B) $M2D = -26.915 + 1.026PEI$
$\qquad\qquad\qquad (3.8)$
$\qquad\qquad\qquad + 0.317YE$
$\qquad\qquad\qquad\quad (79.71)$

$r^2 = 0.9973$
$F = 3184.0$

(13C) $M3D = -53.165 + 2.375PEI$
$\qquad\qquad\qquad (3.0)$
$\qquad\qquad\qquad + 0.527YE$
$\qquad\qquad\qquad\quad (46.7)$

$r^2 = 0.9973$
$F = 1092.7 .$

Exports

Exports in developing countries are usually considered to be exogenous. Since a large proportion of Mexican exports are for the United States market and since the peso-dollar exchange rate was constant during the 1956-1976 period, however, exports were made a function of United States demand:

$$(14) \quad E = a + b_1 US + b_2 OV + M(L) \ ,$$

where US is the United States gross national product in 1970 prices, and OV is the degree of peso overvaluation.

Imports lagged one year are included to account for the dependency of Mexican industry on imported capital goods.

The results confirm the dependence of Mexican exports on the growth of the United States economy and the price competitiveness of Mexican exports:

$$
\begin{aligned}
(14A) \quad E \ &= -27.943 - 0.1980 OV \\
& (2.4) \qquad r^2 = 0.9458 \\
&+ 0.050 US + 0.6241 M(L) \qquad F = 93.0 \ . \\
& (2.9) \qquad\quad (16.2)
\end{aligned}
$$

The Balance-of-Payments Current Account

The current account of the balance of payments reflects the degree of competitiveness of Mexican exports, the imports required for income growth, and the ability of the Mexican economy to meet external demand. These are reflected in the relationship:

$$(15) \quad BC = a + b_1 OV + b_2 \Delta US + b_3 YE + \Delta M1 \ ,$$

where BC is the current account of the balance of payments, OV is the percent of peso overvaluation, ΔUS is the incremental change in real United States gross national product from year $t\text{-}1$ to year t, and $\Delta M1$ is the change in Mexico's domestic money supply between year $t\text{-}1$ and year t.

$$
\begin{aligned}
(15A) \quad BC \ &= 13.291 - 19.822 OV \\
& (9.4) \\
&+ 14.254 \Delta US - 0.0035 YE \quad r^2 = 0.9403 \\
& (8.9) \qquad\quad (7.5) \qquad\quad F = 59.1 \ . \\
&- 106.490 \Delta M1 \\
& (3.4)
\end{aligned}
$$

Long-Term Capital Account

The long-term capital account in Mexico has been influenced largely by Mexican policy through: (1) the ability of the government to encourage private foreign investment; (2) the ability of the government to borrow in international capital markets; and (3) the government's efforts to keep the current account balance of payments in deficit in order to increase the resources available for the country's development effort. These policies are partially captured in:

$$(16) \quad LTC = a + b_1 YE + b_2 GD + b_3 BC \ ,$$

where *YE* is expected income, *GD* is government expenditures (*GE*) minus tax revenues (*T*), and *BC* is the current account of the balance of payments. For 1956-1975 the results were:

$$(16A) \quad LTC = 32.436 - 1.092 YE$$
$$(17.7)$$
$$r^2 = 0.9632$$
$$+ 14.411 GD - 1.053 BC \qquad F = 139.6 \ .$$
$$(7.8) \qquad (6.8)$$

Short-Term Capital Flows

One of the recent problems in Mexico has been the large outflow of private short-term capital. This is in marked contrast to the 1960s, when short-term capital (including "errors and omissions") flows were largely high and positive. The stabilizing development strategy of the 1955-1970 period led to substantial net inflows of short-term capital to take advantage of relatively higher real rates of interest on Mexican financial assets under conditions of negligible exchange risk. The 1970s were quite a different story, and shrewd short-term investors began to divest themselves of peso holdings as world interest rates rose relative to those in Mexico, as Mexican inflation became greater than the nominal interest rate on Mexican *financiera* bonds and deposits, and as the risk of devaluation mounted.

Short-run capital flows are assumed to be a function of changes in the Mexican interest rate, the United States interest rate, gross national product, and changes in the income of the United States:

$$(17) \quad \Delta SRC = a + b_1 \Delta (i) MEX + b_2 \Delta (i) US$$
$$+ b_3 \Delta GDP + b_y \Delta US.$$

The function states that an increased rate of change in the Mexican interest rate and income leads to an increased inflow of short-term capital, and that an increase in the rate of change of the corresponding U.S. variables leads to an outflow.

Unfortunately, the estimates of (9) were unsatisfactory. The large size in some years of the "errors and omissions" term may explain part of the problem. Psychological factors, such as the fear of a devaluation of the peso, undoubtedly played an important role. Because of these estimation problems, short-run capital flows are determined as a residual in the model.

Change in Reserves

The balance of payments in an open economy such as Mexico's plays an important role in determining changes in the stock of domestic money. International reserve inflows, for example, will increase the domestic stock of money if they are added directly to the money balances of residents of Mexico or if they are exchanged for domestic currency at the central bank. In Mexico, reserve flows are an important factor, and occasionally were a dominant one, in determining changes in the domestic stock of money. This observation raises the question as to the major determinants of Mexican reserve flows and the role—if any—the policy actions of the Mexican authorities can play in affecting the country's reserve flows.

Models of open economies that include a market for money suggest two equivalent ways of describing a reserve flow. One asserts that reserves flow into the country when its residents demand fewer goods, fewer services, and fewer nonmonetary assets from nonresidents (than nonresidents demand from them) and of course the converse. The other approach stresses the fact that if residents desire to accumulate money balances faster than the rate at which the authorities and other domestic factors are increasing the stock of money, their reserves will flow into the country. This highly simplified characterization implies that reserve flows result from the states of equilibrium in all nonmonetary markets or equivalently from the state of equilibrium in the money market.

In this section the latter, and simpler, approach is taken, i.e., flows are related to factors determining growth in demand for money, government policies, and other domestically determined factors that contribute to growth in the stock of money.

Since the monetary authorities in Mexico during this period (1955-1975) were willing to buy or sell international reserves at a fixed price, private citizens and businesses played a central role in determining the amount of high-powered money. If, under these conditions, the domestic supply of money exceeded demand, outlays would rise above receipts, and part of the increased outlays would be directed at foreign goods, services, and assets. Residents could acquire the reserve currencies to pay for the increased purchases from foreigners or by buying reserves from the central bank in exchange for domestic money, thus generating a decline in the domestic money stock. This process can be formally stated in terms of a money supply identity:[5]

$$M = aH$$

M = stock of domestic money
a = money multiplier
H = stock of high-powered money.

The amount of high-powered money is derived from the consolidated balance sheet of the monetary authorities. In simplified form, this balance sheet contains the following items in addition to high powered money:

Monetary Authorities Balance Sheet

R	H
OA	OL

where
R = official holdings of international reserves
OA = all other assets of the monetary authorities such as domestic bonds, bank buildings, etc.
OL = all liabilities of the monetary authorities other than high-powered money.

High-powered money can be defined in terms of the balance sheet items:

$$H = R + (OA - OL) = R + D \ .$$

Every change in high-powered money is thus asociated with changes in R and/or changes in all domestic influences on the balance sheet summarized by the variable D.

Substituting equations gives the money supply formula:

$$M = a(R + D) \ .$$

As a first approximation, the central bank's reserves were specified as:

$$(18) \quad RES = a + b_1 (i) + b_2 (PW) + YE,$$

where RES = the reserves of the central bank; (i) = the short-term Mexican interest rate; PW = the wholesale price index (1960 = 100.0); and YE = expected income. The results confirmed the above research flow hypothesis:

$$(18A) \quad RES = 4.010 - 0.496(i)$$
$$(10.2)$$
$$r^2 = 0.9368$$
$$+ 0.057PW + 0.0103YE \qquad F = 79.1 \ .$$
$$(11.4) \qquad (2.1)$$

The results conform to the hypothesized reserve flow mechanism. Several points do need elaboration. The negative sign on the interest rate indicates that an increase in interest rates results in a net outflow of international reserves. The increase in the interest rate would result in a decrease in the demand for money, which in turn is mirrored by a decrease in the demand for money reserves, *ceteris paribus*.

Of course, if domestic interest rates were allowed to differ from the world rate, then two forces with respect to reserves would be at work: a negative influence through the money demand function and a positive effect through the interest rate differential.

Incremental Capital Output Ratio

Several recent discussions of the capital output ratio—the investment in year t divided by the increase in output (GDP) in year $t+1$—have concluded that it should be expected to be lower at higher rates of growth.[6] At least three reasons have been given for this phenomenon.

1. During periods of rapid growth, capacity is likely to be utilized faster than it is created; during slow growth, it is often created faster than it is utilized.
2. Increases in factors other than capital—labor, available resources, and technology—play a large part in determining the growth of output, and to some extent these elements may vary independently of investment.
3. When higher growth rates are based on greater investment, the part of gross investment used to replace old equipment and to construct social overhead facilities represents a smaller share of the total.

The growth of GDP in Mexico has been fairly stable until the last several years; therefore, time series data were used to examine the behavior of the country's capital output ratio (Table 31). As anticipated, the capital output ratio ($ICOR$) does vary with the rate of GDP growth (Y):

$$(19) \quad ICOR = 6.102 - 0.448Y \qquad r^2 = 0.824$$
$$(9.2) \qquad F = 84.22 \ ,$$

assuming lower values with accelerated *GDP* (constant 1960 prices) expansion.

TABLE 31

MEXICO: INCREMENTAL CAPITAL OUTPUT RATIO, 1955-1975

(Billions 1960 Pesos)

	Investment	Change in GDP	ICOR	Growth Rate GDP (%)		Investment	Change in GDP	ICOR	Growth Rate GDP (%)
1955	18.9	–	–	8.53	1966	45.2	14.7	2.73	6.92
1956	22.3	6.4	2.96	6.79	1967	46.8	14.3	3.16	6.30
1957	23.5	8.8	2.53	7.54	1968	51.2	19.6	2.39	8.12
1958	22.3	5.4	4.34	5.41	1969	57.5	16.5	3.10	6.32
1959	22.8	5.3	4.18	2.95	1970	62.4	19.2	2.99	6.92
1960	30.2	10.5	2.16	8.14	1971	59.9	13.1	4.76	4.42
1961	31.4	7.4	4.08	4.92	1972	67.4	20.0	3.00	6.46
1962	32.7	7.4	4.24	4.69	1973	74.7	23.7	2.84	7.19
1963	34.1	13.2	2.48	7.99	1974	79.6	21.0	3.56	5.94
1964	39.6	20.9	1.63	11.71	1975	85.7	16.4	4.85	4.38
1965	40.2	12.9	3.07	6.47					

Source: Computed from data in: Banco de Mexico, *Informe Anual*, various issues.

Private Investment

Ideally one would like to relate private investment to such variables as the rate of return on capital, the interest rate, and perhaps the interest profits. Since the interest rate in Mexico is set by the Bank of Mexico at a level somewhat below the equilibrium rate, fluctuations in this variable have little meaning in examining changes in private investment.

Furthermore, there are no consistent series for the rate of return on capital or business profits, although some attempts have been made to assemble the relevant data.

In the absence of these data, the capital output ratio was used as a proxy for the profitability of investment.

The results were quite good:

$$(20) \quad IP = -0.058 - 0.766ICOR$$
$$(131.7)$$
$$r^2 = 0.960$$
$$+ 1.052\Delta Y(L) - 0.360GE \quad F = 128.53 \ .$$
$$(12.7) \qquad (2.2)$$

The sign of the *ICOR* coefficient is as expected. *ICOR* is in 1960 prices and would take values such as 3.41 for a 6 percent rate of real *GNP* growth.

The negative sign for the government expenditure coefficient (GE) can be interpreted as a crowding-out process whereby the government's budget deficits are used to substitute private outlays for government outlays. Historically, in Mexico there has been little inflationary pressure exerted on the economy resulting from this transfer.

Private Consumption

The final equation is that for private consumption:

$$(21) \quad CP = 2.737 + 0.006CP(L)$$
$$(131.7)$$
$$r^2 = 0.999$$
$$+ 0.787Y - 0.3696E \qquad F = 5841.0 \ .$$
$$(12.7) \qquad (2.2)$$

Again government expenditures appear to compete with the private sector for funds, and thus expanded government expenditures force the private sector to contract consumption expenditures.

Nominal Income: National Accounts

The level of GDP in current prices is equal to aggregate nominal private expenditures plus the value of exports plus nominal government expenditure and minus the value of imports:

$$GDP = PE + X + GE - M \ .$$

Balance of Payments

The balance-of-payments equation is identically equal to the change in reserves of the central bank:

$$RES = BC + SRC + LTC \ ,$$

where RES = reserves of the Bank of Mexico, BC = balance of payments on current account, SRC = short-term capital movements (including errors and omissions); and LTC = long-term capital flows.

Statement of the Model

Comprising the structural equations for imports, private expenditures, government expenditures, components of the balance of payments, money supply, and national income account identities, the basic monetary model for Mexico for the period 1956-1975 is summarized in Tables 32 and 33.

TABLE 32

MEXICO: STRUCTURAL EQUATION ESTIMATES, 1956-1975

Imports   (P1M)
   (1) IM = -43.779 + 41.880 (PW) + 0.547 1M(L) + 0.056 PE
                  (21.8)   (11.5)   (2.1) r^2 = 0.975; F = 203.85

Private Expenditure
   (2) PE = 3.920 - 0.989 GE + 0.026 YE + 8.325 M1
               (60.5)   (9.4)   (5.4) r^2 = 0.996; F = 1258.40

Government Expenditure
   (3) GE = 2.002 + 0.158 BMGC + 0.814 T + 0.555 GE(L)
               (41.1)   (11.0)   (2.5) r^2 = 0.991; F = 604.56

Exports
   (4) E = -27.943 + 0.624 IM(L) - 0.198)V + 0.050 US
              (16.3)   (2.4)   (2.9) r^2 = 0.946; F = 93.03

Private Consumption
   (5) CP = 2.737 + 0.006 PC(L)+ 0.787 Δ Y   - 0.360GE
              (131.7)   (12.7)   (2.2) r^2 = 0.999; F = 5841.10

Private Investment
   (6) IP = -0.058 - 0.766 ICOR + 1.052 Δ Y(L) + 0.659GE
              (4.6)   (16.0)   (10.3) r^2 = 0.960; F = 128.53

Money Supply
   (7) M = -1.003 + 0.380 MB + 0.850 M(L)
              (89.3)   (9.1) r^2 = 0.998; F = 4030.78

Balance of Payment Current Account
   (8) BC = 13.291 - 19.82ZOV + 14.254 ΔUSGDP - 0.004YE - 106.490ΔM
              (9.4)   (9.0)   (7.5)   (3.4) r^2 = 0.940; F = 59.06

Long Term Capital Account Balance of Payments
   (9) LTC = 32.436 - 1.092 YD + 14.411GD - 1.053BC
              (17.7)   (7.8)   (6.8) r^2 = 0.963; F = 139.62

Change in Reserves Balance of Payments
   (10) RES = 4.010 - 0.469(i) + 0.057 PW + 0.010 YE
              (10.2)   (11.4)   (2.1) r^2 = 0.937; F = 79.12

Gross Domestic Product Deflator
   (11) PGDPD = -1.404 + 0.140W + 1.156PEX + 0.059M
              (10.7)   (6.8)   (2.7) r^2 = 0.909; F = 53.6

Incremental Capital Output Ratio
   (12) ICOR = 6.102 - 0.448Y
               (9.2) r^2 = 0.824; G = 84.22

Source: Computed by author.
Note: See text for definition of symbols.

TABLE 33

DEFINITIONS AND IDENTITIES

Gross Domestic Product

(1) GDP = PE + GE + E - M

Short-Run Capital Balance of Payments

(2) RES = BC - LTC

Government Deficit

(3) GD = GE - T

Permanent Income

(4) YE = 0.1GDP + (0.9) (1.0936) GDP(L)

Expected Rate of Inflation

(5) PEX = 0.4 $\left[PGDP + (1-.4) \, PGDP(L) + (1-.4)^2 \, PGDP(L2) \right]$

Government Investment

(6) GI = 0.526

Total Investment

(7) IT = PI + GI

Total Consumption

(8) CT = GC + PC

Savings

(9) X = GNP - CT

Gross Domestic Product

(10) GNP = 0.982GDP

Domestic Gap

(11) GAPD = S - IT

Note: See text for complete explanation of symbols.

Realistically, this model can only provide knowledge of the consistency of forecasts made by more informal subjective methods. Clearly, however, the method of forecasting used here and the judgments of Mexican policymakers are not mutually exclusive since the judgments that have to be made about the behavior of exogenous variables will be reflected in the forecasts produced by the model. In fact, both methods should be used together. There is no reason to forecast mechanically if it is believed that changes from previous trends will take place.

Simulation of Actual Data

The macroeconomic relationships are useful mainly for simulation and forecasting. They were first used to simulate the behavior of the national income accounts and the balance of payments during the period 1957-1975 and to make forecasts of the basic macroeconomic indicators for the 1976-1990 period.

A comparison of the simulated and actual values of the national income accounts (Tables 34 and 35) for the 1957-1975 period shows the model gives a close approximation to the historical data. The model is not as accurate in depicting the actual values for the balance of payments, particularly such volatile items as short-run capital movements. But it does capture the magnitude and direction of change of these items for most years.

Forecasts of the Model

Several forecasts of the Mexican economy were made using the basic macroeconomic relationships summarized above. For this purpose, impact multipliers were first calculated.

The reduced form of the model (Table 36), expressing the endogenous variables in terms of the lagged endogenous and exogenous variables, was calculated from the estimated structural equations.

In dynamic analysis terms, the reduced-form coefficients are called "impact multipliers," and they measure the immediate response of the endogenous variables to changes in the exogenous (policy-determined) variables. From the reduced form of the present model (derived by increasing each of the exogenous variables by ten units while holding all other exogenous variables constant), for example, the immediate effect of a change in monetary policy (through the Bank of Mexico's altering the money base) on private expenditure or imports can easily be determined. These reduced-form equations, of course, do not directly determine how the system would behave under the continuous impact of changes in exogenous variables, yet they can illustrate in convenient

TABLE 34

MEXICO: SIMULATED AND ACTUAL NATIONAL INCOME ACCOUNTS, 1957-1968

	1957 Actual	1957 Predicted	1960 Actual	1960 Predicted	1961 Actual	1961 Predicted	1962 Actual	1962 Predicted	1965 Actual	1965 Predicted	1968 Actual	1968 Predicted
Gross National Product	-	-	149.4	130.6	162.1	163.5	174.6	177.2	249.8	270.3	335.0	329.4
Gross Domestic Product	114.7	109.7	150.5	132.9	163.3	166.4	176.0	180.5	252.0	275.2	339.1	335.4
Private Expenditure	91.6	97.9	132.9	114.9	142.6	140.3	152.4	153.2	217.5	228.8	290.8	278.1
Government Expenditure	9.1	12.9	19.9	15.4	21.7	21.8	28.2	23.2	36.1	39.4	52.0	44.5
Private Consumption	93.6	84.8	113.1	102.4	127.1	126.4	136.5	137.1	187.2	205.9	243.4	251.8
Government Consumption	5.2	6.2	9.5	7.4	10.4	10.5	12.3	11.1	17.7	18.9	25.9	21.4
Total Consumption	98.8	91.0	122.6	109.8	137.5	136.9	148.8	148.2	204.9	224.9	269.3	273.2
Private Investment	13.4	13.3	19.8	12.7	15.5	22.4	15.9	19.9	30.3	45.6	47.4	42.6
Government Investment	-	-	10.4	8.0	11.3	11.3	11.4	11.1	18.4	20.5	26.1	23.1
Total Investment	-	-	19.8	20.7	26.8	33.7	27.3	31.9	48.7	66.1	73.5	65.8
Savings	-	16.7	26.8	20.8	24.6	26.5	25.8	29.0	44.9	45.4	65.7	56.3
Domestic Gap	-	-	-3.4	0.1	-2.2	-7.2	-1.5	-2.9	-3.8	-20.7	-7.8	-9.5
Exports	12.4	12.9	17.0	12.6	18.0	15.1	19.3	16.6	24.4	24.2	29.5	33.1
Imports	17.6	14.9	19.3	15.8	19.0	18.0	19.3	20.4	26.0	28.8	33.3	32.1

Source: Computed by author.

TABLE 35

MEXICO: SIMULATED AND ACTUAL NATIONAL INCOME ACCOUNTS, 1970-1975

(Billions of Pesos)

	1970		1971		1972		1973		1974		1975	
	Actual	Predicted	Actual	Predicted	Actual	Predicted	Actual	Predicted	Actual	Predicted	Actual	Predicted
Gross National Product	411.6	433.3	444.4	475.7	504.6	525.7	605.5	650.8	798.3	810.8	954.7	982.9
Gross Domestic Product	418.7	441.2	452.2	484.4	513.7	535.4	617.9	662.7	812.9	825.7	972.2	1000.9
Private Expenditure	371.5	373.3	403.5	416.0	447.9	457.9	532.0	575.8	710.9	712.9	804.3	846.6
Government Expenditure	55.7	59.7	53.9	61.7	69.5	69.0	93.4	89.0	123.2	122.5	166.8	168.1
Private Consumption	312.6	329.8	345.4	363.2	380.9	400.9	453.9	494.0	602.0	610.4	717.9	732.5
Government Consumption	32.6	28.6	29.8	29.6	35.3	33.1	42.6	42.7	58.4	58.8	80.4	80.7
Total Consumption	345.2	358.4	375.2	392.9	416.2	434.0	496.5	536.8	660.4	669.3	798.3	813.2
Private Investment	58.9	54.5	58.1	57.3	67.0	57.0	78.1	77.6	108.9	103.0	119.4	129.2
Government Investment	23.1	31.0	24.1	32.1	34.2	35.9	50.8	46.3	64.8	63.7	86.4	87.4
Total Investment	82.0	85.4	82.2	89.3	101.2	92.9	128.9	123.9	173.7	166.7	205.8	216.6
Savings	66.4	74.8	69.2	82.8	88.4	91.7	109.0	114.0	137.9	141.6	156.4	169.7
Domestic Gap	-15.6	-10.6	-13.0	-6.6	-12.8	-1.3	-19.9	-9.9	-35.8	-25.2	-49.4	-46.9
Exports	34.0	37.8	39.3	43.1	46.4	47.0	56.6	54.4	75.8	60.7	74.6	80.2
Imports	42.4	41.8	42.6	48.8	50.6	54.6	63.6	68.3	97.0	83.9	106.5	108.1

Source: Computed by author.

TABLE 36

MEXICO: IMPACT MATRIX OF STRUCTURAL EQUATIONS

Endogenous Variable \ Exogenous Variable	$\frac{PIM}{PW}$	IM(L)	YE	BMCG	T	GE(L)	MB	M(L)	OV	OSGDP	Δ OSGDP
Imports (IM)	418.8	5.4	0.014	-0.088	-0.45	-0.31	1.77	3.96	–	–	–
Private Expenditure (DE)	–	–	0.258	-1.563	-8.05	-5.49	31.55	70.76	–	–	–
Government Expenditure (GE)	–	–	–	1.58	8.14	5.55	–	–	–	–	–
Money Supply (M)	–	–	-3(-4)	-2(-4)	1.5(-5)	–	3.79	8.49	–	–	–
Exports (E)	–	6.2	–	–	–	–	–	–	1.98	0.50	–
Balance of Payments Government Account (BC)	–	–	-0.04	–	4.8(-3)	–	–	–	-198.22	–	142.54
Long-Term Capital (LTC)	–	–	-10.88	22.77	-26.84	79.98	⸱	–	208.73	–	-150.01
Reserves (RES)	–	–	0.103	–	–	–	–	–	–	–	–
Gross Domestic Product (GDP)	-418.8	0.77	0.243	0.105	0.54	0.37	29.78	66.80	1.98	0.50	7.55
Short-Run Capital Flows (SHB)	–	–	11.021	-22.77	26.80	-79.98	–	–	-10.51	–	–
Government Deficit (GD)	–	–	–	1.58	-1.86	5.55	–	–	–	0.40	–
Private Consumption (PC)	-329.7	0.60	0.192	-0.50	-2.58	-1.76	23.45	52.60	1.56	0.39	–
Private Investment (PI)	–	–	–	1.04	5.37	3.66	–	–	–	–	–
Government Consumption (GC)	–	–	–	0.76	3.91	2.66	–	–	–	–	–
Government Investment (GI)	–	–	–	0.82	4.23	2.89	–	–	–	–	–
Gross National Product (GNP)	-411.3	0.76	0.24	0.10	0.53	0.36	29.25	65.59	1.94	0.49	–
Domestic Gap (GAPD)	-81.5	0.15	0.047	-2.02	-10.40	-7.09	–	13.00	0.39	0.01	–
Savings (S)	-81.5	0.15	0.047	-0.15	-0.80	-0.54	5.80	13.00	0.39	0.1	–

Source: Computed by author.

Note: Derived by increasing exogenous variables by 10.

form the workings of the economy. Of particular interest is the strong negative effect the Bank of Mexico's credit to the government (*BMGC*) has on private and government expenditures—government expenditures of course increased, but the private expenditures are negative by nearly as much as government expenditures are positive, suggesting that both the private and government sectors have been competing for resources.

Consider also a rise in the value of taxes by 10 million pesos. This would enable government expenditures to increase by 8.14 million pesos, and would reduce imports by 0.45 million pesos. The stimulating effect on private investment (increasing by 5.37 million pesos) and the reduction in private consumption (of 2.58 million pesos) have obvious policy implications.

The forecasts to 1990 are described in Chapter 11. In forecasting the economy, several assumptions were made concerning the values of key variables. These include:

PIM/PW = 1.2266
BMGC = 15 percent annual increase
T = 20 percent annual increase
MB = 15 percent annual increase
OV = 10 percent (the peso was assumed to remain 10 percent overvalued)
USGDP = 3 percent (the U.S. economy is assumed to grow at an annual real rate of 3 percent)
PW = 5 percent.

Clearly, an infinite number of forecasts are possible by varying these (and possibly other) values. The model was primarily intended to trace out a feasible path based on past trends and on possible government action in the area of tax reform and inflation control. The results in Chapter 11 indicate that in this regard an 8 percent of real GNP growth with an implied 12 percent nominal growth is probably the maximum feasible rate the authorities can strive for.

Notes

Preface

1. Robert Looney, *Income Distribution Policies and Economic Growth in Semi-Industrialized Countries: A Comparative Study of Iran, Mexico, Brazil and South Korea* (New York: Praeger, 1975).
2. Particularly the so-called "structuralist school." See particularly A. Moriega, "Las Devaluaciones Monetarias de México, 1938-1954," *Investigación Económica* 15 (1955): 149-177; E. Lobato, "La Política Monetaria Mexicana," *Investigación Económica* 23 (1968): 557-581; H. Flores de la Peña, "La Mexánica de la Inflación," *Investigación Económica* 13 (1953): 461-481; idem, "Crecimiento Demográfico, Desarrollo Agrícola y Desarrollo Económico," *Investigación Económica* 14 (1954); 519-539; idem, "Agricultura Mexicana,"*Comercio Exterior* 4 (1948): 376-379; Manuel Gollas and Adalberto García Rocha, "El Desarrollo Económico Reciente de México," in *Contemporary Mexico*, ed. James Wilkie (Berkeley: University of California Press, 1976); and Carlos Monsivais, "Clasismo y Novela en México, *Latin American Perspectives* 2 (1975): 164-178.
3. For example, Alan Riding, "Why Something Had to Give in the Mexican Economy," *Financial Times*, September 7, 1976, p. 3; idem, "The Headache Is Just Beginning," *Financial Times*, January 25, 1977, p. 5; David Felix, "Income Inequality in Mexico," *Current History* 72 (March 1977): 111-114; and Luis Pazos, *Devaluación y Estatismo en Mexico* (Mexico City: Editorial Diana, 1976).

Chapter 1

1. See Adolfo López Mateos, *The Economic Development of Mexico during a Quarter of a Century (1934-1959)* (Mexico City: Nacional Financiera, S. A., 1968); and Gustavo Romero Kolbeck, "Economic Development of Mexico," in Committee for Economic Development, *Economic Development Issues: Latin America* (New York: Praeger, 1967), pp. 177-214.
2. The best are Clark Reynolds, *The Mexican Economy: Twentieth-Century*

Structure and Growth (New Haven: Yale University Press, 1970); B. Griffiths, *Mexican Monetary Policy and Economic Development* (New York: Praeger, 1972); William Freithgler, *Mexico's Foreign Trade and Economic Development* (New York: Praeger, 1968); David Barkin and Timothy King, *Regional Economic Development: The River Basin Approach in Mexico* (Cambridge: Cambridge University Press, 1970); Raymond Vernon, ed., *Public Policy and Private Enterprise in Mexico* (Cambridge, Mass.: Harvard University Press, 1964); Raymond Vernon, *The Dilemma of Mexico's Development: The Roles of the Private and Public Sectors* (Cambridge, Mass.: Harvard University Press, 1965); Timothy King, *Mexico: Industrialization and Trade Policies since 1940* (New York: Oxford University Press, 1970); John Ross, *The Economic System of Mexico* (Stanford, Calif.: California Institute of International Studies, 1971); Louis Goreux and Alan Manne, *Multi-Level Planning: Case Studies in Mexico* (Amsterdam: North Holland, 1973); Morris Singer, *Growth Equality and the Mexican Experience* (Austin: University of Texas Press, 1969); Tom Davis et al., *Mexico's Recent Economic Growth: The Mexican View* (Austin: University of Texas Press, 1967); and Roger D. Hansen, *Mexican Economic Development: The Roots of Rapid Growth* (Washington, D.C.: National Planning Association, 1971).

3. This is particularly evident in Goreux and Manne, *Multi-Level Planning*.

4. The author is aware of only one other study on Mexico that takes this approach: John Koehler, *Economic Policy Making with Limited Information: The Process of Macro-Control in Mexico* (Santa Monica, Calif.: Rand Corporation, 1968).

5. Leopoldo Solís, "Mexican Economic Policy in the Post-War Period: The Views of Mexican Economists," *American Economic Review* 61 (June 1971), supplement, p. 5.

6. Fausto Zapata, *Development in Freedom: The Policy of Change in Mexico* (Mexico City: Secretaría de la Presidencia, 1972), p. 6.

7. A terse summary of Echeverría's final days in office and the policy initiatives made at that time are given in Calvin Blair, "Echeverría's Economic Policy," *Current History* 72 (March 1977): 124-127.

8. This classification was first suggested by Clark Reynolds in his "Mexico and Brazil: Models for Leadership in Latin America?" in *Contemporary Mexico*, ed. James W. Wilkie (Berkeley: University of California Press, 1976), pp. 452-468. The following closely follows Reynolds' analysis.

9. This is not a recent phenomenon. It is quite likely that the material lot of the poorest 40 percent of Mexican families has not changed significantly since 1910; that although material gains since the revolution have been substantial for the upper 60 percent of families, the relative gains have been far greater for the top 20 percent. It is often contended that there was a marked deterioration in the income distribution in the late 1960s, but there is not hard evidence to support this view.

10. Mexico has four duly registered national political parties, but by far the predominant party is the PRI. This "official" party has been the foundation of Mexican political stability since about 1930, after contending political factions

in choosing a new president had been welded into a more or less solid group that eventually constituted the party. Although the constitution, as amended, provided for a rudimentary kind of proportional representation, the other three parties up to now can be said to constitute only token opposition.

11. Reynolds, "Mexico and Brazil," p. 467.

Chapter 2

1. Unless otherwise indicated, the national income accounts data referred to in the text are from various issues of the Bank of Mexico (Banco de México), *Informe Anual*; and the bank's *Indicadores Económicos*.

2. This is a relatively controversial point. For a detailed analysis of the period, see Timothy D. Sweeney, "The Mexican Balance of Payments," *International Monetary Fund Staff Papers* 1 (1953):132-154.

3. Dwight Brothers and Leopoldo Solís, *Mexican Financial Development* (Austin: University of Texas Press, 1966), pp. 55-68.

4. Joseph S. La Cascia, *Capital Formation and Economic Development in Mexico* (New York: Praeger, 1969), pp. 39-42. La Cascia notes that the Organic Law of December 30, 1940, further allowed Nacional Financiera to regulate the national stock exchanges and long-term credits; to promote the investment of capital in the organization and expansion of industrial enterprises; and to act as fiduciary and agent for the federal government in the issue contraction and conversion of public securities. The Reform Law of December 30, 1947, confirmed the function of Nacional Financiera to obtain and manage foreign credits for economic development so as to contribute to the financing of productive investments. La Cascia, *Capital Formation*, p. 39. See Nacional Financiera, *Nacional Financiera, S.A. en el Desarrollo Económico de México* (Mexico City: Nacional Financiera, 1964), pp. 12-13, for a detailed description of these developments.

5. L. Antonio Aspra, "Import Substitution in Mexico: Past and Present," *World Development* 5 (January/February 1977); 118-120.

6. A good summary is given in Bernard S. Katz, "Mexican Fiscal and Subsidy Incentives for Industrial Development," *American Journal of Economics and Sociology* 31 (1972):353-358. Lamarid notes that industrial location factors such as communications and transport, power, electricity, fuel and water, which predominate either singly or in combination according to types of industries, have played a secondary role as determining factors in the siting of Mexican industries. In fact, to date (mid-1970s), owing to government policy regarding industry and public investment, this combination of factors has favored certain regions, thereby aggravating the present inadequate distribution of manufacturing activities. A. Lamarid, "Industrial Location Policy in Mexico," in United Nations, *Industrial Location and Regional Development — Proceedings of an Interregional Seminar, Minsk 14-26 August 1968* (New York: United Nations, 1972), p. 557.

7. Presumably one of the reasons for persistent budget deficits during this period. Cf. Marnie W. Mueller, "Structural Inflation and the Mexican

Experience," *Yale Economic Essays* 5 (1965): 187-188.

8. The term *stabilizing development* probably originates with Antonio Ortiz Mena. See his *Stabilizing Development: A Decade of Economic Strategy in Mexico* (Mexico City: Ministry of Finance, 1969).

9. The following summary is derived from Raymond Goldsmith, *The Financial Development of Mexico* (Paris: Organization for Economic Co-operation and Development, 1966), pp. 29-32.

10. See Edward Denison, *Accounting for United States Economic Growth 1929-1969* (Washington, D.C.: The Brookings Institution, 1974), for a detailed outline of this methodology.

11. An excellent overview is given in Benjamin Higgins, *Economic Development* (New York: Norton, 1968), pp. 635-653.

Chapter 3

1. John B. Ross, *The Economic System of Mexico* (Stanford, Calif.: California Institute of Intenational Studies, 1971), p. 65.

2. Eprime Eshag, "The Relative Efficacy of Monetary Policy in Selected Industrial and Less-Developed Countries," *Economic Journal* 81 (1971): 294-505. Cf. Tom Mayer, "The Relative Efficacy of Monetary Policy in Selected Industrial and Less-Developed Countries; A Comment," *Economic Journal* 82 (1972): 1368-1371.

3. J. Noyola, "Existe una Politica de Precios?" *Revista de Económia* 11 (1948): 8-10; and idem, "El Desarrollo Económico y la Inflación en México y Otros Paises Latinoamericanos," *Investigación Económica* 16 (1956): 603-606.

4. A. Griffiths, *Mexican Monetary Policy*, Chapter 2.

5. Milton Friedman, "Monetary Policy for a Developing Society," *Bank Markzai Iran Bulletin* 10 (1971): 700-712.

6. An excellent summary of the present structure of the Mexican banking system is given in Gilberto Escobedo, "The Response of the Mexican Economy to Policy Actions," *Federal Reserve Bank of St. Louis Review* 55 (1973): 21.

7. For a detailed description of this early period, see Virgil Bett, *Central Banking in Mexico: Monetary Policies and Financial Crises, 1864-1940* (Ann Arbor: University of Michigan, 1957).

8. Mario Ramón Betteta, "The Central Bank: Instrument of Economic Development in Mexico," in *Mexico's Recent Economic Growth: The Mexican View*, ed. Tom E. Davis et al. (Austin: University of Texas Press, 1967), pp. 72-103.

9. Robert L. Bennet, *The Financial Sector and Economic Development: The Mexican Case* (Baltimore: Johns Hopkins University Press, 1965), p. 45.

10. Manuel Espinosa Yglesias, "Private Banking Sector," in *Business Mexico*, ed. Redvers Opie (Mexico City: American Chamber of Commerce of Mexico, 1973), pp. 61-66.

11. Brothers and Solís, *Mexican Financial Development*, Chapter 3.

12. Ross, *Economic System of Mexico*, p. 67.

13. John S. de Beers, "Mexico's Balance of Payments: Some Tentative Conclusions on the Adjustment Process," *Inter-American Economic Affairs* 6 (1951): 3-46.

14. Ariel Buira, "Development and Price Stability in Mexico," *Weltwirtschaftliches Archiv*, 1968, p. 50.

15. Leopoldo Solís, "The Financial System in the Economic Development of Mexico," in Davis, *Mexico's Recent Economic Growth.*

16. Robert F. Emery, "Mexican Monetary Policy since the 1954 Devaluation," *Inter-American Economic Affairs* 12 (1958): 72-85.

17. David Shelton, "Private Sector Liquidity and Output Growth in Post-War Mexico," *Southern Economic Journal* 36 (1969): 27-39.

18. Brothers and Solís, *Mexican Financial Development*, p. 53.

19. Goldsmith, *The Financial Development of Mexico*, p. 15.

20. Griffiths, *Mexican Monetary Policy*, p. 34. The following sections draw heavily on Griffiths' summary of monetary policies pursued during this period. See also Solís, "The Financial System," pp. 44-47.

21. High-powered money, as defined in this study, would be coins and currency in circulation plus bank deposits at the central bank. It is determined by the following equation: $H = R + (OA - OL) = R + D$, where $D = OA - OL$, $OA =$ assets of the monetary authority other than R, $R =$ international reserves, and OL = liabilities other than high-powered money. See Dwaine Sykes Wilford, "The Open Economy in a Monetized World: The Mexican Case" (Ph. D. diss., Tulane University, 1976), p. 17.

22. Bennet, *The Financial Sector and Economic Development*, pp. 59-60.

23. Griffiths, *Mexican Monetary Policy*, p. 35.

24. Solís, "The Financial System," p. 45.

25. Ibid., p. 46.

26. Griffiths, *Mexican Monetary Policy*, p. 35.

27. As in the case of the national income accounts, data on the financial system of Mexico are taken from Banco de México, *Informe Anual*, various issues.

28. Koehler, *Economic Policy Making with Limited Information*, p. 25.

29. The following sections are based on ibid., pp. 8-15.

30. Ibid., p. 11.

31. Wilford, "The Open Economy," Appendix A.

32. Griffiths, *Mexican Monetary Policy*, pp. 125-128.

Chapter 4

1. Ifigenia M. de Navarrete, "The Tax Structure and the Economic Development of Mexico," *Public Finance* 19 (1964): 158.

2. Clark Reynolds has elaborated on this point at length for the Latin American countries. See his "Social and Political Interaction in the Economic Development of a Disequilibrium System: Some Latin American Examples," *Food Research Institute Studies* 15 (1976): 89-108.

3. Koehler, *Economic Policymaking with Limited Information*, pp. 25-27.

4. Clark Reynolds, "Public Finance in Postrevolutionary Mexico," in *Government and Economic Development*, ed. Gustav Ranis (New Haven: Yale University Press, 1971), p. 334.

5. Ibid., p. 333.

6. In September 1973, for example, substantial changes were introduced in the presentation of Mexico's balance of payments. The change in methodology led to a number of significant changes in the recorded figures of imports and exports. The data on income distribution are—as is the case in many countries— notoriously bad, and the Bank of Mexico has not kept statistics on changes in inventories since the mid-1960s (the change in inventories is now included with the investment figures).

7. The best account of this early period is given in James Wilkie, *The Mexican Revolution: Federal Expenditure and Social Change since 1910* (Berkeley: University of California Press, 1970).

8. For example, D. Sykes Wilford and Walton T. Wilford, "Fiscal Revenues in Mexico: A Measure of Performance, 1950-1973," *Public Finance* 31 (1976): 103-114.

9. The Structuralist argument as expressed by A. Navarrete. See his "El Sector Público en el Desarrollo Económico," *Investigación Económica* 17 (1957): 43-61; and idem, *Estabilidada de Cambios, el Ciclo, y el Desarrollo Económico. Una Investigación Sobre los Problemas de la Balanza de Pagos de México 1929-1946* (Mexico City, 1951). The monetarist argument summarized was espoused by Barry Siegel, in his *Inflación y Desarrollo: Las Experiencias de México* (Mexico City: C.E.M.L.A., 1960).

10. Reynolds, "Public Finance in Postrevolutionary Mexico," p. 342.

11. For example, Escobedo feels that as the public sector's financial requirements were increasing, mainly because of its incapacity to increase tax revenues at the same rate as public expenditures, and as the balance of payments was increasing, the Bank of Mexico had to tolerate greater increases in the money supply. Cf. Gilberto Escobedo, "Ahorro y Desarollo Económico," (unpublished manuscript), p. 12.

12. The following results are from Jorge R. Lotz and Elliot R. Morss, "Measuring Tax Effort in Developing Countries," *International Monetary Fund Staff Papers* 14 (1967).

13. *The Mexican Economy: Analysis—76* (Mexico City: Publicaciones Ejecutivas de México, S.A., 1976), p. 149.

14. The conclusion come to by Raymond Vernon in *The Dilemma of Mexico's Development*.

15. Ibid.

16. A term apparently first coined by John Koehler in his *Economic Policy Making with Limited Information*.

17. Early attempts at coordination of public sector expenditures are described in Miguel Wionczek, "Incomplete Formal Planning: Mexico," in *Planning Economic Development*, ed. Everett E. Hagen (Homewood, Illinois: Richard D. Irwin, 1963).

18. James Wilkie, "Recentralization: The Budgetary Dilemma in the Economic Development of Mexico, Bolivia, and Costa Rica," in *Fiscal Policy for Industrialization and Development in Latin America*, ed. David T. Geithman (Gainesville: University of Florida Press, 1974), p. 210.

19. A similar approach was taken by Wilford and Wilford, "Fiscal Revenues

in Mexico." See also Wilford, "The Open Economy."

Chapter 5

1. Redvers Opie, "Mexico's President Plans for Progress," *Banking* 68, no. 9 (1971): 42-43.
2. Calvin Blair, "Mexico in the World Economy," *Current History* 66 (1974): 217-219.
3. Quoted in Thomas G. Sanders, "Mexico in 1975," *American Universities Field Staff North American Series* 3 (1975): 10-12.
4. "As described for the first time" by Koehler, *Economic Policy Making with Limited Information.* See also Wilkie, *The Mexican Revolution*, pp. 105-114.
5. Blair, "Mexico in the World Economy," p. 219.
6. The Economist Intelligence Unit, *Quarterly Economic Review of Mexico*, 1972, pp. 11-12.
7. See Business International, *Mexico* (Mexico City: Business International, 1976), for an excellent critique of the laws; Price Waterhouse, *Doing Business in Mexico* (New York: Price Waterhouse, 1975), contains an outline of the laws.

Chapter 6

1. Based on the accounts given in Banco Nacional de Comercio Exterior's *Comercio Exterior de México*, various issues.
2. Mexico's import elasticity had averaged 0.8 during the latter 1960s and early 1970s. In 1974, however, it rose to 3.2.
3. The price indexes in Mexico are not considered to be a particularly accurate measure of inflation since they contain a number of goods whose price is controlled by the authorities.
4. Eduardo Venezian and William Gamble, *The Agricultural Development of México: Its Structure and Growth since 1950* (New York: Praeger, 1969), Chapter 4.
5. "Measures to Combat Inflationary Pressures," *Comercio Exterior de México* 19 (August 1973): 3.
6. Lic. Flores de la Peña, the minister of national property, in a news conference following the announcement of the anti-inflation program.
7. A brief statement of President Etcheverría's views on private (especially private foreign) investment is given in "Statement by the President of Mexico to Local and Foreign Investors," *Comercio Exterior de México* 17 (January 1971): 7.

Chapter 7

1. Richard Shaffer, "Mexican Peso is Allowed to Sink Again, the Second Time in Less Than 2 Months," *The Wall Street Journal*, October 28, 1976, p. 2.
2. Marvin Alisky, "Mexico's Population Pressures," *Current History* 72

(1977): 106-110; and idem, "Mexico Versus Malthus: National Trends," *Current History* 69 (1974): 200-203.

3. The country's population, even assuming a moderate decline in the birthrate is likely to double between 1975 and 2000. See Chapter 12.

4. For a sympathetic evaluation of Etcheverría's programs in this area, see Sanders, "Mexico in 1975".

5. See for example, P. A. Olaiz, ed., *Precios del Agua en Irrigacion*, SRH, Subscretaria de Planeacion, "Documentation del Plan Nacional Hidráulico," Mexico City (forthcoming) for an application to the pricing of irrigation water.

6. If this strategy has been prepared, it has not been published or made publicly available.

7. The Economist Intelligence Unit, *Quarterly Economic Review of Mexico*, p. 6.

Chapter 8

1. This is certainly the position taken in the financial press. See Banco Cremi, Cremi Indicador, *Sobre la Económia Mexicana*, 1975, special issue.

2. The following account of the government's policy has been culled from various issues of *Comercio Exterior de México*.

3. The events immediately following the devaluation were given extensive coverage in the press. The following draws heavily on Alan Riding, "Peso Devalued Sharply and Dealings Resume," *Financial Times*, September 3, 1976, p. 32; idem, "Why Something Had to Give in the Mexican Economy," *Financial Times*, p. 3; idem, "Adjusting to Devaluation," *Financial Times*, October 1, 1976, p. 5; idem, "Mending the Broken Bridges," *Financial Times*, October 30, 1976, p. 7; Shaffer, "Mexican Peso is Allowed to Sink Again, p. 2.

4. Quoted in *Comercio Exterior de México* 22 (1976): 385.

5. See "A Long, Long Month," *Comercio Exterior de México* 22 (October 1976): 385-392, for this statement and accounts in the Mexican press concerning the devaluation.

6. "Sixth State of the Nation Address," ibid., pp. 368-384.

7. An excellent critique of the president's last state of the nation address and of the devaluation is given in Redvers Opie, "The Last Informe of President Echeverría: Inflation and Devaluation," *Economic Report American Chamber of Commerce of Mexico*, September 10, 1976. The following draws heavily on Dr. Opie's deep insights on the economic situation of Mexico.

Chapter 9

1. Background and accounts are excellently summarized in Riding, "The Dangers of Dismantling a Myth," p. 5; idem, "Controversial Move," *Financial Times*, October 24, 1976, p. 7. See also "Huge Mexico Left Gift to Peasants," *San Francisco Chronicle*, October 26, 1976.

2. Quoted in John Huey, "Mexico's Economic Ills Could Topple Coalition of Workers, Poor Rebel," *The Wall Street Journal*, August 8, 1977, p. 1.

3. Based on references cited in note 3, Chapter 8.

4. "IMF Puts Together Mexico Loan Package of $963 Million to Reinforce Confidence," *The Wall Street Journal,* October 29, 1976, p. 4. See also "The Great Mexican Dream for a Few Barrels More," *Euromoney,* May 1977, pp. 89-93.

Chapter 10

1. Richard Shaffer, "Mexico: More Troubles Ahead?" *The Wall Street Journal,* November 23, 1976, p. 4.

2. "Silence Can Be Golden," *The Economist,* January 15, 1977, p. 63; Alan Riding, "A New President of Mexico," *New York Times,* December 2, 1976, p. 1. idem, "Mexico's New Chief, Sworn in, Appeals for End to Conflict," *New York Times,* December 2, 1976; p. 3; Richard Shaffer, "Mexico's Economic Ills Expected to Force New President to Seek Capitalist Solution," *The Wall Street Journal,* May 21, 1976, p. 18; "A New President Inherits the Wind," *San Francisco Examiner,* December 1, 1976, p. 36.

3. Bits and pieces can be gleamed from Alan Riding, "Mexico's New President Is Turning Back to Traditional Business Circles for Aid to Revive Economy," *New York Times,* December 26, 1976, p. 17; John B. Oakes, "Mexican Leader, Outlining Plans, Sees a Challenge in National Crisis," *New York Times,* February 1, 1977, p. 1; Alan Riding, "Mexico's Conservatives Regaining Strength since Lopez Took Office," *New York Times,* May 27, 1976, p. 5; "Mexico: The Road Back to Confidence," *Time,* February 21, 1977, pp. 33-36; Grayam Hovey, "Mexican Chief Takes Side of Poor," *New York Times,* February 16, 1977, p. 3; John Huey, "United States Businessmen See Easier Mexican Climate under New President," *The Wall Street Journal,* December 24, 1976, p. 1.

4. See "Economic Aspects of the Mexican President's Inaugural Address," *Comercio Exterior de México* 23 (January 1977): 11-18; "Finance Sector: Recent Fiscal Reform," ibid., pp. 43-47.

5. "Alliance for Production," ibid., pp. 54-57.

6. "Federal Budget for 1977," ibid., pp. 47-52.

7. The following draws heavily on Redvers Opie, *The 1977 Budget of Mexico,* Economic Report, American Chamber of Commerce of Mexico, January 3, 1977.

Chapter 11

1. The model is of the so-called two-gap variety. However, it does differ from this class of models in that it incorporates a number of monetary factors. The basic two-gap framework and the assumptions upon which it is based can be found in Hollis Chenery and Peter Eckstein, "Development Alternatives for Latin America," *Journal of Political Economy* 77 (1970), supplement, pp. 966-1016; Vijay Joshi, "Saving and Foreign Exchange Constraints," in *Unfashionable Economics—Essays in Honour of Thomas Blough* (London: Weidenfeld and Nicolson, 1970); Luis Landau, "Saving Functions for Latin America," in

Studies in Development Planning, ed. Hollis Chenery (Cambridge, Mass.: Harvard University Press, 1971); Constantine Michalopoulos, "Imports, Foreign Exchange and Economic Development: The Greek Experience," in *The Open Economy,* ed. Peter Kennen (New York: Columbia University Press, 1968).

2. In the context of the Colombian economy, Jaroslav Vanek discusses possible adjustment processes. See his *Estimating Foreign Resource Needs for Economic Development* (New York: McGraw-Hall, 1967). For Panama, see Robert Looney, *The Economic Development of Panama* (New York: Praeger, 1976). A version somewhat different from that adopted here was applied by John Stewart, "An Analysis of the Two Gap Theory of Economic Development with Empirical Applications for the Mexican Economy (Ph. D. diss., University of North Carolina, 1975), Chapter 7.

Chapter 12

1. See Alan Riding, "Illegal Migration to U.S. Gives Mexico an Economic Safety Valve," *New York Times,* June 19, 1977, p. 4.

2. Alan Riding, "Oil Riches Down Mexico Way," *Financial Times,* April 18, 1977, p. 6; "The Great Mexican Dream for a Few Barrels More," pp. 89-93.

3. John Isbister, "Birth Control, Income Redistribution, and the Rate of Saving: The Case of Mexico," *Demography* 16 (February 1973): 85-98.

4. Jacques May and Donna McLellan, *The Ecology of Malnutrition in Mexico and Central America* (New York: Hafter Publishing Co., 1972), p. 5.

5. R. Banks, "Water Resources for Development in Mexico," (Mimeographed, International Bank for Reconstruction and Development, Washington, D.C., 1971) gives an excellent overview of Mexico's water problems.

6. The forecasts of water needs are taken from the Plan Nacional Hidráulico (Mexico City, 1957). For general background, see Ronald Cummings, *Water Resource Management in Northern Mexico* (Baltimore: Johns Hopkins Press, 1972); Mercedes Escamilla et al., "Water as a Social Solvent? Alternative Development Strategies for Mexico's Subsistence Agricultural Sector," in *Water for Human Needs: Proceedings of the Second World Congress on Water Resources* (New Delhi: Central Board of Irrigation and Power, 1975), pp. 571-590; and Villarreal Gonzales, "Mexican National Water Plan: Organization and Preliminary Assessment," *American Journal of Agricultural Economics* 55 (December 1973).

7. Osorio Reyes et al., *Estructura Agaria y Desarrollo Agrícola en México* (Mexico City: Fondo de Cultura Económica, 1974).

8. Riding, "Oil Riches Down Mexico Way."

9. Richard Ensor, "Sovereign Borrowers in the Euromarkets in 1977?," *Euromoney,* October 1976, pp. 105-120; S. Yassukovich, "The Growing Political Threat to International Lending," *Euromoney,* April 1966, pp. 10-15. With particular regard to Mexico's chances for increased borrowing as seen by its leading officials, see William Clarke, "President López Portillo: Guiding Mexico through Its Crisis Year," *Euromoney,* August 1977, pp. 10-14; and

Padraic Fallon, "Kolbeck's Road Show: Selling Confidence in Mexico to the Intenational Banks," *Euromoney*, August 1977, pp. 16-17.

10. For the issues in the capital shortage debate, see Henry Wallisch, "The Impending Capital Shortage," *Challenge* 19 (1976): 45; Chauncey Schmidt, "Assessing the Risk of a Capital Shortage," *Euromoney*, February 1977, pp. 66-68.

11. Pierre-Paul Schweitzer, "On the Financing Problems of the Third World," *Euromoney*, March 1976, pp. 14-19.

12. For example, "Should International Banks Continue to Lend to Brazil?" *Euromoney*, May 1976, pp. 16-19; and Stephen Goodman, "How the Big U.S. Banks Really Evaluate Sovereign Risks," *Euromoney*, February 1977, pp. 105-111.

13. See the responses in the excellent survey of U.S. firms in Mexico conducted by Stanford Research Institute, *The Impact of Foreign Private Investment on the Mexican Economy* (Menlo Park, Calif.: Stanford Research Institute, 1976).

14. A breakdown of these is given in Business International Roundtable, *Mexico: Background* (Mexico City: Business International, June 6-9, 1976).

Chapter 13

1. "Mexico's Long-Term Strategy," *Financial Times*, September 3, 1976, p. 6.

2. Alan Riding, "Mexico's Head Reports Economy Improves but Problems Persist," *New York Times*, September 1, 1977.

3. "Mexican Headache for International Banks," *The Economist*, January 22, 1977, p. 99.

4. See Alan Riding, "Mexico's Inflation Fight: Stomach vs. Program," *New York Times*, April 16, 1977, p. 33, for an early assessment of the labor sector's response to the government's new austerity programs.

5. Recent empirical work by Clark Reynolds and Jaime Corredor indicates that (based on a survey in Monterrey) if credit facilities and financial assets were made available to low-income households in a more accessible manner and with attractive yields, the net effect might well be to increase the net financial savings of such households while simultaneously increasing their share of financial wealth. They note that since the cost of providing financial competitive intermediation services to the poor often makes such programs unprofitable for competitive financial institutions, consideration might be given to the use of fiscal subsidies, incentives, and other policies to induce the development of such services. Cf. Clark Reynolds and Jaime Corredor, "The Effects of the Financial System on the Distribution of Income and Wealth in Mexico," *Food Research Institute Studies* 15 (1976): 87.

6. The role of the government in this area is somewhat controversial. See Roger Johnston, "Should the Mexican Government Promote the Country's Stock Exchange?" *Inter-American Economic Affairs* 26, no. 3 (1972): 45-60.

7. This account draws heavily on the recent analysis of Mexican monetary policy by Wilford, "The Open Economy."

8. This mechanism has been outlined in some detail by Gilberto Escobedo.

See his "Mexican Stabilization Policy, Fiscal or Monetary" (mimeographed, no date); "The Response of the Mexican Economy to Policy Action," *Federal Reserve Board of St. Louis Review* 55 (1973): 15-23; and "Ahorro y desarrollo económico" (mimeographed, no date).

9. A number of complaints can be found in various issues of Business International, *Business Latin America*. The picture is not as bad as this source usually leads one to believe. For a more optimistic picture, see Richard Shaffer, "Multinationals Discover Profits in Mexico Despite Peso Problems, Ownership Rules," *The Wall Street Journal*, November 5, 1976, p. 32; and Huey, "U.S. Businessmen See Easier Mexican Climate under New President," p. 1.

10. John Hennessy, "Ratings and Other Factors in Approaching the U.S. Capital Market," *Euromoney*, January 1976, pp. 60-69.

Appendix

1. For an earlier period, Charles Schotta concluded that the multiplier or Keynesian theory of income determination explained between 44 and 50 percent of the variance of money national income in Mexico. In contrast, the quantity theory or monetary approach to income determination explained 70 percent of the variance in money national income. See Charles Schotta, "The Money Supply, Exports, and Income in an Open Economy: Mexico, 1939-63," *Economic Development and Cultural Change* 14 (1966): 458-470.

2. J. J. Polack, "Monetary Analysis of Income Formulation and Payments Problems," *International Monetary Fund Staff Papers* 65 (1957): 1-50; and S. J. Prais, "Some Mathematical Notes on the Quantity Theory of Money in an Open Economy," ibid., 69:212-226.

3. Gilberto Escobedo, on the other hand, finds that the quantity theory yields better results and concludes that the Keynesian model is inferior, because in the *GDP* equation a number of regression coefficients are not significant. Escobedo used data that have subsequently been revised. This may explain some of the differences between his results and the ones here. Nevertheless, the forecasting model was designed primarily as a monetary model to avoid any possible weakness in the Keynesian approach. See Gilberto Escobedo, "Formulating a Model of the Mexican Economy," *Federal Reserve Bank of St. Louis Review* 55 (1973): 15.

4. The validity of using a monetary approach is not only confirmed by the work of Schotta and Escobedo, but by several recent studies as well. See Wilford, "The Open Economy," and D. Sykes Wilford and Walton Wilford, "Monetary Approach to Balance of Payments: On World Prices and the Reserve Flow Equation," *Weltwirtschaftliches Archiv*, 1976, pp. 31-39.

5. See Wilford, "The Open Economy," Chapter 2, for an in-depth description of this process.

6. As noted in Chenery and Peter Eckstein, "Development Alternatives for Latin America," pp. 970-973.

Selected Bibliography

Alisky, Marvin. "Mexico's Population Pressures," *Current History* 72 (1977): 106-110.

"Alliance for Production." *Comercio Exterior de México* 23 (1977): 54-57.

Arronte, R. Carillo. *An Empirical Test on Interregional Planning: A Linear Programming Model for Mexico*. Rotterdam: Rotterdam University Press, 1970.

Aspra, L. Antonio. "Import Substitution in Mexico: Past and Present." *World Development* 5 (1977): 113-120.

Baerresen, Donald W. "Unemployment and Mexico's Border Industrialization Program." *Inter-American Economic Affairs* 29 (1975): 79-90.

Baklanoff, Eric N. *Expropriation of U.S. Investments in Cuba, Mexico, and Chile*. New York: Praeger, 1975.

Banco de México. *Informe Anual*.

_____. *Indicadores Económicos*.

_____. *Informe Anual* (1975), Statistical Appendix.

Banco Nacional. "The Economic Structure." *Review of the Economic Situation of Mexico* 53 (1973): 304-305.

Banco Nacional de Comercio Exterior, S.A. "Reflections in Agricultural Development Policy." *Comercio Exterior de México* 21 (1975): 70-71.

Banks, R. "Water Resources for Development in Mexico." Mimeographed. Washington: International Bank for Reconstruction and Development, 1971.

Barkin, David, and King, Timothy. *Regional Economic Development: The River Basin Approach in Mexico*. Cambridge: Cambridge University Press, 1970.

_____. "Agricultural Development in Mexico: A Case Study of Income Concentration." *Social Research* 37 (1971): 306.

Bennet, Robert L. *The Financial Sector and Economic Development: The*

Mexican Case. Baltimore: Johns Hopkins University Press, 1965.

Bett, Virgil M. *Central Banking in Mexico: Monetary Policies and Financial Crises, 1964-1970.* Ann Arbor: University of Michigan Press, 1957.

Betteta, Mario Ramón. "The Central Bank: Instrument of Economic Development in Mexico." In *Mexico's Recent Economic Growth: The Mexican View,* edited by Tom E. Davis et al. Austin: University of Texas Press, 1967.

Blair, Calvin. "Echeverría's Economic Policy." *Current History* 72 (1977): 124-127.

―――. "Mexico in the World Economy." *Current History* 66 (1974): 217-219.

Blomquist, A. B. "Empirical Evidence on the Two Gap Hypothesis: A Revised Analysis." *Journal of Development Economics* 3 (1976): 181-194.

Brothers, Dwight, and Solís, Leopoldo. *Mexican Financial Development.* Austin: University of Texas Press, 1966.

Bruton, Henry J. "The Two Gap Approach to Aid and Development." *The American Economic Review* 59 (1969): 439-446.

Bueno, Gerardo. "Estructura de la Protección en México." In *La Estructura de la Protección Países in Desarrollo,* edited by B. Balassa et al. Mexico City: CEMLA, 1972.

Buira, Ariel. "Development and Price Stability in Mexico." *Weltwirtschaftliches Archiv,* 1968, pp. 50-62.

Business International. *Mexico.* Mexico City: Business International, 1976.

Business International Roundtable. *Mexico: Background.* Mexico City: Business International, June 6-9, 1976.

Calvert, Peter. *Mexico: Nation of the World.* New York: Praeger, 1973.

Carnoy, Martin. "Earnings and Schooling in Mexico." *Economic Development and Cultural Change* 15 (1967): 408-419.

Chenery, Hollis. "The Structuralist Approach to Economic Development." *The American Economic Review* 65 (1975).

―――. "The Structuralist Theory of Economic Development." *The American Economic Review* 65 (1975).

Chenery, Hollis B., and Eckstein, Peter. "Development Alternatives for Latin America." *Journal of Political Economy* 77 (1960): 966-1016.

Chenery, H. B., and Strout, A. M. "Foreign Assistance and Economic Development." *The American Economic Review* 56 (1966): 679-733.

Clarke, William. "President López Portillo: Guiding Mexico Through Its Crisis Years." *Euromoney,* August 1977, pp. 10-14.

The Combined Mexican Working Party. *The Economic Development of Mexico.* Baltimore: Johns Hopkins University Press, 1953.

Crosson, Pierre. "Economic Consequences of Urbanization in Mexico." University of Wisconsin–Milwaukee Center for Latin American Studies, Center Discussion paper no. 33 (1971).

Cummings, Ronald. *Water Resource Management in Northern Mexico.* Baltimore: Johns Hopkins University Press, 1972.

Davis, Tom, et al. *Mexico's Recent Economic Growth: The Mexican View.* Austin: University of Texas Press, 1967.

De Alcantara, Cynthia Hewitt. "The 'Green Revolution' as History: The Mexican Experience." *Development and Change* 4 (1973): 25-44.

De Beers, John S. "Mexico's Balance of Payments: Some Tentative Conclusions on the Adjustment Process." *Inter-American Economic Affairs* 6 (1951): 3-46.

De la Peña, H. Flores. "Agricultura Mexicana." *Comercio Exterior* 4 (1958): 376-379.

———. "Crecimiento Demográfico, Desarrollo Agrícola y Desarrollo Economico." *Investigacion Económica* 14 (1954): 519-539.

———. "La Elasticidad de la Oferta y el Desarrollo Económico." *Trimestre Económico* 22 (1955): 1-22.

———. "La Mecánica de la Inflación." *Investigación Económica* 13 (1953): 461-481.

De la Peña, Lic. Flores. Minister of national property, in a news conference following the announcement of the anti-inflation program.

De Onís, Joan. "Birth Control in Latin America Making Little Headway as Population Pressures Grow." *New York Times,* June 21, 1977.

Denison, Edward. *Accounting for United States Economic Growth 1929-1969.* Washington: The Brookings Institution, 1974.

Dovring, Folks. *Land Reform in Mexico.* Washington: Agency for International Development, 1970.

"Economic Aspects of the Mexican President's Inaugural Address." *Comercio Exterior de México* 23 (1977): 11-18.

The Economist Intelligence Unit. *Quarterly Economic Review of Mexico,* 1972, pp. 11-12.

Edel, Matthew. *Food Supply and Inflation in Latin America.* New York: Praeger Publishers, 1969.

El Colegio de México. *Dinámica de la Población de México.* Mexico City: El Colegio de México, 1970.

Emery, Robert G. "Mexican Monetary Policy since the 1954 Devaluation." *Inter-American Economic Affairs* 12 (1958): 72-85.

Ensor, Richard. "Sovereign Borrowers in the Euromarkets in 1977?" *Euromoney,* October 1976, pp. 105-120.

Escamilla, Mercedes, et al. "Water as a Social Solvent? Alternative Development Strategies for Mexico's Subsistence Agricultural Sector." *Water for Human Needs, Proceedings of the Second World Congress on Water Resources.* New Delhi: Central Board of Irrigation and Power, 1975

Escobedo, Gilberto. "Ahorro y Desarrollo Economica." (Unpublished manuscript), p. 12.

———. "Formulating a Model of the Mexican Economy." *Federal Reserve Bank of St. Louis Review* 55 (1973): 15-23.

———. "Mexican Stabilization Policy, Fiscal or Monetary." Mimeographed. No date.

_____. "The Response of the Mexican Economy to Policy Actions." *Federal Reserve Bank of St. Louis Review* 55 (1973): 15-23.

Eshag, Eprime. "The Relative Efficacy of Monetary Policy in Selected Industrial and Less-Developed Countries." *Economic Journal* 81 (1971): 294-505.

Fallon, Padraic. "Kolbeck's Road Show: Selling Confidence in Mexico to the International Banks." *Euromoney*, August 1977, pp. 16-17.

"Federal Budget for 1977." *Comercio Exterior de México* 23 (1977): 47-52.

Felix, David. "Income Inequality in Mexico." *Current History* 72 (1977): 111-114.

_____. "Monetarists, Structuralists and Import-Substituting Industrialization: A Critical Approach." *Studies in Contemporary International Development*, 1965.

"Finance Sector: Recent Fiscal Reform." *Comercio Exterior de México* 23 (1977): 43-47.

Flores, Antonio Carrillo. "El Desarrollo Económico de México: Reflectiones Sobre un Caso Latino-Americano." *Cuardernos Americanos*, September-October, 1948, p. 48.

Freebairn, Donald. "The Dichotomy of Prosperity and Poverty in Mexican Agriculture." *Land Economics* 69 (1969): 35.

Freithgler, William. *Mexico's Foreign Trade and Economic Development.* New York: Praeger, 1968.

Friedman, Milton. "Monetary Policy for Developing Society." *Bank Markazi Iran Bulletin* 10 (1971): 700-712.

Fundación para Estudios de la Población. *Perfil Demográfico de México.* Mexico City: Fundación para Estudios de la Población, 1972.

Goldsmith, Raymond W. *The Financial Development of Mexico.* Paris: Organization for Economic Cooperation and Development, 1966.

Gollas, Manuel, and García, Adalberto. "El Desarrollo Económico Reciente de México." In *Contemporary Mexico*, edited by James Wilkie. Berkeley: University of California Press, 1976.

Gonzales, Villarreal. "Mexican National Water Plan: Organization and Preliminary Assessment." *American Journal of Agricultural Economics* 55 (1973).

Goodman, Stephen. "How the Big U.S. Banks Really Evaluate Sovereign Risks." *Euromoney*, February 1977, pp. 105-111.

Goreux, Louis, and Manne, Alan. *Multi-Level Planning: Case Studies in Mexico.* Amsterdam: North Holland, 1973.

"The Great Mexican Dream for a Few Barrels More." *Euromoney*, May 1977, pp. 89-93.

Griffiths, B. *Mexican Monetary Policy and Economic Development.* New York: Praeger, 1972.

Griffin, Keith. "Policy Options for Rural Development." *Oxford Bulletin of Economics and Statistics* 35 (1973), p. 243.

Hansen, Roger D. *Mexican Economic Development: The Roots of Rapid Growth.* Washington: National Planning Association, 1971.

Hennessy, John. "Ratings and Other Factors in Approaching the U.S. Capital Market." *Euromoney*, January 1976, pp. 60-69.

Hicks, W. Whitney. "A 'Reproduction Function' for Young Women in Mexico." *Social and Economic Studies* 17 (1968): 121-125.

_____. "Economic Development and Fertility Change in Mexico 1950-1970." *Demography* 11 (1974): 407-421.

_____. "Comments on Daniel A. Siever's 'Recent Fertility in Mexico: Measurement and Interpretation.' " *Population Studies* 30 (1976): 175-177.

Higgins, Benjamin. *Economic Development*. New York: Norton, 1968.

Hollerman, Leon. "Mexico's Dilemma in Economic Development and the Japanese Solution." *Banca Nacional del Lavoro Quarterly Review* 88 (1969): 66-90.

Hovey, Grayam. "Mexican Chief Takes Side of Poor." *New York Times*, February 16, 1977.

Huey, John. "United States Businessmen See Easier Mexican Climate Under New President." *The Wall Street Journal*, December 24, 1976.

Hurtado, Ernesto Fernández. Director general of the Bank of Mexico, an address to the Money Marketeers of New York University, March 26, 1976.

United Nations. *Income Distribution in Latin America*. New York: United Nations, 1971.

Inter-American Development Bank. *Urban Population Growth in Mexico*. Washington: IDB Technical Department, 1972.

International Reports. *The Future of the Mexican Peso*. New York: International Reports, 1974.

Isbister, John. "Birth Control, Income Redistribution, and the Rate of Saving: The Case of Mexico." *Demography* 16 (1973): 85-98.

_____. "Urban Employment and Wages in a Developing Economy: The Case of Mexico." *Economic Development and Cultural Change* 20 (1971): 24-46.

Izquierdo, R. "Protectionism in Mexico." In *Public Policy and Private Enterprise in Mexico*, edited by R. Vernon. Cambridge, Mass.: Harvard University Press, 1964.

Johnston, Roger D. "Should the Mexican Government Promote the Country's Stock Exchange?" *Inter-American Economic Affairs* 26, no. 3 (1972): 45-60.

Joshi, Vijay. "Saving and Foreign Exchange Constraints." *Unfashionable Economics: Essays in Honour of Thomas Blough*. London: Weidenfeld and Nicholson, 1970.

Katz, Bernard S. "Mexican Fiscal and Subsidy Incentives for Industrial Development." *American Journal of Economics and Sociology* 31 (1972): 353-358.

King, Timothy. *Mexico: Industrialization and Trade Policies since 1940*. London: Oxford University Press, 1970.

Kirk, Dudley. "A New Demographic Transition?" In *Rapid Population Growth*. Vol. 2. Washington: National Academy of Sciences, 1971.

Kitamura, Hiroshi. "Trade and Capital Needs of Developing Countries and Foreign Assistance." *Weltwirtschaftliches Archiv*, 1966, pp. 303-324.

Koehler, John E. *Economic Policy Making with Limited Information: The*

Process of Macro-Control in Mexico. Santa Monica, Calif.: Rand Corporation, 1968.

Kolbek, Gustavo Romero. "Economic Development of Mexico." In Committee for Economic Development, *Economic Development Issues: Latin America.* New York: Praeger, 1967.

La Cascia, Joseph S. *Capital Formation and Economic Development in Mexico.* New York: Praeger, 1969.

Ladman, Jerry. "A Model of Credit Applied to the Allocation of Resources in a Case Study of a Sample of Mexican Farms." *Economic Development and Cultural Change* 23 (1974): 279-301.

Lamadrid, A. "Industrial Location Policy in Mexico." In United Nations, *Industrial Location and Regional Development—Proceedings of an Interregional Seminar, Minsk, 14-26 August 1968.* New York: United Nations, 1972.

Landau, Luis. "Saving Functions for Latin America." In *Studies in Development Planning,* edited by Hollis Chenery. Cambridge, Mass.: Harvard University Press, 1971.

Lavell, A. M. "Regional Industrialization in Mexico: Some Policy Considerations." *Regional Studies* 6 (1972): 343-362.

Ley General de Población. Mexico City: Editores Mexicanos Unidos, 1975.

Lobato, E. "La Política Monetaria Mexicana." *Investigación Económica* 23 (1968): 557-581.

Looney, Robert. *The Economic Development of Iran.* New York: Praeger, 1973.

———. *The Economic Development of Panama.* New York: Praeger, 1976.

———. *Income Distribution Policies and Economic Growth in Semi-Industrialized Countries: A Comparative Study of Iran, Mexico, Brazil and South Korea.* New York: Praeger, 1975.

Lotz, Jurgen R., and Morss, Elliot R. "Measuring Tax Effort in Developing Countries." *International Monetary Fund Staff Papers* 14 (1967): 478-499.

Maizels, A. *Exports and Economic Growth of Developing Countries.* Cambridge: Cambridge University Press, 1968.

Mateos, Adolfo López. *The Economic Development of Mexico During a Quarter of a Century (1934-1959).* Mexico City: Nacional Financiera, S.A., 1968.

May, Jacques, and McLellan, Donna. *The Ecology of Malnutrition in Mexico and Central America.* New York: Hafter Publishing Co., 1972.

Mayer, Tom. "The Relative Efficacy of Monetary Policy in Selected Industrial and Less-Developed Countries: A Comment." *Economic Journal* 82 (1972): 1368-1371.

McKinnon, Ronald. "Foreign Exchange Constraints in Economic Development and Efficient Aid Allocation." *Economic Journal* 74 (1964): 285-409.

"Measures to Combat Inflationary Pressures." *Comercio Exterior de México* 19 (1973): 3.

Mena, Antonio Ortiz. *Stabilizing Development: A Decade of Economic Strategy in Mexico.* Mexico City: Ministry of Finance, 1969.

————. "Contenido y Avances de la Política Fiscal." *Actividad Económica en Latinoamérica,* 1966, pp. 597-605.

The Mexican Economy: Analysis—76. Mexico City: Publicaciones Ejecutivas de México, S.A., 1976.

"Mexican Headache for International Banks." *The Economist,* January 22, 1977, p. 99.

"Mexico: The Limits of State Capitalism." *Latin American Perspectives,* Summer 1975.

"Mexico: The Road Back to Confidence." *Time,* February 21, 1977, pp. 33-36.

"Mexico's Long-Term Strategy." *Financial Times,* September 3, 1976, p. 6.

Meyer, Victoria Junco. "Women in Mexican Society." *Current History* 72 (1977): 120-123.

Michalopoulos, Constantine. "Imports, Foreign Exchange and Economic Development: The Greek Experience." In *The Open Economy,* edited by Peter Kennen. New York: Columbia University Press, 1968.

Miró, Carmen A. "Some Misconceptions Disproved: A Program of Fertility Studies in Latin America." In *Family Planning and Population Programs: A Review of World Developments,* edited by Bernard Berelson. Chicago: University of Chicago Press, 1966.

Monsivais, Carlos. "Clasismo y Novela en México." *Latin American Perspectives* 2 (1975): 164-178.

Moriega, A. "Las Devaluaciones Monetarias de México, 1938-1954." *Investagación Económica* 15 (1955): 149-177.

Mueller, Marnie W. "Changing Patterns of Agricultural Output and Production in the Private and Land Reform Sectors in Mexico, 1940-1960." *Economic Development and Cultural Change* 16 (1968): 262.

————. "Structural Inflation and the Mexican Experience." *Yale Economic Essays* 5 (1965): 187-188.

Nacional Financiera. *Nacional Financiera, S.A. en el Desarollo Económico de Mexico.* Mexico City: Nacional Financiera, 1964.

————. "Nacional Financiera y el Desarrollo del Sector de Bienes de Capital en México." *Mercado de Valores* (1975), pp. 3-30.

Navarette, A. "El Sector Público en el Desarrollo Económico." *Investigación Economica* 17 (1957): 43-61.

————. *Estabilidad de Cambios, el Ciclo, y el Desarrollo Económico. Una Investigación Sobre los Problemas de la Balanza de Pagos de México 1929-1946.* Mexico City, 1951.

Needler, Martin C. "Mexico's Growing Pains." *Current History* 66 (1974): 193-194.

"A New President Inherits the Wind." *San Francisco Examiner,* December 1, 1976, p. 36.

Noyola, J. "El Desarrollo Económico y la Inflación en México y Otros Paises Latinoamericanos." *Investigación Económica* 16 (1956): 603-606.

————. "Existe una Politica de Precios?" *Revista de Economia* 11 (1948): 8-10.

Oakes, John B. "Mexican Leader, Outlining Plans, Sees a Challenge in

National Crisis." *New York Times,* February 1, 1977.

Opie, Redvers. "The Economic Outlook in Mexico." Mimeographed. July 14, 1974.

———. "Mexico's President Plans for Progress." *Banking* 68, no. 9 (1971): 42-43.

———. *The 1977 Budget of Mexico,* Economic Report, American Chamber of Commerce of Mexico, January 3, 1977.

Pazos, Luis. *Devaluación y Estatismo en México.* Mexico City: Editorial Diana, 1976.

Perfil Demográfico de México. Mexico City: Foundacion para Estudios de la Poblacion, 1972.

"Plan Nacional Hidráulico." Mexico City, 1957. Mimeographed.

Polack, J. J. "Monetary Analysis of Income Formulation and Payments Problems." *International Monetary Fund Staff Papers* 65 (1957): 1-50.

Prais, S. J. "Some Mathematical Notes on the Quantity Theory of Money in an Open Economy." *International Monetary Fund Staff Papers* 9 (1961): 212-226.

"Reflections in Agricultural Development Policy." *Comercio Exterior de México* 21 (1975): 70-71.

Price Waterhouse. *Doing Business in Mexico.* New York: Price Waterhouse, 1975.

Reyes, Osorio, et al. *Estructura Agraria y Desarrollo Agrícola en México.* Mexico City: Fondo de Cultura Economica, 1974.

Reyes, Saul Trejo. *Industrialización y Empleo en México.* Mexico City: Fondo de Cultura Económica, 1971.

Reynolds, Clark. *The Mexican Economy: Twentieth-Century Structure and Growth.* New Haven: Yale University Press, 1970.

———. "Mexico and Brazil: Models for Leadership in Latin America?" In *Contemporary Mexico,* edited by James W. Wilkie. Berkeley: University of California Press, 1976.

———. "Public Finance in Postrevolutionary Mexico." In *Government and Economic Development,* edited by Gustav Ranis. New Haven: Yale University Press, 1971.

———. "Social and Political Interaction in the Economic Development of a Disequilibrium System: Some Latin American Examples." *Food Research Institute Studies in Agricultural Economics Trade and Development* 10 (1971): 89-108.

———. "Why Mexico's 'Stabilizing Development' Was Actually Disstabilizing (With Some Implications for the Future)." Paper presented to the Congress of the United States, Joint Economic Committee, Subcommittee on Inter-American Economic Relationships hearing on *Recent Developments in Mexico and Their Economic Implications for the United States.* Washington, January 17, 1977.

Reynolds, Clark, and Corredor, Jaime. "The Effects of the Financial System on the Distribution of Income and Wealth in Mexico." *Food Research Institute Studies* 15 (1976): 87.

Riding, Alan. "The Dangers of Dismantling a Myth." *Financial Times,* September 7, 1966.
_____. "The Headache is Just Beginning." *Financial Times,* January 25, 1977, p. 5.
_____. "Illegal Migration to U.S. Gives Mexico an Economic Safety Valve." *New York Times,* June 19, 1977, p. 4.
_____. "Mexico's Conservatives Regaining Strength Since López Took Office." *New York Times,* May 27, 1976, p. 5.
_____. "Mexico's Head Reports Economy Improves but Problems Persist." *New York Times,* September 1, 1977, p. D4.
_____. "Mexico's Inflation Fight: Stomach vs. Program." *New York Times,* April 16, 1977, p. 33.
_____. "Mexico's New Chief, Sworn In, Appeals for End to Conflict." *New York Times,* December 2, 1976, p. 3.
_____. "Mexico's New President is Turning Back to Traditional Business Circles for Aid to Revive Economy." *New York Times,* December 26, 1976, p. 17.
_____. "A New President of Mexico." *New York Times,* December 2, 1976.
_____. "Oil Riches Down Mexico Way." *Financial Times,* April 18, 1977, p. 6.
_____. "Why Something Had to Give in the Mexican Economy." *Financial Times,* September 7, 1976, p. 3.
Rodríguez, Ernesto Quintanilla. "Interstate Labor Force Migration in Mexico: 1960-1970." Ph.D. dissertation, University of Pittsburgh, 1976.
Ross, John B. *The Economic System of Mexico.* Stanford, Calif.: California Institute of International Studies, 1971.
Sanders, Thomas G. "Mexican Women." American Universities Field Staff, *North American Series* 3 (1975): 1-10.
_____. "Mexico in 1975." American Universities Field Staff, *North American Series* 3 (1975): 10-12.
_____. "Mexico 1974: Demographic Patterns and Population Policy." American Universities Field Staff, *North American Series* 2 (1974): 1-3.
Sarames, George N. "Third System in Latin America: Mexico." *Inter-American Economic Affairs* 7 (1953): 59-72.
Schmidt, Chauncey. "Assessing the Risk of a Capital Shortage." *Euromoney,* February 1977, pp. 66-68.
Schotta, Charles. "The Money Supply, Exports, and Income in an Open Economy: Mexico, 1939-63." *Economic Development and Cultural Change* 14 (1966): 458-470.
Schweitzer, Pierre-Paul. "On the Financing Problems of the Third World." *Euromoney,* March 1976, pp. 14-19.
Secretaría de Industria y Comercio. *Anuario Estatístico Compendiad de los Estados Unidos Mexicanos, 1970.* Mexico City: Dirección General de Estadística, n.d.
_____. Mexico: *VIII Censo de la Población, 1960.* Mexico City: Dirección General de Estadística, 1960.
_____. Mexico: IX *Censo de la Población, 1970.* Mexico City: Dirección

General de Estadística, 1970.

Seiver, Daniel A. "Recent Fertility in Mexico: Measurement and Interpretation." *Population Studies* 29 (1975): 343-353.

―――. "A Reply to W. Hicks' Comments." *Population Studies* 29 (1975): 176-177.

Shaffer, Richard. "Mexico: More Troubles Ahead?" *The Wall Street Journal,* November 23, 1976.

―――. "Mexico's Economic Ills Expected to Force New President to Seek Capitalist Solution." *The Wall Street Journal,* May 21, 1976.

―――. "Multinationals Discover Profits in Mexico Despite Peso Problems, Ownership Rules." *The Wall Street Journal,* November 5, 1976.

Shelton, David. "Private Sector Liquidity and Output Growth in Post-War Mexico." *Southern Economic Journal* 36 (1969): 27-39.

"Should International Banks Continue to Lend to Brazil?" *Euromoney,* May 1976, pp 16 19.

Siegel, Barry. *Inflacion y Desarrollo: Las Experiencas de México.* Mexico City: C.E.M.L.A., 1960.

"Silence Can Be Golden." *The Economist,* January 15, 1977, p. 63.

Simpson, Lesley Byrd. *Many Mexicos.* 4th ed. Berkeley: University of California Press, 1966.

Singer, Morris. *Growth Equality and the Mexican Experience.* Austin: University of Texas Press, 1969.

Solís, Leopoldo. "The Financial System in the Economic Development of Mexico," pp. 44-47. In *Mexico's Recent Economic Growth: The Mexican View.* Edited by Tom Davis et al. Austin: University of Texas Press, 1967.

―――. "Mexican Economic Policy in the Post-War Period: The Views of Mexican Economists." *The American Economic Review* 61 (1971), supplement, p. 5-67.

Stanford Research Institute. *The Impact of Foreign Private Investment on the Mexican Economy.* Menlo Park, Calif.: Stanford Research Institute, 1976.

―――. *Mexico.* Menlo Park, Calif.: Stanford Research Institute, 1975.

"Statement by the President of Mexico to Local and Foreign Investors." *Comercio Exterior de México* 17 (1971): 7.

Stewart, John. "An Analysis of the Two Gap Theory of Economic Development with Empirical Applications for the Mexican Economy." Ph.D. dissertation, University of North Carolina, 1975.

Sweeney, Timothy D. "The Mexican Balance of Payments." *International Monetary Fund Staff Papers* 1 (1953): 132-154.

Tello, Carlos. "Agricultural Development and Land Tenure in Mexico." *Weltwirtschaftliches Archiv,* 1968, p. 22.

Tuchman, Barbara. "The Green Revolution and the Distribution of Agricultural Income in Mexico." *World Development* 4 (1976): 17-24.

Unikel, Luis. "The Process of Urbanization in Mexico: Distribution and Growth of Urban Population." In *Latin American Urban Research.* Edited by Francine F. Rabinovitz and Felicity M. Trueblood. Beverly Hills, Calif.: Sage Publications, 1975.

Urquidi, Victor. "An Overview of Mexican Economic Development." *Weltwirtschaftliches Archiv,* 1978, pp. 8-12.

Urquidi, Victor; Araud, G.; et al. *Studies on Employment in the Mexican Housing Industry.* Paris: OECD, 1973.

Vanek, Jaroslav. *Estimating Foreign Resource Needs for Economic Development.* New York: McGraw-Hill, 1967.

Venezian, Eduardo, and Gamble, William. *The Agricultural Development of Mexico: Its Structure and Growth since 1950.* New York: Praeger, 1969.

Vernon, Raymond, ed. *The Dilemma of Mexico's Development.* Cambridge, Mass.: Harvard University Press, 1963.

————. *The Dilemma of Mexico's Development: The Roles of the Private and Public Sectors.* Cambridge, Mass.: Harvard University Press, 1965.

————. *Public Policy and Private Enterprise in Mexico.* Cambridge, Mass.: Harvard University Press, 1964.

Wacher, Susan M. *Latin American Inflation.* Lexington, Mass.: Lexington Books, 1976.

Wallisch, Henry. "The Impending Capital Shortage." *Challenge* 19 (1976): 45.

Watanabe, Susumu. "Constraints on Labour-Intensive Export Industries in Mexico." *International Labor Review* 107 (1972): 23-45.

Weckstein, R. S. "Evaluating Mexican Land Reform." *Economic Development and Cultural Change* 8 (1970): 391-409.

Weisskopf, T. E. "An Econometric Test of Alternative Constraints on the Growth of Underdeveloped Countries." *Review of Economics and Statistics* 54 (1972): 67-78.

————. "The Impact of Foreign Capital Inflow on Domestic Savings in Underdeveloped Countries." *Journal of International Economics* 2 (1972): 25-38.

Wilford, Dwaine Sykes. *The Open Economy in a Monetized World: The Mexican Case.* Ph.D. dissertation, Tulane University, 1976.

Wilford, Dwaine Sykes, and Wilford, Walton T. "Fiscal Revenues in Mexico: A Measure of Performance, 1950-73." *Public Finance* 31 (1976): 103-114.

————. "Monetary Approach to Balance of Payments: On World Prices and the Reserve Flow Equation." *Weltwirtschaftliches Archiv,* 1976, pp. 31-39.

Wilkie, James. *The Mexican Revolution: Federal Expenditure and Social Change since 1910.* Berkeley: University of California Press, 1970.

————. "Recentralization: The Budgetary Dilemma in the Economic Development of Mexico, Bolivia, and Costa Rica." In *Fiscal Policy for Industrialization and Development in Latin America.* Edited by T. Geithman. Gainesville: University of Florida Press, 1974.

Wionczek, Miguel. "Incomplete Formal Planning: Mexico." In *Planning Economic Development.* Edited by Everett Hagan. Homewood, Illinois: Richard D. Irwin, 1963.

Yassukovich, S. "The Growing Political Threat to International Lending." *Euromoney,* April 1966, pp. 10-15.

Yglesias, Manuel Espinosa. "Private Banking Sector." In *Business Mexico.* Edited by Redvers Opie. Mexico City: American Chamber of Commerce of Mexico, 1973.

Zapata, Fausto. *Development in Freedom: The Policy of Change in Mexico.* Mexico City: Secretaría de la Presidencia, 1972.

Index

Agrarian law (new; 1971), 74-75
Agricultural policies, 89-92, 107
Alemán, Miguel, 9, 14
Alliance for Production, 134-135
Argentina, 49, 166, 172
Ávila Camacho, Manuel, 9, 14

Baja California, 164
Balance of payments, 6, 12, 14, 16,
    18, 19, 28, 31, 33, 41, 62, 65,
    69, 71, 72, 74, 76, 77, 83, 84,
    85, 88, 94, 96-99, 106, 114,
    115, 119, 120, 121, 129, 143,
    145, 146, 153, 154, 181, 182,
    183, 185, 186; strengthening,
    111-113
Bank of America, 128
Bank of Mexico (Banco de Méxi-
    co), 25, 29-30, 31, 32, 34, 35,
    38, 55, 75, 84, 90, 117, 127,
    181, 182; discount rate, 35;
    Monetary Policy Commis-
    sion, 29; Organic Law of, 29
    [Article 71, 30]; peso floated
    by, 105, 125; reserve require-
    ments, 35-36, 37, 39, 40-41,
    42, 53-54, 95, 110-111, 182
Banks, 29, 34-41, 75, 77, 110, 127,
    178; foreign, and investment
    climate, 174-175; reserve re-
    quirements, 35-36, 39, 40-41,
    42, 95, 110-111

Bond issues, increasing, 186-187;
    ratings, need for, 187
Borrowing, government, 46, 51,
    53, 55, 58, 59, 65, 69, 72, 78,
    84, 85, 99, 100, 101, 108, 115,
    137, 155, 178, 181
Bravo region, 162
Brazil, 49, 166, 172
Budget Expenditures Law, 137
Budget overruns, 102
Budgets, 136-142; inflationary or
    deflationary, 141-142; 1977,
    136-138, 139 [effects of, on
    economy, 138-141]

Capital, flight of, 114, 118, 123,
    127, 133
Capital formation, 16, 24, 154
Capital goods, index of volume
    of, 12
Capital imports, 12, 13, 16, 86,
    112-113
Capital investment needs, of de-
    veloped nations, 170
Cárdenas, Lázaro, 9, 56, 62, 64
CETENAL, 106
Chiapas, 158, 164
Chihuahua, 164
Chile, 49
Chiquasen, hydro scheme at, 107
Class struggle, 106
Coahuila, 164

Coatzacoalcos River, 161
Colombia, 49
CONASUPO (National Company for Popular Subsistence), 49, 89-91, 93, 102, 116, 141, 179
Confederation of Chambers of Industry, 135, 136
Constitution of 1917, 28
Consumer price index, 77; Mexico City (MCCPI), 94
Consumption, 154, 155; controlling private, 179-180
Cotaxtla (Veracruz), 158, 164
Credit, 4, 14, 26, 27, 31-32, 33, 35, 36, 38, 41, 42, 76-77, 86, 89, 94-95, 100, 107, 181; expansion, reducing, 109-111, 117; trade, 166
Crisis of 1976, 4-5, 6, 8

Death rate, 17
Debt maturities, longer, 186
Debt-service ratio, 18, 178
Deficit financing, 14, 19, 26, 31, 32, 40, 42, 69, 85, 139, 180, 182
Deficit, government, 65
Demand, long-term management of, 179-182; monetary authorities, role of, 180-182 [need for greater freedom, 181-182]; private consumption, controlling, 179-180
Denison method, 22-24
Deputies, Chamber of, 138
"Destabilizing development," 108
Devaluation, currency, 109
Devaluations, of the peso, 15, 30-31, 32, 46, 71, 95, 100, 105, 143, 145, 148; aftereffects of, 125-129; as import control, 154; 1976, 114-121, 125, 171; problems from, 129-130; rationale for, 115, 120-121
Development;   "destabilizing,"

180; government role in, 45-47, 59; long-term strategy for, 177-187 [foreign direct investment, attracting, 182-187, management of demand, long-term, 179-182; reforms, necessary, 177-178]; "shared," 62, 72, 108
Development planning, French or "indicative" method of, 135
Development with monetary stability (desarrollo estabilizador), 2, 27-28, 33, 38-39, 41, 45, 61, 76, 101
Díaz Ordaz, Gustavo, 5, 9, 72, 74
Disequilibrium in Mexican economy, 43-44, 147; 1974-75 period, 83-103 [corrective measures against, 84-85; imports, growth of, 86; ineffectiveness of anti-inflationary measures, 92-94]; in 1976-90 projections, 147, 152
Dollar, 112, 125-126; devaluations of, 78, 96
Domestic value added, increasing, 136
Durango, 164

Echeverría, Luis, 3, 4, 6, 7, 19, 61-82, 83, 85, 89, 92, 95-96, 99, 101, 105-108, 121, 123, 124, 126, 128, 129, 130, 133, 188; disequilibrium under, 83-103; goals of, 62; growth during administration, 64-82 [of expenditures and inflation, 65-71; in GDP, 64-65; patterns of, 71-82]; overview of administration, 105-108; peso devaluation, reasons for, 118; priorities of, 63-64; stabilization, final proposals for, 116-120; State of the Union Message, Sixth, 118

Economic growth; with coercion, 5; with co-optation, 6; patterns of 1970-73, 61-82 [1971, 72-76, 81; 1972, 76-77, 81; 1973, 77-82]; projected, 1976-90, 145-156 [major deterrents to, 156, 158-176; physical resources for, 157-158]

Economic policy, 1, 2, 3, 33; approaches to, 5-8 [through foreign investment, 8; growth for all classes, 6-7; growth with coercion, 5; growth with co-optation, 6; revolutionary reform, 7-8]; Echeverría's approach to, 63

Education, Ministry of, 102

Education, reform of, 63

Ejidos, 75

Employment, 4, 15, 54, 61, 62, 72, 93, 135, 136, 153, 155, 160

Energy shortages, 163-165

Eurocurrency, 166, 167

Eurodollars, 77

Euromarkets, 166, 167, 169, 170

Excess profits tax, 117

Exchange rates, 32-33, 42, 154, 178, 181; floating, 78, 169

Expenditures; government, 51, 54-55, 65-69, 71, 72, 74, 76, 78, 81, 84, 100-101, 102, 119, 124, 137, 139, 142, 146, 155, 182 [public expenditures control commission, 107-108]; private, 54, 83

Exports, 12, 13, 18, 63, 69, 76, 78, 85, 87, 89, 96-99, 111, 114, 120, 130, 146, 147, 152, 155; agricultural, 90, 93, 113, 114; measures promoting, 112-113, 115, 154, 155, 178; oil, 164-165

FDRs, 128

Federal Budgeting Accounting and Public Spending Law, 137

Federal Reserve Act (1913), 29

Federal Reserve Bank, New York, 78

Federal Reserve System, U.S., 29

Finance, Ministry of, 55, 112

Financial system, 32; evolution of, 28-30; growth of, through savings, 37-38, 40; liquidity of, 143; strains on, 42

Financieras. See Investment banks

Fiscal policy, 43-59; government role in, 45-47; inflationary, 46; objectives of, 43-44; problems of applying, 44-45; for stabilization, difficulties of using, 54-59

Fiscal (tax) incentives, 55-56, 113, 184

FOGAIN, 113

FOMEX, 113

FONACOT (National Fund for Workers Consumption), 106

FONEI, 113

Food resources, 159

Foreign capital; difficulties of obtaining, 156, 159, 165, 170-172, 176, 178; in direct investment, 172-175, 178, 182-187 [bond issues, increasing, 186-187; and relation to borrowing, 174-175; uncertainty of investors, 172-174, 183, 184-185]; to non-OPEC developing countries, 166-168; from private sources, 166 [greater recent volume of, 168-170, 175]

Foreign exchange controls, 114, 127

Foreign exchange reserves, 39, 110, 115

France, 49

Gaps in projected model of Mexican economy, 147-152, 153, 154, 155
GDP, 9, 14, 16, 17, 18, 19, 24, 37-38, 43, 46, 51, 53, 58, 59, 64-65, 71, 74, 76, 77, 78, 85, 86, 87, 99, 100, 119, 128, 133, 141, 152, 155, 160. *See also* GNP
Germany, 3. *See also* West Germany
GNP, 14, 15, 16, 49, 76, 143, 147, 148, 152, 153, 154, 155, 157, 159, 170, 179. *See also* GDP
Government bonds, 50, 182
Government stabilization policies, 1954-70, 15-26; industrialization an attraction, 22; investment, importance of, 22-24, 25; negative results of, 18-22 [balance-of-payments deficits, 18; other problems, 19-22; public sector deficits, 18-19]
Grijalva River, 161
Gross domestic product. *See* GDP
Gross national product. *See* GNP
Guadalajara, 162
Guatemala, 164
Gulf of Mexico, 164
Gulf States (Persian), 169

Hacienda y Crédito Público (Treasury), Secretaria de, 29-30, 33, 115
Hidalgo, 163

Illiteracy, 17
IMF. *See* International Monetary Fund
Import controls, 112, 113, 153-154; elimination of, 183-184; greater flexibility in, 183
Imports, 12, 13, 16, 18, 69, 78, 83, 85, 86, 88, 96-99, 111, 147, 153, 154; agricultural, 90, 93, 123, 129; essential, 129; restriction of, 112, 113, 114, 153-154
Import substitution, 111, 112, 113, 155
Income distribution, 5, 26, 45, 61, 62, 63, 64, 76, 89, 101, 103, 130, 153, 159
Income, growth of, 16-17, 42, 179
Industrialization, 13-15, 16, 22
Industry and Commerce, Ministry of, 80, 112, 113, 125
Inflation, 4, 9, 14-15, 26, 28, 30, 31, 33, 38, 39, 46, 47, 53, 59, 64, 65, 69, 71, 72, 74, 76, 77, 78, 81, 83, 84, 85, 86, 87, 88, 93, 103, 106, 108, 109, 111, 119, 120, 123, 124, 133, 137, 139, 141, 142, 145, 147, 154, 155, 172, 180, 182, 185; budgetary, 141-142; factors leading to (1974-75), 88-103 [agricultural policy, 89-92; government ineptness, 99-103; ineffective policies against, 92-94; international conditions, 96-99; private-sector uncertainty, 94-96; wage increases, 94, 96]; world, 78, 85, 92, 96, 105, 119
INFONAVIT (Workers Housing Fund), 106
Infrastructure, 14, 19, 24, 25, 43, 46, 89, 107, 117, 136, 184
Institutional Party of the Revolution (PRI), *See* Partido Revolucionario Institucional
Inter-American Development Bank, 92, 165
Interest rates, 38, 53, 71, 76-77, 78, 95, 116-117, 181, 182; fixed, 76, 180-181; on foreign funds, 110, 115, 127, 167-168, 171, 186; negative differential in, 77; 1974 increases in, 84
International Monetary Fund

(IMF), 17, 126, 127-129, 133, 143, 159, 166; "Extended Fund Facility," 128

Investment, 53-54, 77, 84, 120, 121, 135, 147, 152, 159, 160; domestic, 7, 31; encouraging, 6, 133, 155; foreign, 6, 8, 17, 58, 69, 80-81, 120, 121, 123, 124, 172-175; for infrastructure, 24, 25, 43, 46; López Portillo program for industrial, 135-136; private sector, 4, 5, 13, 15, 17, 26, 39, 42, 47, 54, 56, 58, 64, 74, 81-82, 84, 87, 92, 94-96, 99, 110, 124, 143, 146; public, 14, 19, 24, 25, 26, 33, 39, 43, 46, 53, 54, 64, 65, 71, 75, 87, 92, 124, 146

Investment banks (*Financieras*), 37, 38, 42, 59, 71, 110-111

Italy, 3

Japan, 3, 78

La Angostura, hydro scheme at, 107

Labor Law (1970), 75

Land expropriation, 123, 124

Land Reform Law (new; 1972), 106

Latin America, 17, 41, 49, 120, 172; exports to, 12

Law to Promote Mexican Investment, 80-81

Law on the Transfer of Technology and the Use and Exploitation of Patents and Trademarks, 80

Lerma Basin, 162

Life expectancy, 17

London Inter-Bank Offer Rate (LIBOR), 167

López Mateos, Adolfo, 9, 121

López Portillo, José, 5, 7, 107, 121, 123, 126, 133, 143, 145, 152, 164, 177; budget-making activities, 136-142 [effects of, 138-141; 1977, 136-138, 139, 142]; priorities, enforced, 133; problems facing, 124-125, 126, 129-131; programs, proposed, 134-136 [Alliance for Production, 134-135; industrial investment, 135-136]

Marxist views, 95

"Mexdollars," 127

Mexican Bankers' Association, 79

Mexican economy; at end of 1976, 123-124; growth of, 9, 13, 26 [investment's role in, 22-24]; growth patterns, 1976-90, projected, 145-156, 177 [assumptions made, 147, 148; gaps in, 147-152, 153, 154, 155; macroeconomic module to explore, 146-156]; 1940-70 period, 9-26 [economic take-off in 1940-45, 12-13; at end of 1976, 123-124; industrialization in 1945-54, 13-15; stabilization in 1954-70, 15-17, 31, 32, 61]; 1976 crisis, 4-5, 6, 8; phenomena to be analyzed, 1 [methodology, 2]; policy for 5-8 [approaches available, 5-8]; problem of, 3-5 [characteristics of, 4]

Mexicanization, 63

Mexican Labor Congress, 125

Mexico City, 125, 162

Mexico City Chamber of Commerce 79

México, State of, 163

Minimum wages, increases in, 94, 116, 129-130

Monetary and credit policy, 27-42, 94, 120; aim of, 27; changes post–World War II, 30-42 [1945-54, 31-32; 1955-

70, 32-42]; development with
stability, 27-28, 33, 38-39, 41,
45; institutional basis of, 29-
30
Money supply, 33, 35, 36, 39, 65,
74, 76, 78, 86, 93, 94, 100, 110,
120, 155, 181, 182

Nacional Financiera, 13, 29
National banking system, 12-13
Nationalization, 183
National Manufacturing Cham-
ber, 79
National Railways System, 49,
141
National Water Plan (PNH), 106
Natural resources, study of (CE-
TENAL), 106
New Workers' Housing Fund
Payroll Tax, 78
Nixon, Richard M., 96
Non-OPEC developing coun-
tries, 166-167
North Sea, 164
North Slope of Alaska, 164
Noyola, J., 28

Oil, 83, 88, 114, 126, 143, 153, 157,
158, 164, 178, 183
OPEC, 169
Organic Law of the Federal Public Administration, 137

Papaloapán River, 161; basin, 162
Parenthood, responsible, 106
Partido Revolucionario Institucional (PRI), 7, 17, 54, 136
PEMEX, 83, 88, 102, 135, 164,
165, 187
Peru, 49, 166
Peso, 61, 74, 96; convertibility of,
32; decline of, 4, 5; devaluations of, 15, 30-31, 32, 46, 71,
95, 100, 105, 143, 145, 148
[aftereffects of, 125-129; 1976,

114-121, 125, 171; problems
from 129-130; rationale for,
115, 120-121]; overvaluation
of, 114, 115, 153, 154; stabili-
zation of, necessary, 133, 185
Petroleos Mexicanos. *See* PE-
MEX
Petroleum. *See* Oil
Philippines, 166
PIDER (National Rural Develop-
ment Program), 106
Pollution, 160, 162
Population; growth of, 115, 156,
158; problems in, 159-160,
175-176; reduction of, 106
Poza Rica, 164
Pragmatism, in Mexican policy,
25
Presidency, Ministry of the, 55,
107
Presidential Act (1971), 107
Presidential cycle, 55, 72, 74, 81
PRI. *See* Partido Revolucionario
Institucional
Price controls, 116, 126, 127, 129,
184; elimination of, 184
Price increases, 86-87, 92, 96, 126,
127, 141, 148, 154, 182
Price level, 14, 16, 32, 33, 78, 89
Private sector, 13-14, 15, 17, 24, 25,
26, 31, 32, 36, 39, 40, 42, 43,
45, 69, 76, 79-80, 83, 86, 87,
88, 94-96, 99, 100, 101, 105,
112, 117, 124, 125, 133, 134,
135, 137, 138, 141, 152, 174,
181, 182
Public Debt Law, 137
Public expenditure control commission, 107-108
Public Investment Financing,
Subcommittee for, 55
Public sector, 13, 14, 17, 18-19, 24,
25-26, 36, 37, 40, 41, 43, 45, 46,
47, 49, 53, 64, 71, 75, 83, 84,
85, 86, 88, 92, 99, 100, 105,

107, 108, 110, 112, 117, 118, 119, 124, 128, 138, 139, 141, 181, 182

Public utility industries, 24, 25, 183

Public Works, Ministry of, 102; industrial parks projects of, 102

Puebla, 163

Quasimoney, 17, 100
Querétaro, 162

Recession, world, 96

Rediscounting, by Bank of Mexico, 35, 37

Reforma, 164

Reserve requirements, 35-36, 37, 39, 40-41, 42, 53-54, 95, 110-111, 182

Revenues; government, 47-51, 56, 65, 130 [underestimating, 55, 139]; tax, 49-51, 55-58, 75, 88, 110, 152, 153, 179, 182

Roosevelt, Franklin, 62

Ruiz Cortines, Adolfo, 9

Rural sector, 16, 63

Savings, 37-38, 42, 46, 47, 53-54, 77, 95, 99, 100, 101, 147-148, 153, 154-155, 160, 165, 179, 180, 181, 182; in U.S. and Western Europe, 170-171

"Shared development," 62, 72, 108

Social policy, 1, 5, 6, 14; curtailed by economic priorities, 62

Social welfare, 89, 92, 93, 155; indicators of, 17

Sonora, 164

South Korea, 166

Spain, 187

Spheres of activity, allocation of, 17

Stabilization, government measures toward; after devaluation, 125, 126; Echeverría's proposals for, 116-118, 126 [evaluation of, 119-120]; 1974-75, 84-88, 94, 99, 105; 1975-76, 109-121 [balance of payments, strengthening, 111-114; credit expansion, reducing, 109-111, 113]

Stock market, 181

Support prices, agricultural, 89-91, 107

Tabasco, 158, 164

Tamaulipas, 164

Tariffs, 14, 58, 112, 130, 153, 154, 184

Taxes, 45, 46, 47, 49-51, 53; ad valorem, 130; commodity, 179-180; import and export, 49, 51, 56, 88, 113, 116, 130; income, 49-51, 56, 58, 65, 75, 88, 139, 179; other, 51, 65, 78-79, 88, 139-141; reforms in (1975), 88; sales, 49, 56-58, 88

Tax incentives. *See* Fiscal (tax) incentives

Tax rebate certificates (CEDIS), 113, 116

Tax reform law (December 1971), 75; corporate taxes, 75; fixed-interest securities, 76; personal taxes, 75

Tax system, 55-58, 99, 148; inflexibility of, 182; reforms needed in, 182, 184

Third World, 8

Tlaxcala, 163

Toluca, 162

Tonata River, 161

Tourism, 12, 16, 39, 47, 96, 107, 113-114, 117, 120, 136, 138, 153, 164

Treasury. *See* Hacienda y Crédito

Público, Secretaria de
Treasury Accounting Law, 137
Treasury, United States, 78, 126

Unemployment, 115, 120, 133,
    160
United Kingdom, 78
United Mexican States, bond is-
    sue of, 187
United States, 4, 12, 14-15, 16, 22,
    25, 29, 33, 69, 78, 82, 83, 96,
    114, 115, 118, 119, 120, 133,
    147, 157, 164-165, 170, 172,
    186, 187
Urbanization, 16
Uruguay, 49
Usumacinta River, 161

Valle de México, 162
Venezuela, 1, 165

Villahermosa, 164

Wage increase (1973), 79-80
Wage and salary adjustments,
    116, 119, 124, 125, 126-127,
    133
Water Law (new; 1971), 106
Water shortages, 156, 158-159,
    160-163, 175; agricultural,
    163; recycling of water, 162-
    163; urban-industrial, 161-
    163
Western Europe, 170
West Germany, 78. *See also* Ger-
    many
Wholesale price index, 87
World Bank, 92, 165, 166
World War II, 12, 16, 25, 29, 30

Yucatán Peninsula, 164